Making
CONNECTIONS

1

Skills and Strategies for Academic Reading

Second Edition

*for the people that say
IDK we

or you don't know how*

Jessica Williams

CAMBRIDGE
UNIVERSITY PRESS

CAMBRIDGE
UNIVERSITY PRESS

University Printing House, Cambridge CB2 8BS, United Kingdom

One Liberty Plaza, 20th Floor, New York, NY 10006, USA

477 Williamstown Road, Port Melbourne, VIC 3207, Australia

314–321, 3rd Floor, Plot 3, Splendor Forum, Jasola District Centre, New Delhi – 110025, India

79 Anson Road, #06–04/06, Singapore 079906

Cambridge University Press is part of the University of Cambridge.

It furthers the University's mission by disseminating knowledge in the pursuit of
education, learning and research at the highest international levels of excellence.

www.cambridge.org
Information on this title: www.cambridge.org/9781108583688

© Cambridge University Press 2013

This publication is in copyright. Subject to statutory exception
and to the provisions of relevant collective licensing agreements,
no reproduction of any part may take place without the written
permission of Cambridge University Press.

First published 2011
Second edition 2013
20 19 18 17 16 15 14 13 12 11 10 9 8 7 6

Printed in the United Kingdom by Latimer Trend

A catalogue record for this publication is available from the British Library

ISBN 978-1-108-58368-8 Student's Book with Integrated Digital Learning
ISBN 978-1-107-61023-1 Teacher's Manual

Cambridge University Press has no responsibility for the persistence or accuracy
of URLs for external or third-party internet websites referred to in this publication,
and does not guarantee that any content on such websites is, or will remain,
accurate or appropriate.

TABLE OF CONTENTS

SCOPE AND SEQUENCE

Making CONNECTIONS

MAKING CONNECTIONS 1 is a low intermediate academic reading and vocabulary skills book. It is intended for students who need to improve their strategic reading skills and build their academic vocabulary.

Finding the Meanings of Words

Writers sometimes use words that a reader may not know. To help readers understand a difficult word, writers may explain what the word means by giving its definition. Writers often use clues to do this. These clues can be other words, phrases, or punctuation. They can signal, or show you, that a definition is coming next. Good readers pay attention to these clues. This helps them find the meanings of words.

Examples & Explanations

Computers can scan, **or** take pictures of, travelers' faces.

Sometimes writers give the definition of a difficult word immediately after the word. They may use the word or to signal, or show you, that a definition is coming next.

scan = take pictures of

Governments want to be able to use their countries' natural resources, **that is,** the natural materials in the water, on land, and underground.

Writers may use phrases, such as *that is* or *in other words*, to explain the meaning of a word or a phrase.

natural resources = materials in the water, on land, and underground

National borders **–** the places where one country ends and another country begins **–** can be physical or political.

Writers may also use punctuation around definitions. They may use parentheses, dashes, and commas. Here the writer uses dashes (–).

national borders = the places where one country ends and another begins

Computer chips are an important development in technology. These very small electronic parts can store large amounts of information.

Sometimes writers don't give a signal. They just give a definition in a sentence that follows.

computer chips = very small electronic parts that can store large amounts of information

> Each unit begins with an in-depth study of key skills and strategies for reading academic texts, helping students to learn how and when to use them.

> Students learn strategies for approaching academic texts and skills for consciously applying the strategies.

Strategies

These strategies will help you find the meanings of words while you read.

- Look for words and phrases that signal, or show you, that a definition for a difficult word is coming next. Read the definition carefully.
- Pay attention to punctuation. Look for parentheses, commas, and dashes.
- If there is no definition immediately after the difficult word, look for it in a sentence that follows. Writers sometimes also repeat the word before they give the definition.

Skill Practice 1

Read the following sentences, and find the clues that signal the meaning of each word in bold. Highlight the clues. The first one has been done for you.

1 Gold and sugar are two of Mexico's important **exports** (items sold by one country to another country).

2 The officials told the travelers about the dangerous **infection** – a disease or sickness in a person's body – in South America.

3 It is important to use different **strategies**, or plans for success, when you play chess.

4 The speaker talked for 15 minutes, and then he gave his **conclusion**. It was this last part of the talk that was most exciting.

5 At international soccer matches, fights are quite **frequent**; in other words, they occur often.

6 Since we do not know how much the tickets cost, we have to **guess**, that is, give an answer that we are not sure about.

7 The man was not sure of the **value** of the painting. In other words, he was not sure how much money to pay for it.

8 Some toys are dangerous. They can seriously **injure**, or harm, the children who play with them.

FEATURES

- Critical thinking skills
- Real-time practice of skills and strategies
- Study of the Academic Word List
- Audio files of all readings available online

Before You Read

Connecting to the Topic

Discuss the following questions with a partner.

1 Where are some famous border walls? Think about the past and more recent times.
2 Why do you think countries built walls on their borders in the past?
3 Why do you think countries build walls on their borders today?

Previewing and Predicting

> Reading the title and the first few sentences of a reading can give you a good idea of what the whole reading will be about.

A Read the first four sentences of Reading 2 below and the title of the reading on page 13.

> Today, most national borders are lines on a map. Two countries agree on the line between them. However, in the past, some countries had walls or fences on their borders. Walls had several purposes.

B After reading the title and the four sentences, what do you think this reading will be about? Circle four answers.

a Border walls that were built a long time ago
b Famous walls
c How to build a strong border wall
d The reason that countries build walls at their borders
e Walls that are at the border of some countries today
f Walls that protect homes

C Compare your answers with a partner's.

While You Read

As you read, stop at the end of each sentence that contains words in **bold**. Then follow the instructions in the box in the margin.

12 • UNIT 1

Predicting the content of a text is critical for reading college books, and students practice this skill extensively before beginning each reading.

Each unit contains 3 readings, providing students with multiple opportunities to practice applying the skills and strategies.

Students learn how to use the skills and strategies by applying them to each text while they read it.

READING 2

Walls as Borders

1   Today, most national borders are lines on a map. Two countries agree on the line between them. However, in the past, some countries had walls or fences on their borders. Walls had several purposes. They helped prevent invasions, that is, the arrival of enemies. Walls were also a good way to make money. There were often only a few entrances in a wall. People had to pay taxes when they went through these entrances. In more **recent** times, walls also have had other purposes. These days, some walls prevent people from leaving their country. Other walls stop people from entering a country. These people are often looking for jobs and are hoping for a better life on the other side of the wall.

2   Two of the most famous walls in history are the Great Wall of China and Hadrian's Wall. The Great Wall of China is 5,500 miles (8,850 kilometers) long and more than 29.5 feet (9 meters) wide in some places. The Chinese built it to stop invaders from entering China. Along the top of the wall, there were thousands of **guards**. These guards were men who could see anyone who came near the wall. In England, the Romans built Hadrian's Wall in the second century CE. Like the Great Wall of China, its major purpose was also to stop invaders. However, that was not its only purpose. The other reason was money: People had to pay a tax to the Romans when they came through Hadrian's Wall.

3   The most famous wall in recent history was the Berlin Wall. After World War II, East and West Germany became separate, that is, they became two different countries. The Soviet Union controlled East Germany and the eastern part of Berlin. At first, people could still travel between East and West Berlin. However, the Soviet Union wanted to stop this, so in 1961, it built the Berlin Wall. The purpose of this wall was not to stop invaders or get money from taxes. It was

WHILE YOU READ ①
Look in the next sentence for a definition of *recent*. Highlight it.

WHILE YOU READ ②
Look in the next sentence to help you guess the meaning of *guards*. What do guards do?
a) Keep people safe
b) Build walls

The Great Wall of China stopped invaders from entering China.

READING 2   **13**

vii

FROM THE SERIES AUTHORS

"Reading is an interactive process, in which readers use their knowledge of language, text organization, and the world to understand what they read."

"Reading is goal-oriented and strategic; good academic readers know when to use the right reading skills."

---

6 Match the name of the wall in the left column to the purpose of the wall in the right column. One wall has two purposes.

Wall

_____ 1 The Great Wall of China

_____ 2 Hadrian's Wall

_____ 3 The Berlin Wall

_____ 4 Fences on the Mexico-United States border

Purpose

a to stop people from leaving

b to stop people from entering without permission

c to stop enemy invaders

d to make money from taxes

Skill Review

In Skills and Strategies 1, you learned that different clues can help you figure out the meaning of new words. You also learned that sometimes you need to look in a sentence after the new word to find its meaning.

A The sentences with the words in **bold** are from Reading 2. Which sentences have clues that signal the meaning of the words in **bold**? Which sentences give the definition in the next sentence without a clue? Choose the correct answer.

1 They helped prevent **invasions**, that is, the arrival of enemies. Walls were also a good way to make money.
   a First sentence has a clue
   b Second sentence has a definition

2 However, that was the not its only **purpose**. The other reason was mor
   a First sentence has a clue
   b Second sentence has a definition

3 After World War II, East and West Germany became **separate**, that is, t
   two different countries. The Soviet Union controlled East Germany and
   part of Berlin.
   a First sentence has a clue
   b Second sentence has a definition

4 East German guards **shot** some of these people. More than 100 people
   trying to cross the border before the Berlin Wall came down in 1989.
   a First sentence has a clue
   b Second sentence has a definition

B Highlight the definition for each word in **bold** in A above.

Students continually review the skills and strategies, helping them build up a valuable set of tools for reading academic texts.

(Vocabulary Development)

Definitions

Find the words in Reading 3 that complete the following definitions.

1 A/An _____ is an official piece of paper. (n) Par. 1

2 Your _____

3 To _____
   (v) Par

4 If som

5 Two b
   are __

6 A/An _____
   (n) Par

7 To _____

8 When

Words in

Comple

| brief |
| citizens |

1 Wh
   enter
   is, pe
   visitin
   reasor
   be __
   same

2 Trav
   use ne
   carefu
   can re
   _____

Students expand their vocabularies by studying key words from each reading and academic words from each unit.

Academic Word List

The following are Academic Word List words from all the readings in Unit 1. Use these words to complete the sentences. (For more on the Academic Word List, see page 260.)

| areas (n) | features (n) | major (adj) | requires (v) | technology (n) |
| documents (n) | identification (n) | physical (adj) | resources (n) | unique (adj) |

1 She put important _____, such as her passport, under her bed.

2 The country's most important natural _____ are oil, gas, and gold.

3 _____, especially the use of computers, has changed many things in business, government, and education.

4 A trip to Antarctica _____ a lot of warm clothes.

5 Scientists said the fish was _____. It was the only one in the world.

6 There were different _____ in the classroom. Some were for quiet work, and others were for discussion.

7 All citizens must carry a/an _____ card when they leave the country.

8 One of the most famous _____ of Egypt is the Nile River.

9 During the twentieth century, there were several _____ wars.

10 As children grow, their _____ abilities increase. They can run, jump, and throw things.

THE APPROACH

The *Making Connections* series offers a skills-based approach to academic reading instruction. Throughout each book, students are introduced to a variety of academic reading and vocabulary-building skills, which they then apply to high-interest, thematically-related readings.

Beyond the Reading

Critical Thinking

In Reading 3, the writer says that in the future, there will be powerful technology at borders, borders will become easier to cross, and one day, borders may even disappear.

> **EVALUATING INFORMATION**
>
> Critical thinkers ask themselves if there is enough information to support the points a writer makes in a text.

A Work with a partner and decide if there is enough information to support the writer's point by answering the following questions. Give reasons for your answers, and take notes on your discussion.

1 Does the writer explain what type of powerful technology there might be at the borders in the future? What type do you imagine there will be?

2 Does the writer explain why it will become easier to cross borders in the future? Do you think it will become easier to cross borders in the future or more difficult?

3 Does the writer explain why borders might disappear in the future? Do you think there will be a time in the future when borders disappear?

B Work with another pair of students. Compare your answers and the reasons you gave for your answers.

Research

Find out about border control in your country or a country that you know well. Find answers to the following questions.

- Who needs a visa to visit this country?
- Do citizens of the country need a visa to visit other countries?
- What sort of technology is used at the borders of the country?

Writing

Write a short summary of your research. Describe border control in the country you researched.

Improving Your Reading Speed

Good readers read quickly and still understand most of what they read.

A Read the instructions and strategies for Improving Your Reading Speed in Appendix 3 on page 273.

B Choose one of the readings in this unit. Read it without stopping. Time how long it takes you to finish the text in minutes and seconds. Enter the time in the chart on page 274. Then calculate your reading speed in number of words per minute.

Each unit develops students' higher level thinking skills, such as evaluating and synthesizing information.

Students also learn to read more quickly, a valuable skill for extended academic texts.

The units end with a study of academic connectors, helping students learn how to navigate dense academic text.

MAKING CONNECTIONS

PRONOUN CONNECTORS

Writers use pronouns to connect words and ideas within and across sentences. Pronouns make the writing shorter and less repetitive. However, pronouns give the reader extra work to do because the reader has to find the words and ideas that the pronouns refer to.

Some common pronouns are

| he | she | it | they | this | that | these | those |

When you see a pronoun, ask yourself: *What does this pronoun refer to?*

In the following example, the pronoun is in **bold**, and the noun it refers to is underlined. The arrow shows the connection.

Government officials work at the border. **They** check all passports.

In the next example, the pronoun is in **bold**, and the idea it refers to is underlined. The arrow shows that the pronoun refers to the whole idea in the first sentence.

There was a long line of trucks and cars at the border crossing. **This** delayed the tour bus for 3 hours.

Exercise 1

Read the following groups of sentences. Highlight the pronoun in the second sentence in each group. Underline the noun or ideas the pronoun refers to. Draw an arrow from the pronoun to the underlined items. The first one has been done for you.

1 I gave my passport to the official. He examined the photo carefully.

2 Everyone is required to show some kind of identification. The guard at the entrance will ask for it.

3 All the documents are electronic. They are stored on one computer.

4 There were three attempts to guess the password. They all failed.

5 Each person's iris is unique. That is the reason irises are good forms of identification.

6 There were separate lines for visitors and citizens. This made it faster for citizens to come back into the country.

Acknowledgments

Many people have helped shape this second edition of *Making Connections 1*. I am grateful to all of the supportive and professional staff of Cambridge University Press for the opportunity to create this new edition. There are many others who did so much to make this project successful, including Don Williams for page design and composition; and especially Bernard Seal, my project manager, who has provided guidance and wisdom for all of the *Making Connections* books.

Thanks to Poyee Oster, photo researcher; Mandie Drucker, fact-checker and copyeditor; Patricia Egan, proofreader; and as always, Karen Shimoda, freelance development editor, whose dedication and attention to detail know few limits. And, as in the first edition, I want to acknowledge the contribution of Daphne Mackey for writing key portions of the text, and of Ken Pakenham, the author of the first *Making Connections* book, for inspiring the creation of the series.

Finally, textbooks are only as good as the feedback that authors receive on them. Many thanks to the following reviewers whose insights helped shape the new editions of the entire *Making Connections* series: Macarena Aguilar, Lone Star College-CyFair, Texas; Susan Boland, Tidewater Community College, Virginia; Inna Cannon, San Diego State University, California; Holly Cin, University of Houston, Texas; Stacie Miller, Community College of Baltimore County, Maryland.

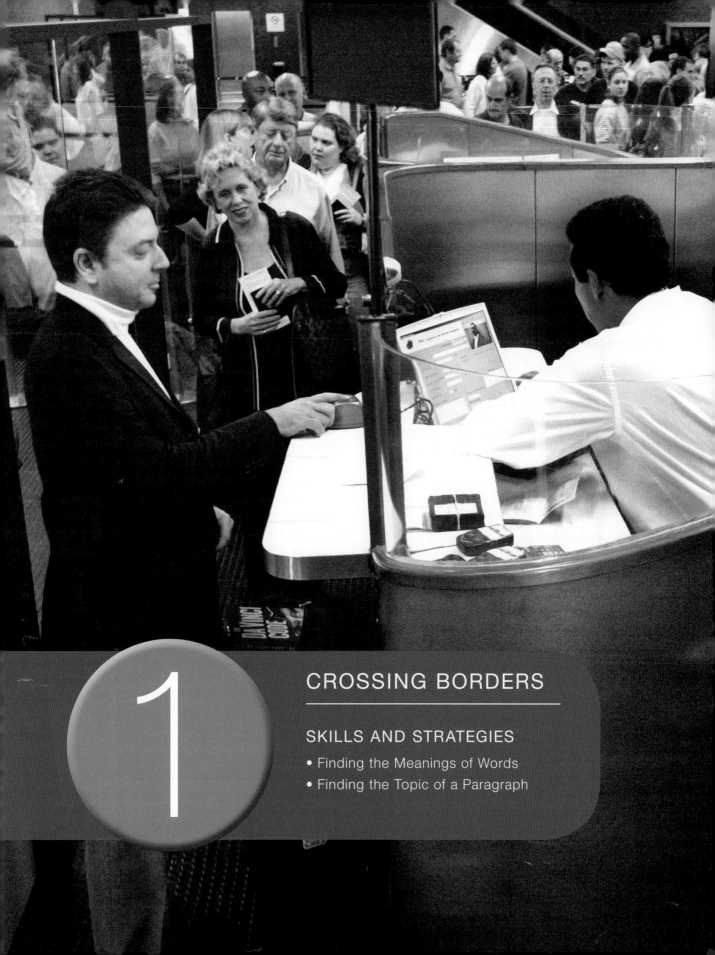

1 CROSSING BORDERS

SKILLS AND STRATEGIES

- Finding the Meanings of Words
- Finding the Topic of a Paragraph

Finding the Meanings of Words

Writers sometimes use words that a reader may not know. To help readers understand a difficult word, writers may explain what the word means by giving its definition. Writers often use clues to do this. These clues can be other words, phrases, or punctuation. They can signal, or show you, that a definition is coming next. Good readers pay attention to these clues. This helps them find the meanings of words.

Examples & Explanations

Computers can scan, **or** take pictures of, travelers' faces.

Sometimes writers give the definition of a difficult word immediately after the word. They may use the word or to signal, or show you, that a definition is coming next.

scan = take pictures of

Governments want to be able to use their countries' natural resources, that is the natural materials in the water, on land, and underground.

Writers may use phrases, such as *that is* or *in other words*, to explain the meaning of a word or a phrase.

natural resources = materials in the water, on land, and underground

National borders – the places where one country ends and another country begins – can be physical or political.

Writers may also use punctuation around definitions. They may use parentheses, dashes, and commas. Here the writer uses dashes (–).

national borders = the places where one country ends and another begins

Computer chips are an important development in technology. These very small electronic parts can store large amounts of information.

Sometimes writers don't give a signal. They just give a definition in a sentence that follows.

computer chips = very small electronic parts that can store large amounts of information

Strategies

way to do something →

These strategies will help you find the meanings of words while you read.

- Look for words and phrases that signal, or show you, that a definition for a difficult word is coming next. Read the definition carefully.
- Pay attention to punctuation. Look for parentheses, commas, and dashes.
- If there is no definition immediately after the difficult word, look for it in a sentence that follows. Writers sometimes also repeat the word before they give the definition.

Skill Practice 1

Read the following sentences, and find the clues that signal the meaning of each word in **bold**. Highlight the clues. The first one has been done for you.

1 Gold and sugar are two of Mexico's important **exports** (items sold by one country to another country).

2 The officials told the travelers about the dangerous **infection** – a disease or sickness in a person's body – in South America.

3 It is important to use different **strategies**, or plans for success, when you play chess.

4 The speaker talked for 15 minutes, and then he gave his **conclusion**. It was this last part of the talk that was most exciting.

5 At international soccer matches, fights are quite **frequent**; in other words, they occur often.

6 Since we do not know how much the tickets cost, we have to **guess**, that is, give an answer that we are not sure about.

7 The man was not sure of the **value** of the painting. In other words, he was not sure how much money to pay for it.

8 Some toys are dangerous. They can seriously **injure**, or harm, the children who play with them.

Skill Practice 2

Read the sentences in Skill Practice 1 again. Look at the clues you highlighted for each sentence. Use the clues to figure out the meaning of each word in bold. Write a short definition or synonym – a word that means the same or almost the same thing – on the blank lines. The first one has been done for you.

1 Gold and sugar are two of Mexico's important **exports** (items sold by one country to another country).

   exports = _items sold by one country to another country_

2 The officials told the travelers about the dangerous **infection** – a disease or sickness in a person's body – in South America.

   infection = _____

3 It is important to use different **strategies**, or plans for success, when you play chess.

   strategies = _____

4 The speaker talked for 15 minutes, and then he gave his **conclusion**. It was this last part of the talk that was most exciting.

   conclusion = _____

5 At international soccer matches, fights are quite **frequent**; in other words, they occur often.

   frequent = _____

6 Since we do not know how much the tickets cost, we have to **guess**, that is, give an answer that we are not sure about.

   guess = _____

7 The man was not sure of the **value** of the painting. In other words, he was not sure how much money to pay for it.

   value = _____

8 Some toys are dangerous. They can seriously **injure**, or harm, the children who play with them.

   injure = _____

Connecting to the Topic

Look at a map of the world or of a continent. Then discuss the following questions with a partner.

1 What is a national border? Point to a border between two countries on the map.

2 Where are the borders in your country? Are there any mountains or rivers along the border?

3 Look at other countries and their borders. Are any of the borders straight lines?

4 Who do you think decides where national borders should be?

Previewing and Predicting

It is a good idea to look at parts of a reading quickly before you read it carefully. This is called *previewing*. Previewing gives you information about what you are going to read. One way to do this is to read the title and the first few sentences of a reading. This can help you predict what the whole reading will be about.

A Read the first few sentences of Reading 1 below and the title on page 6. Then answer the questions that follow. Write your answers on the blank lines.

Long ago, there were no national borders. People moved freely from place to place. Today, countries have national borders. National borders are where one country ends and another country begins. There are two kinds of national borders. The first kind is a physical border. Physical borders between countries are physical features like rivers or mountains. *2 kinds, the one we can see and the ones we can't see*

1 What is the definition of *national border*? *→*

National borders are where one country ends and another country begins

2 What do you think this reading will discuss next?

the second part of the physical borders *ocean, lakes or mountains*

3 What do you think the whole reading will be about?

About the things that moving around our world like everything in nature, for example plants, lakes, weather.

B Compare your answers with a partner's.

While You Read

As you read, stop at the end of each sentence that contains words in bold. Then follow the instructions in the box in the margin.

↓ is basically, a line that separates one thing from another (Area, state, country)

Borders on the Land, in the Ocean, and in the Air

1   Long ago, there were no national borders. People moved freely from place to place. Today, countries have national borders. National borders are where one country ends and another country begins. There are two kinds of national borders. The first kind is a **physical border**. Physical borders between countries are physical features like rivers or mountains. You can see them. The Rio Grande is a physical border between Mexico and the United States. The Pyrenees Mountains are a physical border between Spain and France.

2   The second kind of border is a **political border**. When there is no physical border between countries, governments must decide on one. Political borders are also lines between countries like physical borders, but governments decide where these borders will be. The political borders of many North African countries are a good example of this. In the nineteenth and early twentieth centuries, European countries had power over many parts of Africa. They decided on the borders. Many of these borders were just straight lines on a map. They were not physical features like rivers or mountains. (See Figure 1.1.)

3   Governments want to control their borders. They want to decide *who* is coming into their country. Government officials at the borders **check**, that is, take a careful look at, everyone who enters. Only people who have permission to enter the country may come in. The government also wants to know *what* is entering the country, so officials also

WHILE YOU READ ❶

Look in the next sentence for a definition of *physical border*. Highlight it.

WHILE YOU READ ❷

Look in the third sentence for a definition of *political border*. Highlight it.

WHILE YOU READ ❸

Find a clue in this sentence that signals a definition of *check*. Highlight the clue and the definition.

Figure 1.1 Countries of North Africa

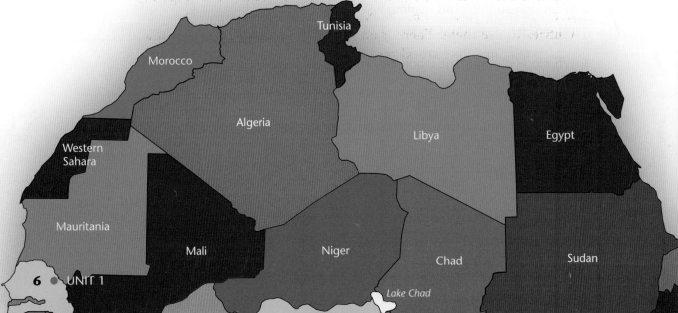

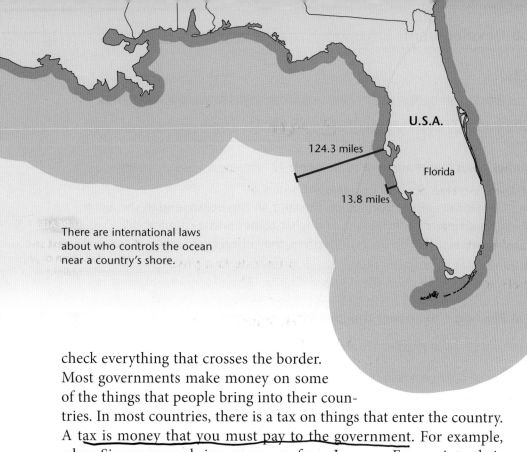

U.S.A.

124.3 miles

Florida

13.8 miles

There are international laws
about who controls the ocean
near a country's shore.

Figure 1.2
The Area in the
Ocean that a
Country Controls

check everything that crosses the border.
Most governments make money on some
of the things that people bring into their coun-
tries. In most countries, there is a tax on things that enter the country.
A tax is money that you must pay to the government. For example,
when Singaporeans bring a new car from Japan or Europe into their
country, they have to pay money to the Singapore government.

4   Governments also want to control the ocean near their borders.
They want to be sure their country is safe, so they do not want dangerous people to come near their country. There is an international
law about this. It says that a country owns the ocean within 13.8 miles
(22.2 kilometers) of that country's **shore** – the country's border with
the ocean. However, there is another important reason why countries
want to control the ocean near their shores. The ocean and the land
under the ocean have many natural resources, such as fish and oil.
Countries want to use these resources, and they do not want other
countries to use them. There is an international law that says that a
country may use the natural resources within 124.3 miles (200 kilometers) of its shore. Other countries may not use them. However, no
country controls the ocean or its resources more than 124.3 miles
from its shore. (See Figure 1.2.)

5   What about the air near a country's border? Can a country control
that, too? The international law about the air around a country is the
same as the law about the ocean. Every country controls the airspace
within 13.8 miles of its borders. A plane must request permission to
fly in that space. International laws like this are another way to control
national borders.

WHILE YOU READ 4

Look in the rest of this
sentence for a definition
of *shore*. Highlight it.

Main Idea Check

> The main idea of a reading is what the whole reading is about.

Which sentence gives the main idea of Reading 1?

a Long ago there were no physical or political borders.
b There are different laws about borders on the land, in the ocean, and in the air.
c Borders help governments control who and what comes into a country.
d If two countries cannot decide on their borders, they often go to war.

A Closer Look

Look back at Reading 1 to answer the following questions.

1 A river can be a physical border. True or False? (Par. 1)

2 How did many of the borders in North Africa begin? (Par. 2)
   a The borders followed the rivers, which are very straight.
   b The borders were physical features.
   c The Europeans who controlled North Africa decided on the borders.
   d North African countries decided on their borders when they became independent.

3 What are fish and oil examples of? (Par. 4)
   a Products that you must pay tax on
   b Products that cross borders
   c Physical features
   d Natural resources

4 Match the beginning of a sentence in Column A with its correct ending in Column B. (Pars. 4 and 5)

Column A	Column B
_c_ 1 No country controls the water that is	a within 13.8 miles of the shore.
_a_ 2 Each country owns the ocean	b within 124.3 miles of the shore.
_d_ 3 Every country controls the airspace that is	c more than 124.3 miles from the shore.
_b_ 4 Every country controls natural resources that are	d within 13.8 miles of the border.

5 According to the whole reading, why do governments want to control their borders? Circle four answers.

(a) They want to know who is entering the country.

b They want to know who is leaving the county.

(c) They want to know what is entering the country.

(d) They want to collect taxes.

(e) They don't want other countries to use their natural resources.

Skill Review ~Habilidades ~stratigis

> In Skills and Strategies 1, you learned several strategies to help you figure out the meaning of new words. You were told to look for words, phrases, and punctuation that signal a definition. You were also told that sometimes you may find the word defined in a sentence that follows.

A Find the words and phrases in the left-hand column of the chart in Reading 1. Put a check (✓) next to the type of clue the writer gave in the text to help readers understand the meanings.

WORD OR PHRASE	OR	THAT IS + DEFINITION / IN OTHER WORDS + DEFINITION	PUNCTUATION	DEFINITION IN A SENTENCE THAT FOLLOWS
physical border (*n*) Par. 1				✓
political borders (*n*) Par. 2				✓
check (*v*) Par. 3		✓		
tax (*n*) Par. 3	✓	✓		
shore (*n*) Par. 4			✓	

B Work with a partner and define the words in the chart. Explain where you found the definitions.

Definitions

Find the words in Reading 1 that complete the following definitions.

1 Something that you can see or touch is _physical_. (adj) Par. 1

2 _features_ are an important part of something and are easy to notice. (n pl) Par. 1

3 A/ An _straigt line_ line is the closest distance from one place to another place. (adj) Par. 2

4 To _control_ something is to have power over it. (v) Par. 3

5 A person who has government responsibility is a/an _officials_ (n pl) Par. 3

6 _resources_ are valuable things that belong to a person, group, or country. (n pl) Par. 4

7 The air or sky above a country is its _air space_. (n) Par. 5

8 If you allow people to do something, you give them _permission_ to do it. (n) Par. 5

Synonyms

Complete the sentences with words from Reading 1 in the box below. These words replace the words or phrases in parentheses, which are similar in meaning.

area ✓	checked ✓	freely ✓	shore ✓
borders ✓	cross ✓	requested ✓	tax ✓

1 The officials (looked over) _checked_ the travelers' papers.

2 There is a/an (place) _area_ in the store where children can play while their parents shop.

3 The children picked up rocks as they walked along the (land by the ocean) _shore_.

4 The student (asked) _requested_ permission to take the test on a different day.

5 You should always look in both directions before you (go to the other side of) _cross_ the street.

6 In some countries people cannot move around (easily) _freely_. They must ask permission to go from one city to another.

7 Some countries have had wars about their (lines between countries) _borders_.

8 In many cities, you must pay a/ an (money for the government) _tax_ on cigarettes.

Critical Thinking

In Reading 1, you learned that most countries today have national borders. However, there is one place in the world that still has no national borders – Antarctica. Antarctica has many natural resources. Perhaps in the future, the most powerful countries at the time may want to divide up Antarctica and divide up its resources.

> **APPLYING INFORMATION**
>
> You use critical thinking skills when you apply information you have just learned to new situations.

A Work in small groups. Imagine it is the future – the year 2200. You have been sent by the four most powerful countries in the world (decide which countries these will be) to help divide Antarctica into physical borders. Decide where the borders should go. Draw lines on the map.

B Explain your group's decision to the other groups in your class.

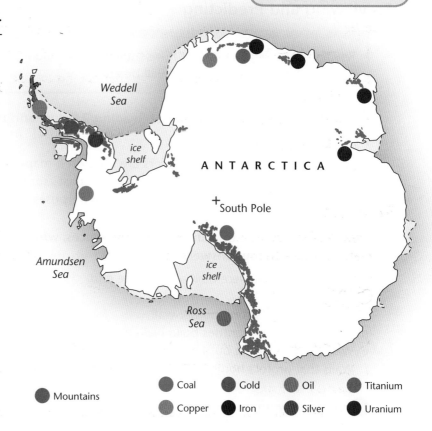

Research

Find a map of your own country or a country you know well. Study the borders. Look for any physical borders, like mountains or rivers. Find answers to the following questions.

- Which countries share a border with the country you chose to research?
- Are there any physical borders? What are they?
- What is the history of the borders?

Writing

Write a short description of the borders in the country you researched.

Connecting to the Topic

Discuss the following questions with a partner.

1 Where are some famous border walls? Think about the past and more recent times.
2 Why do you think countries built walls on their borders in the past?
3 Why do you think countries build walls on their borders today?

Previewing and Predicting

> Reading the title and the first few sentences of a reading can give you a good idea of what the whole reading will be about.

A Read the first four sentences of Reading 2 below and the title of the reading on page 13.

> Today, most national borders are lines on a map. Two countries agree on the line between them. However, in the past, some countries had walls or fences on their borders. Walls had several purposes.

B After reading the title and the four sentences, what do you think this reading will be about? Circle four answers.

a Border walls that were built a long time ago
b Famous walls
c How to build a strong border wall
d The reason that countries build walls at their borders
e Walls that are at the border of some countries today
f Walls that protect homes

C Compare your answers with a partner's.

While You Read

As you read, stop at the end of each sentence that contains words in **bold**. Then follow the instructions in the box in the margin.

Walls as Borders

1   Today, most national borders are lines on a map. Two countries agree on the line between them. However, in the past, some countries had walls or fences on their borders. Walls had several purposes. They helped prevent invasions, that is, the arrival of enemies. Walls were also a good way to make money. There were often only a few entrances in a wall. People had to pay taxes when they went through these entrances. In more **recent** times, walls also have had other purposes. These days, some walls prevent people from leaving their country. Other walls stop people from entering a country. These people are often looking for jobs and are hoping for a better life on the other side of the wall.

2   Two of the most famous walls in history are the Great Wall of China and Hadrian's Wall. The Great Wall of China is 5,500 miles (8,850 kilometers) long and more than 29.5 feet (9 meters) wide in some places. The Chinese built it to stop invaders from entering China. Along the top of the wall, there were thousands of **guards**. These guards were men who could see anyone who came near the wall. In England, the Romans built Hadrian's Wall in the second century CE. Like the Great Wall of China, its major purpose was also to stop invaders. However, that was not its only purpose. The other reason was money: People had to pay a tax to the Romans when they came through Hadrian's Wall.

3   The most famous wall in recent history was the Berlin Wall. After World War II, East and West Germany became separate, that is, they became two different countries. The Soviet Union controlled East Germany and the eastern part of Berlin. At first, people could still travel between East and West Berlin. However, the Soviet Union wanted to stop this, so in 1961, it built the Berlin Wall. The purpose of this wall was not to stop invaders or get money from taxes. It was

WHILE YOU READ ❶
Look in the next sentence for a definition of *recent*. Highlight it.

WHILE YOU READ ❷
Look in the next sentence to help you guess the meaning of *guards*. What do guards do?
a) Keep people safe
b) Build walls

The Great Wall of China stopped invaders from entering China.

to prevent the people of East Berlin from leaving. On August 13, 1961, all travel between East and West Berlin suddenly stopped. No one could cross the border. Some people tried to climb over the wall, but this was dangerous. East German guards shot some of these people. More than 100 people were killed trying to cross the border before the Berlin Wall came down in 1989.

A guard at the Berlin Wall prevents people from crossing the border.

4   Today, the newest walls are electronic. For example, many people attempt to enter the United States from Mexico without permission every year. Many of these people are searching for jobs in the United States. The United States has tried to stop them with fences and walls at the border. However, the border is very long, and in some places there are no physical walls or fences. In some of those places, the government wants to build an electronic fence. An **electronic fence** is a group of computers and cameras that can tell the guards when people are crossing the border, so the guards can stop them.

WHILE YOU READ 3

Look in the rest of this sentence for a definition of *electronic fence*. Highlight it.

5   There are still walls and fences in many countries around the world. They are often in places where there are wars or other problems. Walls and fences **divide** people. Often people with more money and easier lives are on one side. Poorer people with more difficult lives are on the other side. However, walls and fences cannot always prevent people from crossing the border. The fence at the Mexican border does not stop a lot of people. Government officials believe that half a million people enter the United States from Mexico without permission every year. People who want a better life will continue to try to cross borders.

WHILE YOU READ 4

Find clues in the next two sentences for a definition of *divide*. Highlight the clues.

People cross into the United States without permission every day.

Main Idea Check

The main idea of a reading is what the whole reading is about.

Which sentence gives the main idea of Reading 2?

a Walls can stop people from entering a country.

b Walls and fences help governments make money and keep people safe.

c The most famous walls in history are the Great Wall of China and the Berlin Wall.

d In the past and today, walls at borders have had different purposes.

A Closer Look

Look back at Reading 2 to answer the following questions.

1 Which of the following is *not* a purpose for a wall on a border? (Par. 1)

a Walls can give people a better life.

b Walls stop enemies from entering the country.

c Walls stop people from leaving the country.

d Walls help the government collect money from people when they enter the country.

2 Hadrian's Wall protected China in the second century CE. **True or False?** (Par. 2)

3 Which of the following statements is correct? Circle two answers. (Par. 3)

a East German guards killed some people who tried to climb over the wall.

b The Soviet Union killed some Germans who tried to enter East Berlin.

c The wall stopped invaders from the Soviet Union.

d The purpose of the wall was to stop travel between East and West Berlin.

e The Berlin Wall was built during World War II.

4 What is the main reason why many people try to enter the United States from Mexico when they do not have permission? (Par. 4)

a They don't like living in Mexico.

b They think the wall is unfair.

c They don't want to pay taxes in Mexico.

d They want to find jobs in the United States.

5 Which of the following will you find at an electronic fence? Circle two answers. (Par. 4)

a Cameras

b Guns

c Metal wires

d Computers

e Lights

6 Match the name of the wall in the left column to the purpose of the wall in the right column. One wall has two purposes.

Wall

_c_ 1 The Great Wall of China

_d_ 2 Hadrian's Wall

_a_ 3 The Berlin Wall

_b_ 4 Fences on the Mexico-United States border

Purpose

a to stop people from leaving

b to stop people from entering without permission

c to stop enemy invaders

d to make money from taxes

Skill Review

> In Skills and Strategies 1, you learned that different clues can help you figure out the meaning of new words. You also learned that sometimes you need to look in a sentence after the new word to find its meaning.

A The sentences with the words in **bold** are from Reading 2. Which sentences have clues that signal the meaning of the words in **bold**? Which sentences give the definition in the next sentence without a clue? Choose the correct answer.

1 They helped prevent **invasions**, that is, the arrival of enemies. Walls were also a good way to make money.
   (a) First sentence has a clue
   b Second sentence has a definition

2 However, that was the not its only **purpose**. The other reason was money.
   a First sentence has a clue
   (b) Second sentence has a definition

3 After World War II, East and West Germany became **separate**, that is, they became two different countries. The Soviet Union controlled East Germany and the eastern part of Berlin.
   (a) First sentence has a clue
   b Second sentence has a definition

4 East German guards **shot** some of these people. More than 100 people were killed trying to cross the border before the Berlin Wall came down in 1989.
   a First sentence has a clue
   (b) Second sentence has a definition

B Highlight the definition for each word in **bold** in **A** above.

Definitions

Find the words in Reading 2 that complete the following definitions.

1 To _agree_ about something is to think the same thing about it. (v) Par. 1

2 _fences_ are walls made of metal or wood. (n pl) Par. 1

3 _separate_ things are more than two things. (adj) Par. 1

4 People who work against other people and try to hurt them are _enemies_.
(n pl) Par. 1

5 Something that happened a short time ago is _recent_. (adj) Par. 1

6 To _prevent_ something is to stop it from happening. (v) Par. 3

7 When something happens very quickly, it happens _suddenly_. (adv) Par. 3

8 Machines that use computers or parts of computers are _electronic_.
(adj) Par. 4

Words in Context

Complete the sentences with words from Reading 2 in the box below.

attempt	entrance	invasion	purpose
divide	guards	major	searched

1 The _guards_ stood at the door and stopped the people from entering.

2 Dogs _searched_ for the man who was lost in the mountains.

3 The _purpose_ of the new machine is to make our work easier.

4 There was a/(an) _invasion_ by an army of 20,000 men.

5 Mountains _divide_ the country into two parts.

6 She stood at the _entrance_ of her house and said hello to her friends when
they arrived.

7 The teacher explained the two _major_ causes of the war.

8 Travelers should not _attempt_ to climb mountains during the winter.

Critical Thinking

In Reading 2 the writer claims that people cross borders "hoping for a better life."

A Look at these paintings of people climbing over walls and fences. They are on a fence that is on the border between Mexico and the United States. (In the third picture, the word *AMOR* means *love*.) How do these paintings illustrate the writer's claim?

CLARIFYING CONCEPTS

Critical thinking includes exploring an idea in a text by thinking about how it would fit in a different context.

Source: Mark Ehrman *Borders and Barriers*

B Work in a small group and answer the following questions.

1 Do you think people hoping for a better life should be allowed to enter another country?

2 Do you think they can be prevented from doing so? How?

Research

Find out if there are any fences or walls on the border of your country or a country that you know well. Find answers to the following questions.

● What is the purpose of the wall or fence?

● When was it built?

● How successful has it been?

Writing

Write a short summary of your research. Describe the wall or fence and its history.

Finding the Topic of a Paragraph

Most paragraphs have one topic. The topic is the general subject of the paragraph. It is what the paragraph is about. Usually you can find the topic at the beginning of the paragraph. Sometimes, however, you will have to read the whole paragraph to find the topic. Finding the topic of a paragraph is an important reading skill.

Examples & Explanations

Today people cross national borders much more often than they did 100 years ago. Cars and planes help us move easily from one country to another. You can get on a plane and a few hours later arrive in another country on the other side of the world.

The topic is often at the beginning of the paragraph. In this paragraph, the topic is *crossing national borders*.

However, this easy movement can also cause problems. The spread of disease is the most serious problem. When people move around the world, diseases sometimes move with them. As a result, at many borders, government officials check to see if travelers are sick. Sick travelers may have to see a doctor or take some medicine before they can enter the country.

The topic is not always in the first sentence. The first sentence in this paragraph says there are problems, but the second sentence gives the topic: *the spread of disease*. In addition, many of the words in this paragraph, such as *sick*, *doctor*, and *medicine*, give clues to the topic. These words can help you understand that the topic is *the spread of disease*.

One example of this is SARS. In 2003, this serious disease appeared in China. It spread quickly around Asia and to Canada. More than 8,000 people became sick and more than 700 people died. Government officials at borders around the world checked travelers, especially from China and Canada, to see if they were sick. Travelers with SARS were prevented from entering the country.

The topics of the first two paragraphs are *crossing borders* and *disease*. In this paragraph, there are a lot of specific details about one disease. The topic of this paragraph is *the spread of a disease called SARS*.

Strategies

These strategies will help you find the topic of a paragraph while you read.

- As you read the paragraph, ask yourself: *What is this paragraph about?*
- Pay attention to the first sentence. It often gives the topic of the paragraph.
- Look for words and phrases that are all connected to the same topic. They can help you figure out the topic of the whole paragraph.

Skill Practice 1

Read the following paragraphs. Then look at the four possible topic choices for the paragraph. Circle the best choice. Discuss your answers with a partner.

1   In the early 1800s, many people came to the United States from different countries. These people are called immigrants. The United States wanted immigrants to come to work on farms and in factories. The government did not check the immigrants' health. In the 1880s, the number of immigrants increased quickly. The government began to worry about diseases. It worried that the immigrants were bringing diseases.

Topic:
a The history of immigration
b Health and immigration
c Immigrant workers
d Health in the United States

2   In 1891, the government began to check the health of all immigrants. There were doctors and hospitals at the border. The largest number of immigrants – about 70 percent of them – came through New York, so the largest hospital was there. The doctors looked for two kinds of diseases. The first were dangerous diseases that might spread from one person to another. The second were diseases that might prevent the person from working. The government only wanted immigrants who were healthy enough to work hard.

Topic:
a Immigrants in New York
b Checking immigrants' health
c Dangerous diseases
d Government doctors on the U.S. border

3   If immigrants had either of these kinds of diseases, they could not enter the country. If the doctors believed that the people would get better, they sent them to a hospital. They stayed in the hospital until they were healthy again. Their friends and families had to wait for them. If the doctors believed the immigrants would not get better, sometimes they sent them back to their countries.

Topic:
a Immigrants with diseases
b Immigrant families
c Two diseases
d Immigration and immigrants

Skill Practice 2

Read the following paragraphs. After each paragraph, stop and think about the topic. Then write the topic on the blank line.

1   Computer chips are very small, but they can store a lot of information. Many credit cards and passports have computer chips inside of them. These are called *smart cards*. Look at a credit card. It may have a black line on the back. Computers can read this black line. It tells the computer a lot of important information.

Topic: _Computer Chips_

2   Many people use passwords. A password is a secret number, word, or group of letters and numbers. You may use a password to get into your computer, your bank, or the school library. You should never use your telephone number or birthday as your password because other people may know them. You should also choose different passwords for different purposes. Have you ever forgotten a password? When people have a lot of different passwords, they sometimes forget them.

Topic: _Pass word_

3   People often worry about their pet dogs and cats. They worry that their pet will run away or get lost. How will they be able to find their pet? Some pets wear something around their necks that has information about them. For example, the information might give the pet's name and address. What happens if the pet loses this information? The pet may never come home. Because some people worry about this, they put a computer chip under their pet's skin. The chip has the information about the pet. If someone finds the pet, a computer can read the information on the chip. This helps the dog or cat return home.

Topic: _about pets and information_

Connecting to the Topic

Discuss the following questions with a partner.

1 What usually happens when people cross a border into a different country? Do they have to show anything to the officials at the border? Do they have to answer any questions? Can they take what they want with them over the border?

2 Have you or someone you know ever had an unusual experience crossing a border? What happened? *He had to drink water in the desert from some holes that had dirty water*

Previewing and Predicting

> When you preview a reading, look to see if it has sections. Also, look to see if the sections have headings. Read the headings and think about why the writer divided the reading in this way.

He wants to explciand step by step

A Read the section headings in Reading 3. Decide what you will read about in each section. Then write the number of the section (*I–III*) next to the topic that best describes it.

SECTION	TOPIC
II	Using fingerprints to identify people as they cross the border
III	How our grandchildren may go from country to country
III	Using eyes to identify people as they cross the border
I	Passports
I	Documents you may need to enter different countries

B Compare your answers with a partner's.

While You Read

As you read, stop at the end of each sentence that contains words in **bold**. Then follow the instructions in the box in the margin.

◄)) Border Control

I. Documents at the Border

1   What happens when you cross a national border? The answer is not the same in every country. When you enter most countries, you need a **passport** ⊖ a document that governments give to their citizens that allows them to travel to other countries. Passports include important information such as name, birth date, and birthplace. Most passports also include a photograph. When you enter most countries, you must show a passport. However, this is not true for many countries in Europe. When Europeans cross a national border between most countries in the European Union, they do not need to show a passport.

WHILE YOU READ ❶

Find a clue in this sentence that signals a definition of *passport*. Highlight the clue.

Passport control at an airport

2   A passport is not the only type of travel document. A visa is another important travel document. <u>Many countries require travelers to have a visa when they enter</u>. The type of visa depends on which country you come from and the reason for your visit. There are several types of visas. If you go for a brief visit, you may need a tourist visa. If you want to study, you need a student visa. If you want to find a job in the country, **you probably need a business or work visa**.

WHILE YOU READ ❷

What is the topic of paragraph 2? Highlight the word or words that name the topic.

II. New Technology at the Border

3   Government officials at national borders look very carefully at passports and visas. They want to be sure that the people who are entering the country are not dangerous. They use technology to help them decide who may enter the country. For example, when travelers enter the country, officials at the border check their computers for important information about these travelers. They can check if travelers have been in the country before and if they have done anything wrong. Officials also examine the traveler's documents to see if they are real. Some people try to cross the border without permission. They use fake passports or visas. Officials at the border can use computer technology to check whether these documents are real or fake.

4   Technology has been helpful in other ways, too. In the second half of the twentieth century, passports were the major form of identification for travelers. Now there are new forms of identification that use technology. One example is a machine that can read fingerprints. When travelers enter the country, they put their fingers on a machine that **scans** them. In other words, the machine takes a picture of the fingerprints and saves the picture in a computer. It can also send the picture to government officials who are far from the border. Those officials can compare the picture to fingerprints of many other people. If the traveler's fingerprints are the same as fingerprints of a dangerous person, the traveler may not enter the country. This technology is now in use at many airports all over the world.

WHILE YOU READ ❸

Find a clue in the next sentence that signals a definition of *scan*. Highlight the clue and the definition.

A fingerprint

5   One person's fingerprints are different from another person's fingerprints. Therefore, many countries use fingerprints as a good form of identification. However, it is possible to trick the machines that scan them. In 2008, a woman at a Japanese airport put tape on her fingers. The tape had another person's fingerprints on it, so she was able to enter Japan without permission.

6   As a result of these problems, some airports are using another part of the body for identification – **the iris**. The iris is the colored part of the eye. New machines can scan travelers' irises and save the pictures. Several airports are already using this technology, including airports in London and Qatar. Irises work better than fingerprints for identification. The iris has hundreds of very small lines in it. These lines are **unique**. In other words, everyone's iris is different. Even twins have different irises. These new forms of technology have another advantage. They are fast. This makes lines at airports and borders shorter and helps travelers move more quickly.

WHILE YOU READ ❹

Look in the next sentence for a definition of *iris*. Highlight it.

WHILE YOU READ ❺

Find a clue in the next sentence that signals a definition of *unique*. Highlight the clue and the definition.

An iris

III. Crossing Borders in the Future

7   Passports, visas, fingerprint scans, and iris scans are all forms of identification that governments can use today. Sometime in the future, there might be new forms of identification. You will not need paper documents. You may not need to scan your fingers or eyes. You

will store all of your important information on a computer chip. This computer chip will be inside a small card, or perhaps under your skin. Computers will quickly read, save, and send the information on the card when you **cross the border**.

8   Long ago, there were no national borders. People moved around freely. They moved to find food or somewhere to live. They did not think about borders or documents. Some people believe that in the future, national borders will become less important. Some borders may disappear. People will move freely again. They will travel quickly and easily around the world for education, for work, or simply to see new places.

WHILE YOU READ 6

What is the topic of paragraph 7? Highlight the words that name the topic.

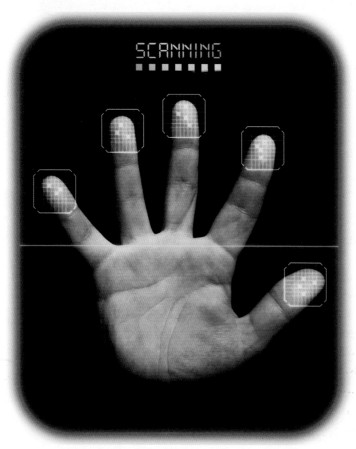

New technology will help travelers cross borders more quickly in the future.

Main Idea Check

The main idea of a reading is what the whole reading is about.

Which sentence gives the main idea of Reading 3?

a Paper documents are not important anymore.

b It is important to have correct documents when you cross a national border.

c In the future, there will be no national borders.

d The way that officials check travelers at the borders is changing.

A Closer Look

Look back at Reading 3 to answer the following questions.

1 Which of the following is *not* information on most passports? (Par. 1)

a Birth date

b Birthplace

c Name

d Address

e Photograph

2 If you want to visit a country for one week, what kind of visa will you probably need? (Par. 2)

a A student visa

b A business visa

c A traveler's visa

d A tourist visa

3 According to section II, how has technology helped government officials? Circle three answers.

a Computers can check if travelers have done anything wrong.

b Machines can scan travelers' eyes.

c Computers can make fake documents.

d Computers can tape travelers' fingerprints.

e Machines can scan travelers' fingerprints.

4 What happens if computers show that a traveler's fingerprints are the same as fingerprints of a dangerous person? (Par. 4)

a The traveler needs a new passport.

b The traveler must have an iris scan.

c The traveler may not enter the country.

d The traveler must give his passport to officials at the border.

5 How did the woman at the Japanese airport trick the fingerprint scanner? (Par. 5)

a Her fingerprints were not on her passport.

b She used a fake passport.

c She taped another person's fingerprints onto her fingers.

d She used the iris scanner instead of the fingerprint scanner.

6 Twins have the same lines in their irises. **True or False?** (Par. 6)

7 Reread paragraphs 5 and 6. What are three reasons why iris scanners may be better than fingerprint scanners?

   a Iris records are easier to store on computers.
   (b) They are harder to trick.
   (c) They are faster.
   d They are cheaper.
   (e) Irises are unique; fingerprints are not.

8 According to paragraph 7, what might be the next step in technology at borders? (Par. 7)

   a Borders will disappear.
   (b) People will store all their information on a computer chip.
   c People will move freely everywhere.
   d Passports will disappear.

• Skill Review

> In Skills and Strategies 2, you learned that every paragraph has a topic. You also learned that it is an important reading skill to be able to identify what the topic of a paragraph is.

A Look back in Reading 3, and then match the topic of paragraphs 1–7 (note that the concluding paragraph 8 is not included) to the list below. Write the number of the correct paragraph on the blank line. Three items in the list will not be used.

1 __1__ Checking documents
2 __7__ Forms of identification in the future
3 __1__ Passports
4 __4__ Countries without border checks
5 __4__ Fingerprint scanning
6 __1__ Visas
7 __2__ Border officials
8 __5__ Someone who tricked the fingerprint scanner
9 _____ Long lines at the border
10 __6__ Iris scanning

B Compare your answers with a partner's.

Definitions

Find the words in Reading 3 that complete the following definitions.

1 (A) An _Document_ is an official piece of paper. (*n*) Par. 1

2 Your _Identification_ is a card or piece of paper that says who you are. (*n*) Par. 4

3 To _trick_ is to make someone believe something that is not true. (*v*) Par. 5

4 If something is _unique_ there is nothing else that is like it. (*adj*) Par. 6

5 Two brothers, two sisters, or a brother and a sister who are born at the same time are _twins_ . (*n pl*) Par. 6

6 A/An _Advantage_ is something that gives you a better chance of success. (*n*) Par. 6

7 To _store_ is to keep something to look at or use in the future. (*v*) Par. 7

8 When things _disappear_ people can no longer see them. (*v*) Par. 8

Words in Context

Complete the passages with words from Reading 3 in the box below.

brief	depends on	fake	technology
citizens	examine	requires	tourists

1   When you arrive at an airport in a different country, often you must wait in line to enter the country. There are usually two lines. The first is for _citizens_ , that
a
is, people who live in that country. The second line is for _tourists_ , who are
b
visiting the country, as well as students and people who have come for business reasons. Sometimes you have to wait a long time, but if you are lucky, your wait will be _brief_ . This _depends on_ the number of planes that land at the
c   d
same time.

2   Travel to another country usually _requires_ a passport. Today's passports
e
use new computer _technology_ . If you _examine_ a passport very
f   g
carefully, you will see very thin lines. These lines have information that a computer can read. The computer uses this information to tell if the passport is real or if it is
fake .
h

Academic Word List

The following are Academic Word List words from all the readings in Unit 1. Use these words to complete the sentences. (For more on the Academic Word List, see page 260.)

areas (n) ✓	features (n)	major (adj) ✓	requires (v) ✓	technology (n) ✓
documents (n) ✓	identification (n) ✓	physical (adj) ✓	resources (n) ✓	unique (adj) ✓

1 She put important _documents_, such as her passport, under her bed.

2 The country's most important natural _resources_ are oil, gas, and gold.

3 _technology_, especially the use of computers, has changed many things in business, government, and education.

4 A trip to Antarctica _requires_ a lot of warm clothes.

5 Scientists said the fish was _unique_. It was the only one in the world.

6 There were different _areas_ in the classroom. Some were for quiet work, and others were for discussion.

7 All citizens must carry a/an _identification_ card when they leave the country.

8 One of the most famous _features_ of Egypt is the Nile River.

9 During the twentieth century, there were several _major_ wars.

10 As children grow, their _physical_ abilities increase. They can run, jump, and throw things.

Critical Thinking

In Reading 3, the writer says that in the future, there will be powerful technology at borders, borders will become easier to cross, and one day, borders may even disappear.

(A) **Work with a partner and decide if there is enough information to support the writer's point by answering the following questions. Give reasons for your answers, and take notes on your discussion.**

> **EVALUATING INFORMATION**
>
> Critical thinkers ask themselves if there is enough information to support the points a writer makes in a text.

1 Does the writer explain what type of powerful technology there might be at the borders in the future? What type do you imagine there will be?

2 Does the writer explain why it will become easier to cross borders in the future? Do you think it will become easier to cross borders in the future or more difficult?

3 Does the writer explain why borders might disappear in the future? Do you think there will be a time in the future when borders disappear?

(B) **Work with another pair of students. Compare your answers and the reasons you gave for your answers.**

Research

Find out about border control in your country or a country that you know well. Find answers to the following questions.

- Who needs a visa to visit this country?
- Do citizens of the country need a visa to visit other countries?
- What sort of technology is used at the borders of the country?

Writing

Write a short summary of your research. Describe border control in the country you researched.

Improving Your Reading Speed

Good readers read quickly and still understand most of what they read.

(A) Read the instructions and strategies for Improving Your Reading Speed in Appendix 3 on page 273.

(B) Choose one of the readings in this unit. Read it without stopping. Time how long it takes you to finish the text in minutes and seconds. Enter the time in the chart on page 274. Then calculate your reading speed in number of words per minute.

PRONOUN CONNECTORS

Writers use pronouns to connect words and ideas within and across sentences. Pronouns make the writing shorter and less repetitive. However, pronouns give the reader extra work to do because the reader has to find the words and ideas that the pronouns refer to.

Some common pronouns are

| he | she | it | they | this | that | these | those |

When you see a pronoun, ask yourself: *What does this pronoun refer to?*

In the following example, the pronoun is in **bold**, and the noun it refers to is underlined. The arrow shows the connection.

Government officials work at the border. **They** check all passports.

In the next example, the pronoun is in **bold**, and the idea it refers to is underlined. The arrow shows that the pronoun refers to the whole idea in the first sentence.

There was a long line of trucks and cars at the border crossing. **This** delayed the tour bus for 3 hours.

Exercise 1

Read the following groups of sentences. Highlight the pronoun in the second sentence in each group. Underline the noun or ideas the pronoun refers to. Draw an arrow from the pronoun to the underlined items. The first one has been done for you.

1 I gave my passport to the official. He examined the photo carefully.

2 Everyone is required to show some kind of identification. The guard at the entrance will ask for it.

3 All the documents are electronic. They are stored on one computer.

4 There were three attempts to guess the password. They all failed.

5 Each person's iris is unique. That is the reason irises are good forms of identification.

6 There were separate lines for visitors and citizens. This made it faster for citizens to come back into the country.

Exercise 2

Make a clear paragraph by putting sentences A, B, and C into the best order after the numbered sentence. Look for pronouns to help you. Write the letters in the correct order on the blank lines.

1 The fence along the border prevents people from entering. ____ ____ ____

| A These help officials see if anyone is trying to come across the fence at night. | B It is very high and has a lot of lights. | C That is the time when most people try to cross the border without permission. |

2 All Americans need to know about recent changes at the Mexican border.

____ ____ ____

| A They began in January. | B The most important change affects American tourists. | C They now have to show passports as identification instead of drivers' licenses. |

3 Tourists should check the government website before they travel. ____ ____ ____

| A These could make travel in those countries difficult for foreign citizens. | B This helps people understand when there are dangerous political situations. | C It has information about safety in different countries. |

4 The invasion was a complete surprise. ____ ____ ____

| A Enemy soldiers crossed the border at night. | B They took control of the major city. | C It happened suddenly, with no warning. |

5 The information is stored on a computer chip in your passport. ____ ____ ____

| A They worry that someone with the right technology can steal the information. | B A computer can then scan it when you go through customs. | C Some people don't like this. |

2 NAMES

SKILLS AND STRATEGIES

- Noticing Parts of Words
- Finding the Main Idea of a Paragraph

Noticing Parts of Words

One way to understand the meaning of a word you don't know is to notice the parts of the word. Sometimes a group of letters is added to the beginning or the end of a word to change its meaning. A group of letters added to the beginning of a word is called a *prefix*. A prefix creates a new word. A group of letters added to the end of a word is called a *suffix*. A suffix can tell you what part of speech a word is. For example, it can tell you if the word is a *noun*, a *verb*, or an *adjective*. Good readers can use prefixes and suffixes to help them figure out a word's meaning.

Examples & Explanations

↳ ___ mechanic ___
Prefix   suffix

I have an **un**usual name. People often **mis**pronounce it.

When a prefix is added to a word, it creates a new word. This new word has a new and different meaning.

unusual = not usual
mispronounce = pronounce the wrong way

The teach**er** asked for his name and checked his identifica**tion**.

Many suffixes help you identify nouns.

teacher = a person who teaches
identification = someone or something used to identify

Many cities are named after other cities that are more fam**ous**. Twenty-three towns in the United States are named after the beauti**ful** city of Paris, France.

Suffixes also help you identify adjectives.

famous = having fame
beautiful = full of beauty

They want to moder**nize** the name of their store. They are going to short**en** it to GT.

Suffixes also help you identify verbs.

modernize = make modern
shorten = make short

The Language of Prefixes and Suffixes

Here are some common prefixes and suffixes and their meanings.

PREFIXES	NOUN SUFFIXES	ADJECTIVE SUFFIXES	VERB SUFFIXES
in-, un-, dis- not	*-er, -ist, -or* a person or thing that does something	*-al, -an, -ish, -ous* related to something or from somewhere	*-en, -ify, -ize* make or cause something to be
inter- between	*-tion, -ment* an action, idea, or process	*-less* without something	
mis- wrong	*-ness* quality or condition	*-ful, -y* full of or having a lot of something	
re- again, back			

Strategies

These strategies will help you notice parts of words. They will help you understand the meanings of words while you read.

- Study and learn the meanings of the prefixes and suffixes in the chart.
- To learn more prefixes and suffixes, find a dictionary or a source on the Internet that lists prefixes and suffixes.
- If you see a word you don't know, notice if the word has a prefix or a suffix.
- If the word has a prefix, see if the prefix helps you understand the meaning of the word.
- If the word has a suffix, see if the suffix helps you identify the word as a noun (a person or thing), an adjective (a description of a person or thing), or a verb (an action).
- Look at the whole sentence. Notice how the word connects to the other words and the general meaning of the sentence.

Skill Practice 1

Read the following sentences, and notice the different parts of the words in bold. Highlight any prefixes or suffixes you see in the words. The first one has been done for you.

1 The **actor** changed his name after he became famous.

2 The baby's parents **disagreed** about what to name their baby.

3 The teacher was **careless** and always called his students by the wrong names.

4 They **renamed** their store last year, but everyone still calls it by its old name.

5 The **unofficial** name of their football team is the "Green Men."

6 Their name was difficult to spell, so they decided to **simplify** it.

7 In some **African** countries, the day when you are born becomes part of your name.

8 Some **interstate** highways in the United States are named after famous people.

Skill Practice 2

Read the sentences in Skill Practice 1 again. Look at the prefixes or suffixes you highlighted in each sentence. Then figure out the definitions for the words in bold. Write the definitions on the blank lines. The first one has been done for you.

1 The **actor** changed his name after he became famous.

   actor = _a person who acts_

2 The baby's parents **disagreed** about what to name their baby.

   disagreed = _____

3 The teacher was **careless** and always called his students by the wrong names.

   careless = _____

4 They **renamed** their store last year, but everyone still calls it by its old name.

   renamed = _____

5 The **unofficial** name of their football team is the "Green Men."

   unofficial = _____

6 Their name was difficult to spell, so they decided to **simplify** it.

   simplify = _____

7 In some **African** countries, the day when you are born becomes part of your name.

   African = _____

8 Some **interstate** highways in the United States are named after famous people.

   interstate = _____

Connecting to the Topic

Discuss the following questions with a partner.

1 What is your full name? *Valeria*

2 Which part of your name is your family name? *I don't have idea*

3 Does your family name come first or last? *first*

4 Does your name mean something? If so, what does it mean? *No*

5 How did you get your name? *My parents*

Previewing and Predicting

> The first thing that you look at before you start reading is usually the title. You should then quickly look at any art, such as photos and drawings. If the art has a caption next to it, read that, too. Also look at any graphic material, such as charts, tables, and graphs. Looking quickly at all these elements helps you predict what a text will be about. This will help you understand the text when you read it more carefully.

A **Look at the title and the photograph on page 38, and read the caption next to the photo. Then put a check (✓) next to the topic or topics that you think might be in the reading.**

_____✓_ a The history and origin of names

_____ b Names of famous people

_____ c How to say people's names

_____✓_ d Common names around the world

_____ e The scientific study of names

_____✓_ f Differences in names around the world

B **Now look at Table 2.1 on page 39. Put a check (✓) next to any other topics in A that you think might be in the reading.**

C **Compare your answers with a partner's.**

While You Read

As you read, stop at the end of each sentence that contains words in bold. Then follow the instructions in the box in the margin.

Where Does Your Name Come From?

1   Naming customs are different around the world. For example, not everyone has the same number of names. In some countries, such as Indonesia, many people have just one name. In most cultures, however, people have at least two names: a family name and a **given name**. Your given name is the name you receive when you are born. Your family name is the name you share with other people in your family.

2   In the United States, the family name is often called the *last name*, and the given name is often called the *first name*. However, the order of the two names is not the same everywhere. For example, in many Asian countries, the family name is first and the given name is second. **When** two people from different cultures meet, sometimes they use the incorrect name. This can cause embarrassment.

3   Family names can show something about a family's early history. The origin of many English family names is a place, like *London*, or a job, such as *Farmer* or *Shoemaker*. A long time ago, these families probably worked as farmers or shoemakers. Swedish and Danish family names often mean son of ___. For example, Johansson means son of Johan. In South Korea, there are only about 250 family names. These names go back hundreds of years to very old **clans**, or large groups of families. About half of all Koreans have one of the three most common family names – Kim, Park, or Lee. This can cause a problem, because many Koreans believe you should not marry a person with the same last name. This means Koreans must be careful whom they fall in love with!

WHILE YOU READ 1

Look in the next sentence for a definition of *given name*. Highlight it.

WHILE YOU READ 2

Look for a word with a prefix in this sentence. Highlight the prefix.

WHILE YOU READ 3

Find a clue in this sentence that signals the definition of *clans*. Highlight the clue and the definition.

People from different countries meet and learn each other's names.

Table 2.1 The World's Most Common Family Names by Country

COUNTRY	MOST COMMON FAMILY NAME	COUNTRY	MOST COMMON FAMILY NAME
Brazil	Silva	Philippines	Cruz
China	Wang	Poland	Nowak
England	Smith	South Korea	Kim
France	Martin	Spain	García
Germany	Müller	Turkey	Öztürk
Japan	Sato	United States	Smith
Mexico	Hernández	Vietnam	Nguyen

Source: Wikipedia

4   **There** is generally no choice about a family name, but there is much more choice about given names. Parents choose their child's name for many different reasons. They may select a name that sounds beautiful or means something special. These names may have meanings like *peaceful* or *happiness*. In some cultures, there may be a connection between children's names and when or how they were born. For example, a Yoruba child in Nigeria might have a name like *Sunday* or *Born on a Sunny Day*. **In** some countries, parents may pay money to a professional baby namer to help them find a good name. They want to find a name that will be lucky for their child.

5   It is also common to give a child a name that is the same as the name of a parent or grandparent. Another common choice is the name of a famous religious person. For example, many Mexicans choose names such as Jesús or María. Many Egyptians have the name of the Muslim leader, Muhammed. Parents may choose the name of a singer or actor. Sometimes names become popular for a short time. For example, some parents in the United States and Kenya chose the name Barack after Barack Obama became the president of the United States. Other parents want a name that is unusual or unique. In China, many people have the same family name, so some parents invent new given names. They want their children to be a little different from other children.

6   There are many different naming customs, and parents all over the world choose their children's names very carefully. Your name may tell something about your history and culture, or it may be unique. It may honor a family member or a famous person. It may have a special meaning. Do you know why your parents chose your name?

WHILE YOU READ 4

What do you think the topic of this paragraph will be?
a) Given names
b) Last names
c) Choosing names

WHILE YOU READ 5

Look for a word with a suffix in this sentence. Highlight the suffix.

Reading Skill Development

Main Idea Check

> The main idea of a reading is what the whole reading is about.

Which sentence gives the main idea of Reading 1?

a The order of names may be different in different countries.
b Parents may have many different ideas when they choose their child's name.
c There are many different naming customs around the world.
d Names have an interesting history.

A Closer Look

Look back at Reading 1 to answer the following questions.

1 Most people have more than two names. **True or False?** (Par. 1)

2 What are two common origins of family names? (Par. 3)
a A job
b A religious leader
c A place
d Something beautiful or special

3 South Korea does not have a lot of family names. Why is this a problem? (Par. 3)
a Soon there will not be enough family names.
b Koreans prefer not to marry a person with the same last name.
c Many Koreans do not like these names.
d Koreans must ask their parents if they want to marry.

4 Some parents pay a professional to help them choose a name. **True** or False? (Par. 4)

5 Why do some parents in China invent new names for the children? (Par. 5)
a They want a name that is easy to remember.
b Many people have the same last name so they want their child's first name to be unusual.
c They don't want to give their children the name of anyone who is famous or well known.
d They want to honor a member of their family.

6 Parents may choose a name for their child for many different reasons. Which reason is *not* given in the reading?
a They want to give the child the name of a religious leader.
b They want to give the child the name of a person in a book.
c They want to give the child a name that sounds beautiful.
d They want to give the child a name of a family member.

Skill Review

In Skills and Strategies 3, you learned that the study of prefixes (at the beginning of words) and suffixes (at the end of words) can often help you figure out the meaning of words you do not know.

A Review the adjective suffixes in the Language of Prefixes and Suffixes box on page 35. Then look back in Reading 1 to find words with an adjective suffix. Fill in the blanks below with the correct words. Highlight the suffixes.

1 from Sweden _Swedish_ (Par. 3)

2 from Korea _Koreans_ (Par. 3)

3 full of care _careful_ (Par. 3)

4 full of peace _peaceful_ (Par. 4)

5 full of sun _Sunny Day_ (Par. 4)

6 related to a profession _proffesional_ (Par. 4)

7 full of luck _lucky_ (Par. 4)

8 from Mexico _Mexicans_ (Par. 5)

9 related to fame _famous_ (Par. 5)

10 related to religion _Religious_ (Par. 5)

B Review the noun suffixes in the Language of Prefixes and Suffixes box on page 35. Then look back in the reading to find words with a noun suffix. Fill in the blanks below with the correct words. Highlight the suffixes.

1 If you don't know the answer to the teacher's question, it can cause _embarrassment_ (Par. 2)

2 The two men had the same last name, but they said there was no family _connection_ between them. (Par. 4)

3 The birth of a child brings parents a great deal of _happiness_ . (Par. 4)

4 The _singer_ on television was only 14 years old! She had a beautiful voice. (Par. 5)

5 The young _actor_ in the movie is very handsome. Girls all over the country want to meet him. (Par. 5)

Vocabulary Development

Definitions

Find the words in Reading 1 that complete the following definitions.

1 To _share_ something is to have the same thing as another person. (v) Par. 1

2 A feeling of discomfort in front of other people is _embarrassment_. (n) Par. 2

3 A/An _common_ name is a very frequent and usual name. (adj) Par. 3

4 If something is _generally_ true, this means it is usually true. (adv) Par. 4

5 To _select_ something is to choose it. (v) Par. 4

6 A/An _professional_ person is someone who uses special knowledge and training in a job. (adj) Par. 4

7 A/An _leader_ is a person who controls a group or country. (n) Par. 5

8 To _invent_ something is to create something new. (v) Par. 5

Words in Context

Complete the sentences with words from Reading 1 in the box below.

clans	customs	lucky	origin
culture	honor	members	popular

1 The most _popular_ girls' name in the United States in 1910 was Mary.

2 My friend named her son Daniel to _honor_ her grandfather.

3 Many English words have a Latin _origin_.

4 Many Native Americans belong to _clans_ that are named after animals, such as bears or spiders.

5 When she went to live in India, she had to learn the rules of a different _culture_.

6 There are many different _customs_ for celebrating the New Year, such as family parties and special food.

7 Many Chinese people like the number eight because they believe it is _lucky_.

8 Many _members_ of her family are doctors, including her mother and her grandfather.

Critical Thinking

In Reading 1, you read about some common ways in which parents choose given names for their children. How would you choose a given name for a child?

> **PERSONALIZING**
>
> Thinking about how new information applies to your own life can help you understand a text better.

A Look at the list of possible reasons below for choosing a child's given name. If you can think of another reason, write it on the blank line for *Other*. Put a check (✓) next to reasons you would use to choose a child's name.

_____ The name has a special meaning in my language.

_____ A member of my family has the same name.

_____ A religious or political figure has the name.

___✓___ The name sounds nice.

_____ The name is lucky

_____ The name is unusual or unique.

_____ The name is popular at the moment.

_____ Other _____

B Work in a small group, and share and explain your answers.

Research

Find out about naming customs in your country or in another country. Find answers to the following questions.

- What are the three most popular family names in the country?
- What is the most popular given name for baby boys in the country today?
- What is the most popular given name for baby girls in the country today?
- What are some of the naming customs in the country?

Writing

Write a short explanation of naming customs in the country you researched. Be sure to give examples.

Connecting to the Topic

Think about the famous people or people you know who have changed their names. Then discuss the following questions with a partner.

1 Why do you think these people changed their names? Write two possible reasons.

a _____

b _____

2 Would you ever change your name? Explain your answer.

Previewing and Predicting

Reading the first sentence in each paragraph can help you to predict what a reading will be about.

A **Below are the first sentences of paragraphs 1–6 in Reading 2. Read these sentences. Then put a check (✓) next to the topics, listed below the sentences, that you think might be in the reading.**

1 Everyone begins life with a name. (Par. 1)

2 Some people change their names when their lives change. (Par. 2)

3 Immigrants may also change their names. (Par. 3)

4 Names that are unusual or different can sometimes make life difficult. (Par. 4)

5 Writers sometimes do not use their own names when they write. (Par. 5)

6 Some people change their names just because they want a change. (Par. 6)

_____ a Famous people who change their names

_____ b Religious reasons for name changes

_____ c How kings choose their names

_____ d Baby names

_____ e Unusual names

_____ f Immigrants' names

_____ g Names in history

B **Compare your answers with a partner's.**

While You Read

As you read, stop at the end of each sentence that contains words in bold. Then follow the instructions in the box in the margin.

◀)) Changing Names

1   Everyone begins life with a name. A name becomes an important part of a person's identity. However, sometimes a person's name changes. There are many reasons for name changes, but the most common reason is marriage. Many women change their family name to their husband's family name when they get married. This has been a tradition in the western part of the world for a long time. However, today it is not unusual for women in those places to want to keep their own family names. Some couples may then use both the husband's and the wife's family name. For example, if Sarah Smith marries William Taylor, she becomes Sarah Smith-Taylor. Her husband becomes William Smith-Taylor.

2   Some people change their names when their lives change. They may take a new name if they change their religion. The American boxer, Muhammad Ali, changed his name from Cassius Clay when he

Jet Li

became a Muslim. Other people change their names when they become famous. Many famous actors have changed their names. They may believe that their name is too ordinary. They want a name that sounds more exciting. Martial arts star Jet Li's original name was Li Lian Jie. Singers often change their names, too. Singer Lady Gaga's original name was Stefani Germanotta.

3   Immigrants may also change their names. (They want their name to sound more like the names in their new country) (They believe it will be easier for them and for their children) to fit in to their new home if their names are not so unusual. During the nineteenth and early twentieth centuries, many immigrants to the United States and parts of Canada gave their children English first names. Some of them also changed their family names. One Polish immigrant with the family name Sochaczewski brought her child to school in New York. The teachers told her the name was too difficult.

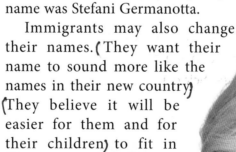

Lady Gaga

> **WHILE YOU READ ①**
> What do you think the topic of this paragraph will be? Highlight a sentence or part of a sentence that gives the topic.

They told her to simplify it or to find a new **name**. She chose her aunt's name, Wachtel, which was easier for the teachers to pronounce. Soon, the entire family changed to the new name.

4   Names that are unusual or different can sometimes make life difficult. Names can reveal a person's religious or ethnic group. As a result, in some places, people with certain names may face **discrimination**. This means it may be difficult for them to get an education, find a job, or find a place to live. During periods of religious or ethnic conflict, some names can become dangerous. Therefore, sometimes people change their name because a different name is safe for them and their family.

5   Writers sometimes do not use their own names when they write. They may not want everyone to know who they are. They want their private lives to stay private. They do not change their names. Instead, they have two different names. They use their real name for their private life and another name – **a pen name** – for writing. Mark Twain, George Orwell, Pablo Neruda, and Voltaire all are pen names.

6   Some people change their names just because they want a change. For example, one person may think his name sounds **childish**. He may want something more serious. Another person may think her name is too serious. She may want a name that sounds more fun and exciting. Finally, there are people who just want to change to silly names. Some recent examples include people who have changed their names to *Superman*, *Happy Birthday*, *Miss Jelly Tots*, *They*, and *Ten Sixty-Nine*.

7   People change their names for many reasons: marriage, a new religion, a new job, a new country, or just for a change. Because a name is an important part of a person's identity, a change in a name can also mean a change in identity.

WHILE YOU READ 2

Look in this sentence for a word with a suffix. Highlight the suffix.

WHILE YOU READ 3

Find a clue in the next sentence that signals the definition of *discrimination*. Highlight the clue and the definition.

WHILE YOU READ 4

Find a clue in this sentence that signals the definition of *pen name*. Highlight the clue and the definition.

WHILE YOU READ 5

Highlight the suffix in *childish*. Is *childish* (a) a noun, (b) a verb, or (c) an adjective?

When a couple gets married, sometimes the woman changes her name.

Main Idea Check

> The main idea of a reading is what the whole reading is about.

Which sentence gives the main idea of Reading 2?

(a) People change their names for many different reasons.
b People need a very good reason to change their names.
c Name changes can happen at different times in life.
d A name change is a serious decision.

A Closer Look

Look back at Reading 2 to answer the following questions.

1 Marriage is the most common reason for a family name change. **True** or False? (Par. 1)

2 What is the reason for a double family name such as Smith-Taylor? (Par. 1)
   a Some women have two family names.
   (b) It includes both the husband's and wife's family names.
   c It shows a family's ethnic or religious group.
   d It shows a wife's identity.

3 Which types of people often change their names? Circle three answers. (Par. 2)
   (a) Immigrants   d Politicians
   (b) Famous actors   (e) Singers
   c Children

4 What are two reasons why an unusual or different name may cause problems?
   (Pars. 3 and 4)
   (a) Other people cannot pronounce unusual names.
   b Other people laugh at people with unusual names.
   (c) People with unusual names may face discrimination.
   d Unusual names are often childish.

5 A name can be dangerous. **True** or False? (Par. 4)

6 What is a pen name? (Par. 5)
   a A name of a famous person   c A name on a writer's pen
   (b) A name that writers use when they write   d A name that stays private

7 According to the whole reading, why do people change their names? Circle four answers.
   (a) People want a name that is more exciting.
   (b) People want a name that is easier to say.
   c People want a name that reveals their identity.
   (d) People want a name that matches their new religion.
   (e) People want a name that is safer than their original name.

Skill Review

In Skills and Strategies 3, you learned about different parts of words, such as prefixes and suffixes. Understanding prefixes and suffixes can help you figure out the meaning of new words. It is important for other reasons, too. When you learn words that have prefixes and suffixes that belong to words that you already know, you can increase the size of your vocabulary.

A The words in **bold** are from Readings 1 and 2. Use the prefixes and suffixes you have learned to create new words from the words in **bold**.

1 Add a suffix to **tradition** to make it an adjective. _traditional_

2 Add a suffix to **help** to make it an adjective. _helpful_

3 Add a prefix to **common** to make it mean the opposite. _uncommon_

4 Add a suffix to **pay** to make it a noun. _payment_

5 Add a prefix to **safe** to make it mean the opposite. _unsafe_

6 Add a suffix to **pronounce** to make a noun. _pronounciation_

7 Add a suffix to **use** to make it an adjective. _useful_

8 Add a prefix to **popular** to make it mean the opposite. _unpopular_

B Use the words you created in **A** to complete the sentences below.

1 The woman at the government office was very _helpful_. She explained exactly what to do.

2 It is _unsafe_ to drive more than 100 miles per hour.

3 The repairman asked for _payment_ after he fixed the television.

4 The website is very _useful_ for new parents. It gives information about first names from all over the world.

5 In 1900, many American women had the name Bertha, but it is _unpopular_ now. Most parents don't like this name.

6 The _pronounciation_ of some words in other languages is often difficult for learners.

7 Fifty years ago it was _uncommon_ for Chinese students to come to the United States, but now there are more than a quarter of a million Chinese students in American universities.

8 Some parents like _traditional_ English names such as Katherine and Michael; other parents prefer more modern English names like Emma and Tyler.

Vocabulary Development

Definitions

Find the words in Reading 2 that complete the following definitions.

1 All of the unique features that make one person different from other people are his or her _identity_ . (n) Par. 1

2 _inmigrants_ are people who come from one country to live in another country. (h pl) Par. 3

3 To _fit in_ is to begin to be accepted by others. (v two words) Par. 3

4 To _reveal_ something is to tell or show others something that was hidden or secret. (v) Par. 4

5 A/An _ethnic_ group is a group of people with the same race or national origin. (adj) Par. 4

6 To _face_ something is to deal with something that is difficult. (v) Par. 4

7 _Discrimination_ is treating people badly because of their religion, race, or age. (n) Par. 4

8 A/An _serious_ idea is an idea that is not silly. It needs a lot of thought. (adj) Par. 6

ESTUDIAR

Synonyms

Complete the sentences with words from Reading 2 in the box below. These words replace the words or phrases in parentheses, which are similar in meaning.

boxers	conflict	entire	period
childish	couple	ordinary	simplified

1 The (husband and wife) _couple_ invented an unusual name for their child. (n) Par. 1

2 (Fighters) _boxers_ sometimes hurt each other during fights. (n pl) Par. 2

3 Mary didn't like her name because she thought it was too (common, usual) _ordinary_ . (adj) Par. 2

4 Last week almost the (whole) _entire_ class was sick so the teacher did not give any homework. Par. 3

5 The teacher (made easier) _simplified_ the directions so the children could understand them. (v) Par. 3

6 The last 5 years has been a difficult (time) _period_ in her life. (v) Par. 4

7 The (fight) _conflict_ between the two countries continued for many years. (n) Par. 4

8 As she grew older, she did not enjoy (silly) _childish_ games anymore. She preferred to read. (adj) Par. 6

Critical Thinking

In Reading 1, you learned why parents choose certain names for their children. In Reading 2, you learned that famous people often change their names.

SYNTHESIZING

Critical thinking includes connecting new information to information you learned in previous readings.

A With a partner, think of some famous people who have changed their names. Make a list. First, discuss why you think their parents gave them their names. Then discuss why you think these people changed their names when they became famous.

B Work with the whole class to discuss the following questions.

1 Why do you think famous people, such as singers, actors, and athletes, are more likely to change their names than people who are not famous?

2 If you had a chance to change the name your parents gave you, what name would you choose? Why?

3 Should people be able to choose their own names, or should they respect the wishes of their parents?

Research

Find some information about an important person who has changed his or her name. Find answers to the following questions.

- What was his or her original name?
- Why did the person change his or her name?
- Do you think it was a good decision? Explain your answer.

Writing

Write a short summary of your research. Describe the reasons for the name change.

Finding the Main Idea of a Paragraph

As you learned in Skills and Strategies 2 on page 19, each paragraph has a topic. However, each paragraph also has a main idea. The main idea is what the writer wants to say about the topic. Sometimes you can find the main idea in the first sentence of the paragraph. Sometimes you must read the whole paragraph before you can find the main idea. Finding the main idea of each paragraph will help you understand what the whole reading is about.

Examples & Explanations

Places get their names in many different ways. Sometimes they have the names of famous people. Sometimes they have the names of a physical feature. For example, Hillside is a common name for a town near a hill.

The topic of this paragraph is *names of places*.

The main idea is what the writer wants to say about names of places. Here, the writer wants to say that places get their names in many different ways.

In this paragraph, both the topic and the main idea are in the first sentence.

Some places have very amusing names – they make people laugh. For example, there is a town in the United States called Boring, Oregon. Another town is called Why, Arizona.

The topic in this paragraph is also *names of places*.

This time the writer's main idea is that some places have very amusing names.

In this paragraph, both the topic and the main idea are also in the first sentence.

Why do some places have unusual names? Sometimes one person calls a place something, and that becomes its name. A town in the U.S. state of Tennessee did not have a name. The people made many suggestions for the name, but they couldn't agree on one. Finally, one person said, "I guess our town will remain nameless." This is how Nameless, Tennessee, got its name.

The main idea is not always in the first sentence. In this case, the first sentence is a question. The answer to the question is the main idea.

The topic of this paragraph is *how places get unusual names*. The topic is in the question that begins the paragraph.

The main idea is the answer to the question, which is in the second sentence: *Sometimes one person calls a place something, and that becomes the name.*

Strategies

These strategies will help you find the main idea of a paragraph while you read.

- As you read a paragraph, ask yourself questions: *What is the topic? What does the writer want to say about this topic?*
- Pay attention to the first sentence and second sentence of a paragraph. One of them often contains both the topic and the main idea.
- Look for the answer to a question. This may tell you the main idea.
- Read the whole paragraph to find out what the writer is trying to say about the topic.

Skill Practice 1

Read the following paragraphs. Then look at the four possible main idea choices for the paragraph. Circle the best choice. Discuss your answers with a partner.

1   Sometimes the names of towns are not amusing to the people who live there. The citizens of Boring, Oregon, do not think the name of their town is amusing. It was named after Mr. Boring, an important man in town.

   Main idea:
   a Many towns are named after important people.
   b Mr. Boring was so important that people named a town after him.
   c Many towns have unusual names.
   d The people who live in a town may not think its name is amusing.

2   How do places get such amusing names? They often happen by accident. Long ago, the town of Why, Arizona, was only a place where a few streets met. The point where the streets met was in the shape of the letter *Y*. Later, the place with the Y became Why.

   Main idea:
   a Arizona has a town called Why.
   b Some places get their names by accident.
   c The town of Why was named after two streets.
   d People in Why, Arizona, changed the name of their town.

3   In the United States, *Jr.* (junior) and *Sr.* (senior) after a name show that the two people are son and father, but in Germany this is not true. The *Jr.* just shows that a person is named after someone else. The two people may not be close relatives.

   Main idea:
   a In the United States, *Jr.* and *Sr.* show that two people are related.
   b Two people with *Jr.* and *Sr.* may not be close relatives in Germany.
   c *Jr.* and *Sr.* may show different things in different countries.
   d Someone named *Jr.* is named after his father.

4   When countries change their names, the governments of other countries do not always use the new name. Myanmar is an example of this. When a new government took over the country of Burma (the old name), the new rulers called it Myanmar. Governments that wanted to work with the new rulers started to call the country Myanmar. Other governments continued to call it Burma.

Main idea:

a Myanmar and Burma are names of the same country.

b Governments sometimes do not like the new rulers of a country.

c The use of a country's name is a big decision for other governments.

(d) Even if a country chooses a new name, other governments sometimes still use the old name.

Skill Practice 2

Read the following paragraphs. Write the main idea of each paragraph on the blank lines.

1   How important is a name in a person's life? A recent study shows that it is very important. Boys with certain names get into trouble and go to jail much more often than boys with other names. The names Alec, Ivan, and Luke are not a good choice of names, according to this research.

Main idea: A recent study shows ^name it is very important in people life

2   People often like to visit towns with unusual names. In the Grand Cayman Islands, you can visit Hell. It is a popular place for tourists to buy postcards. In Germany, a lot of people visit the town of Kissing. They like to take pictures of the official town sign.

Main idea: People often like to visit towns with unusual names

3   In the United States, many small towns are named after famous places in other countries. Some of the towns got their names because people came from those places. Others were just named for beautiful cities. For example, 23 towns in the United States are named Paris.

Main idea: Many small towns are named after famous places in other countries

4   Some towns change their names to attract visitors. The town of Truth or Consequences is named after an old American television game show. In 1950, the TV show asked for a town to change its name in order to host the game show. The 7,300 people in Hot Springs, New Mexico, agreed to change their town's name. Many visitors go to this town just because of its name.

Main idea: Some towns change their names to attract visitors

Connecting to the Topic

Think about the names of products you buy, such as shampoo, jeans, or cell phones. Then discuss the following questions with a partner.

1 Why do you think companies chose those names for the products?

2 Which names do you think are good? Which names do you think are not good? Explain your answers.

3 Do you think the name of a company or product is important? Explain your answer.

Previewing and Predicting

When a reading is divided into sections and the sections have headings, it is important to preview those headings to get a good idea of the organization and content of the reading.

A Read the section headings and the first sentences of each section in Reading 3, and look at the photos on pages 55–57. Then read the questions below. Write the number of the section (*I*, *II*, or *III*) next to the question or questions you think the section will answer.

SECTION	QUESTION
I	Why are names important in business?
III	How do people feel when they hear or read a company or product name?
II	How can a product's name make people want to buy it?
II	How are names connected to companies and products?

B Compare your answers with a partner's.

While You Read

As you read, stop at the end of each sentence that contains words in **bold**. Then follow the instructions in the box in the margin.

◀) Names in Business

I. The Importance of Names

1   The names of companies and products have many different origins. Older companies often got their names from people. Car companies are a good example. Many car companies, such as Ford, Toyota, and Tata[1], all have the names of the men who started them. Other car companies, such as SAAB, FIAT, and BMW have names that are **initials**. For example, BMW are the initials for Bavarian Motor Works. Today, many new companies choose different kinds of names. They know that company and product names are very important, and they spend a lot of time and money on these names.

2   A new company must choose its name carefully. It must also think carefully when it names its products. A name can influence what people think about a company or a product. People will remember a good name. They may choose that company or product because of its name. This means that a company or a product with a good name may not need many advertisements. This can save the company a lot of money.

II. Connecting a Name to a Company

3   Some companies choose their own name. However, because this is a very important decision, other companies ask professionals to help **them**. There are businesses that do just one thing: they think of names for new companies and products. They research names and give advice about how people will respond to them. If it is an international

---

[1] *Tata:* the largest Indian automobile company

WHILE YOU READ ①

Find a clue in the next sentence that signals a definition of *initials*. Highlight the clue. What does *initials* mean?
a) Symbols
b) Abbreviations
c) First letters

WHILE YOU READ ②

What is the topic of this paragraph?
a) Choosing names
b) International names
c) Names

Many car companies have names that are initials.

company, they consider international factors. Companies want to know how people all over the world will respond to their company or product name. International companies have to be careful. Sometimes a good name in one language could also mean something bad or embarrassing in another language.

4   Companies consider many things when they choose a name. They want a name that customers will connect with the company or product. If a company makes shoes for running, it should consider names that are related to feet or shoes. *Green Moon* or *Crazy Cow* would not be good names for shoes. A good name should also be easy to remember. However, the name should not be too ordinary. It is probably not a good idea to choose a name like *Best Shoes* or *The Shoe Company*. These names are boring and do not show how the company is **unique**.

III. Emotional Response to Names

5   Perhaps the most important factor that a company must consider is the emotion that people will feel when they hear the name of the company. What will they think about when they hear the name? When the online company Amazon began, it sold only books. The founder of the company chose the name because the Amazon River is vast and powerful. It is the largest river in the world. He wanted his company to be the biggest bookseller in the world.

6   A good name tells a story. If a shoe company chooses a name like *Fast Feet*, this explains the business to the customers. There is a clear connection between shoes and their purpose, but the name is a little ordinary. Two companies that make running shoes chose names that are more interesting: Nike – the Greek goddess of victory – and Reebok – a large animal from Africa that runs very **fast**. These names tell good stories. The companies probably hope their customers will think about victory and speed when they buy their shoes.

WHILE YOU READ 3

Which sentence gives the main idea of this paragraph?
a) First sentence
b) Second sentence
c) Last sentence

WHILE YOU READ 4

Find a clue in this sentence that signals the definition of *reebok*. Highlight it.

A South African reebok can run very fast.

Nike is the Greek goddess of victory.

7   The names of some electronic and technology products also provide good examples of responses to products. The names for these products should make people think about modern science and technology. Sometimes this choice relates to sounds. For example, words that begin with *e-* or *i-*, like e-mail and iPhone, make people think about technology. In English, words that begin or end with *x*, such as x-ray, often sound very scientific or technical. A good example of a product name is Xerox. It sounds very technical, but it is also easy to remember. Another good example is the company name Google. This name comes from the word *googol*, which means a very large number: 10^{100}. The company's original name was Back Rub, but as it grew, the directors decided it needed a better name. They probably chose the new name because it makes the company sound scientific and powerful. Today, Google is a very **successful company**.

WHILE YOU READ ⑤

What is the topic of this paragraph?
a) Successful products
b) Letters and technology
c) Naming technical products

8   Finally, sometimes businesses want to find a new name. Kentucky Fried Chicken sells lots of fried chicken. Today, many customers worry that they eat too much fat. Kentucky Fried Chicken didn't want its customers to just think about its fried food. The company decided to change its name to KFC. KFC wanted customers to think about its other products, which are not fried. A company may also change its name when something bad happens. For example, there was an airplane crash in Florida in 1997. Many people died in the crash. The company that owned the airplane, Valujet, wanted its customers to forget the crash, so it changed its name to AirTran.

KFC doesn't want customers to think of only fried chicken.

9   Choosing and changing names is an important part of any business. Names can have a **powerful** influence on customers. With a good response from customers, a company can make a lot of money. With a bad response, a company may lose a lot of money.

WHILE YOU READ ⑥

Highlight the suffix in *powerful*. Is *powerful* (a) a noun, (b) a verb, or (c) an adjective?

Main Idea Check

Match the main ideas below to five of the paragraphs in Reading 3. Write the number of the paragraph on the blank line.

_6_ A Product names can tell a story.

_3_ B Many companies hire professionals when they need to choose a name.

_4_ C Customers' emotional response to a name is very important.

_5_ D A name should have a clear connection to a product.

_8_ E Companies sometimes need to change their name.

A Closer Look

Look back at Reading 3 to answer the following questions.

1 Reread paragraph 1. What were two common choices for company names in the past?
  (a) The name of the person who started the company
  b The name of a famous person
  (c) Initials
  d A name that people would remember

2 A good name can save money for a company. (True) or False? (Par. 2)

3 What do some professionals do to find names for new businesses or products? Circle three answers. (Par. 3)
  (a) They do research about how people will respond to a name.
  (b) They give advice about names.
  c They find customers for the company.
  (d) They think about international factors.

4 What is the most important thing that companies must consider when they choose a name for a new product? (Par. 5)
  a International factors
  b Customers' emotional response
  c The connection between the name and the product
  (d) Scientific or technical value

5 What do you think companies hope that customers will think about when they see these product names? Match the product in the left column to an idea in the right column. (Pars. 6 and 7)

Product	Idea
_b_ 1 Nike shoes	a the power of large numbers
_d_ 2 Xerox	b victory
_a_ 3 Google	c speed
_c_ 4 Reebok shoes	d modern technology

6 The name *Google* is a new word that the company invented to sound technical and powerful. True or False? (Par. 7)

7 Which three letters sound technical or scientific in English? (Par. 7)

a i   b z   c x   d e

8 Why do some companies decide to change their name? (Par. 8)

a They want customers to change their ideas about the company or product.

b They think customers will be more interested in a new name.

c They think the old name has become too boring.

d They hope that the new name will save the company money.

Skill Review

In Skills and Strategies 4, you learned that writers express the main idea in different places. Sometimes they put the main idea in the first sentence of a paragraph; sometimes they put it in the second or last sentence. It is important to look at all of these possibilities. However, sometimes you have to read the entire paragraph to understand what the main idea is. This is because no single sentence gives the main idea.

A Look back in Reading 3, and find the main ideas of paragraphs 1–8. Where did you find the main idea in the paragraphs? Put a check (✓) in the correct columns.

PARAGRAPH NUMBER	FIRST SENTENCE	SECOND SENTENCE	LAST SENTENCE	WHOLE PARAGRAPH
1				
2				
3				
4				
5				
6				
7				
8				

B Compare your answers with a partner's.

Vocabulary Development

Definitions

Find the words in Reading 3 that complete the following definitions.

1 _products_ are things that companies make and sell. (*n pl*) Par. 1

2 To _research_ is to study something carefully and find out information about it. (*v*) Par. 3

3 A/An _factor_ is something that is important enough to change a result. (*n*) Par. 3

4 _costumers_ are people who buy things from a store or business. (*n pl*) Par. 4

5 A/An _emotional_ is a strong feeling. (*n*) Par. 5

6 A/An _victory_ is when you win a race or a game. (*n*) Par. 6

7 If something is _modern_, it is based on new ideas. (*adj*) Par. 7

8 Something that has good results is _succesful_. (*adj*) Par. 7

Word Families

> Word families are different *parts of speech*, or word forms, that have similar meanings. Some parts of speech are *verbs, nouns, adjectives,* and *adverbs.* When you learn a word, learn the other words in its word family, too. This will help you increase your vocabulary.

A The words in **bold** in the chart are from Reading 3. The words next to them are from the same word family. Study and learn these words.

NOUN	VERB
advertisement	*advertise*
advice	*advise*
consideration	**consider**
influence	**influence**
response	respond

B Choose the correct form of the words from the chart to complete the following sentences. Use the correct verb tenses and subject-verb agreement. Use the correct singular and plural noun forms.

1 There was a good _respond_ to my idea. Everyone said they liked it very much.

2 A company's sales are often closely related to how much they _advertise_ their products.

3 Television news can _influence_ what people think about important issues.

4 She gave her sister good _advise_ about where to apply for a new job.

5 After months of _consideration_, the couple finally decided what to name their baby.

6 The teacher asked a difficult question, and none of the students _respond_

7 Parents have a lot of _influence_ on what their children think and do.

8 The doctor _advice_ him to stop smoking and get more exercise.

9 She carefully _consider_ all of her choices before she decided to take a job in New York.

10 There was a large _advertisement_ for a new phone in today's newspaper.

Academic Word List

The following are Academic Word List words from all the readings in Unit 2. Use these words to complete the sentences. (For more on the Academic Word List, see page 260.)

conflicts (n)	factor (n)	period (n)	researched (v)	reveal (v)
ethnic (adj)	immigrants (n)	professional (adj)	response (n)	selected (v)

1 _immigrants_ arrived in New York from many different countries in the early twentieth century.

2 The most important _factor_ in their decision to leave their country was safety.

3 She studied for many years and finally became a/an _professional_ musician.

4 The student _researched_ the origins of the city's traditions.

5 There was a strong _response_ to the leader's ideas. Many people did not like them, but other people did.

6 The soldier did not _reveal_ his name. He said nothing.

7 There was a short _period_ of peace between the two wars.

8 He looked at all the computers in the store and finally _selected_ a very expensive one.

9 There are many different _ethnic_ groups in Nigeria. They speak different languages and have different traditions.

10 There are often _conflicts_ between countries about natural resources near their shores. Both countries want to control them.

Critical Thinking

APPLYING INFORMATION

You use critical thinking skills when you apply information you have just learned to new situations.

In Reading 3, you learned about how companies choose names for their businesses and products and how they consider their customers' emotional response to these names.

A Imagine that you work for a company that finds good names for businesses and products. Your company has several new naming projects. With a partner, decide on a good name for the following products or businesses:

a A low-fat snack food (for example, chips)
b An electric car
c A new airline
d A headache medicine
e A store that sells inexpensive clothing for young people

B Present the new names you have chosen for the businesses or products to your class. Explain why you chose the names.

Research

Choose a company or a product. Do some research on the origin of its name. Find answers to the following questions.

- When did the company get its name?
- How did it get its name?
- Has the company or product been successful?

Writing

Write a short summary of your research. Include your opinion of the name.

Improving Your Reading Speed

Good readers read quickly and still understand most of what they read.

A Read the instructions and strategies for Improving Your Reading Speed in Appendix 3 on page 273.

B Choose one of the readings in this unit. Read it without stopping. Time how long it takes you to finish the text in minutes and seconds. Enter the time in the chart on page 274. Then calculate your reading speed in number of words per minute.

Estudiar

ADDITIONAL INFORMATION CONNECTORS

Writers often add to information about an idea, person, or thing that they have already written about. Some words that signal this addition are *another*, *others*, and *also*. When you see these words, look back to see what information the writer is adding to, and look forward to see what the new information is.

In the following example, the word that signals additional information is in **bold**. The earlier idea, person, or thing is underlined. The additional information is also underlined. The arrow shows the connection.

Smith is the most common family name in the United States. **Another** common family name is Williams.

Exercise 1

Read the following groups of sentences. Highlight the word that signals additional information. Underline the original idea, person, or thing in the first sentence. Underline the additional information. Draw arrows from the highlighted word to the underlined items. The first one has been done for you.

1 Some parents name their children after family members. Others name their children after famous people.

2 Names often reveal a person's ethnic group. They sometimes also reveal a person's religious group.

3 One popular name for girls in Japan in the 1990s was Akiko. Another was Tomoko.

4 Some immigrants' names are often difficult to spell. They are also difficult to pronounce.

5 Some immigrants changed the spelling of their names. Others changed their names to something completely new.

6 All the girls in the family have Maria in their names. One daughter is Maria Angela. Another daughter is Anna Maria.

Exercise 2

Make a clear paragraph by putting sentences A, B, and C into the best order after the numbered sentence. Look for pronouns (see page 31) and words that signal addition to help you. Write the letters in the correct order on the blank lines.

1 There are a lot of ways to find out more about family history. ____ ____ ____

| **A** There are also professionals who will do the research for you. | **B** Another possibility is to research the origin of your name on the Internet. | **C** Talking to older family members is a good way to begin. |

2 If you meet an American woman named Linda, she is probably not young.

____ ____ ____

| **A** This is because the name Linda was popular in the United States in the 1950s. | **B** Now, it is not as common as the name Emma. | **C** Another popular modern name is Olivia. |

3 The most common family names in Canada have changed in the last 20 years.

____ ____ ____

| **A** It has a lot more people from different ethnic groups than it used to. | **B** They used to be British names, but now names like Patel and Li are more common. | **C** This shows very clearly the change in the Canadian population. |

4 We have different naming traditions in our family. ____ ____ ____

| **A** Some of us give children religious names such as Sarah and Matthew. | **B** Others like more unusual names for children. | **C** They prefer unique names with uncommon spellings. |

5 Young people need to be careful when they select their e-mail names. ____ ____ ____

| **A** Some are not serious names. | **B** This is a problem when answering an advertisement for a job. | **C** Others are quite childish. |

3

FOOD

SKILLS AND STRATEGIES

- Collocations
- Finding Supporting Details

Collocations

test #3

> When you read in English, you will notice that sometimes the same words often go together. For example, when you see the word *meal*, it often appears in a group of words, such as *make a meal* or *have a meal*. When two or more words often go together, we call this a *collocation*. Many collocations have a verb and a noun. Good readers know these collocations. This helps them read more quickly.

Examples & Explanations

If I **have time** in the mornings, I eat a big breakfast with eggs, toast, and fruit. However, a big breakfast **takes time**, so I usually only eat cereal.

A noun such as *time* may appear with different verbs in collocations. Learn the words together, for example, **have time** and **take time**.

When my family eats dinner together, everyone **makes** a lot of **noise**.

Notice that sometimes there are other words between the words that go together. For example, *a lot of* is in the middle of the collocation **makes noise**. *A lot of* is not part of the collocation.

The Language of Collocation

Here are some common collocations with verbs and nouns.

VERB + NOUN			
have	*make*	*take*	*tell*
• fun	• a difference	• a break	• a lie
• lunch	• a meal	• a shower	• a story
• time	• noise	• time	• the truth

Strategies

These strategies will help you learn collocations.

- When you are reading, try to notice verbs and nouns that often go together. These may be useful collocations. Be careful. Sometimes other words are between the verb and noun. These words may not be part of the collocation.

- When you look up verbs and nouns in a dictionary, pay attention to any verbs and nouns that appear together in example sentences. These could possibly be useful collocations.

- When you make a list of new vocabulary to study, write the collocations. Learn the words that go together, not just the single words.

Skill Practice 1

Read the following paragraphs. Choose words from the box above each paragraph to complete the collocations. Write the words on the blank lines. The first one has been done for you.

follow	make	take	win

1   Learning to cook is easy. You just need to find a recipe and _____*follow*_____
     a
     the directions. ____take____ care when you measure, but don't worry if you
                        b
     ____make____ a mistake. Some cooks ____win____ prizes for recipes that
         c   d
     they made with mistakes.

have	meet	offer	take

2   If you ____have____ trouble learning how to cook, you may want to
                a
     ____take____ a cooking class. Some grocery stores ____offer____ cooking
         b   c
     lessons. This can also be a great way to ____meet____ people.
                                                  d

do	get	spend	take

3   Students ____spend____ a lot of time sitting in classes all day. Then they
                  a
     ____take____ a bus or train home. Most students also need to
         b
     ____do____ homework as soon as they get home. This means that many
        c
     students don't ____get____ enough exercise.
                        d

does	makes	take	tell

4   Many married couples _____*take*_____ turns cooking. Each night one person
    _____*Makes*_____ dinner, and the other person _____*does*_____ the dishes. This
    (b)   (c)
    is a great system. If you don't like what your husband or wife cooks, this is a good
    time *not* to _____*tell*_____ the truth!
    (d)

Skill Practice 2

Read the following paragraphs. Highlight any verb and noun collocations you see. Then write the collocations on the blank lines next to their meanings. The first one has been done for you.

1   In the past, families ate together every night. They were able to have dinner
    at the same time each night. Today, both parents usually have a job. It may be
    difficult for them to have the time to make dinner.

    a work somewhere _____*have a job*_____
    b cook a meal _____*make dinner*_____
    c eat a meal in the evening *have dinner*
    d be available _____*have time*_____

2   Young people often rent a house together to save money. Some people call
    this a "share house." Sometimes sharing the kitchen can cause problems, and
    housemates have arguments.

    a fight _____*have arguments*_____
    b create difficulties _____*cause problems*_____
    c spend less _____*save money*_____
    d pay money for a place to live _____*rent a house*_____

3   When housemates take turns cooking, they often make a mess. Sometimes
    they don't do the dishes. Sometimes they fight over which food is theirs in the
    refrigerator. Housemates need to solve problems like these to make a share
    house successful.

    a cause things to be untidy or dirty _____*make a mess*_____
    b find answers or solutions _____*solve problems*_____
    c go one after another _____*take turns*_____
    d wash things that you use for eating _____*dishes*_____

Connecting to the Topic

Study the map, and discuss the following items with a partner.

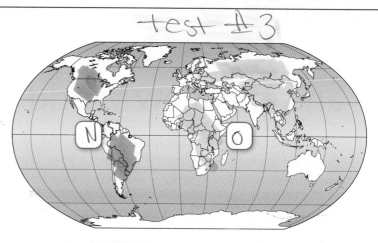

test #3

1 We often call one half of the world "the Old World" and the other half "the New World." Why?

2 Label the map. Label the Old World with an *O*. Label the New World with an *N*.

3 People from the Old World began to visit the New World in the fifteenth century. Name one food or animal that people from the Old World brought to the New World.

4 Name one food or animal that people brought back from the New World to the Old World.

Previewing and Predicting

> Previewing a reading's title, as well as charts, tables, and graphs, can help you predict what the reading will be about.

A Read the title of Reading 1, and look at Table 3.1 on page 71. What do you think this reading will be about? Put a check (✓) next to the topic or topics that you think will be included in the reading.

  ✓   a Foods of the Old World and New World

  ✓   b How foods that begin one part of the world are now in other parts of the world

  ✓   c Why people in the Old World like to eat some foods, and people from the New World like other foods

      d Farms in the Old and New Worlds

B Think about other foods that you know. Do you think they come from the Old World or the New World? Write *O* (for *Old World*) or *N* (for *New World*) on the blank lines.

  O apples   N beef   O grapes   N tea

  N bananas   N corn   O oranges   N tomatoes

While You Read

As you read, stop at the end of each sentence that contains words in **bold**. Then follow the instructions in the box in the margin.

Food from the Old World and the New World

1   When it is time to make breakfast, what do you think of? Coffee and eggs? Perhaps a banana? What about your favorite dinner? Pizza and chocolate cake? Chicken and rice? Meat and potatoes? Today, many people eat foods from all over the world. However, this has not always been possible. In the past, these familiar foods were not available everywhere.

WHILE YOU READ 1

What does *this* refer to? Highlight it.

2   A big change occurred about 500 years ago, when people from the Old World began to explore the New World. They found many unfamiliar kinds of food in the New World. They found potatoes, peanuts, tomatoes, chilies, corn, and chocolate. Today, many of these New World foods are very common in Europe and Asia.

3   The explorers brought food from the Old World with them. There were many foods that the people in the New World did not have at that time. For example, there was no milk, cheese, or bananas. People of the New World did not raise animals for food. Instead, they hunted wild animals as well as birds and insects. They did not raise chickens, cows, pigs, or sheep. These animals came to the New World with **European explorers**.

WHILE YOU READ 2

Look back in paragraph 3 for two collocations with verbs and the noun *animals*. Highlight the collocations.

4   Between the fifteenth and seventeenth centuries, explorers from Europe and Asia brought plants from their countries. They started to grow these plants – wheat, apples, and sugar cane – in the New World. These crops are now very common in North and South America. Today, some countries in the New World are the biggest producers of crops that began in the Old World. For example, Brazil is the world's biggest producer of coffee, a crop that began in the Old World. (See Table 3.1.)

WHILE YOU READ 3

Highlight the suffix in *explorers*. Is it (a) a noun, (b) a verb, or (c) an adjective?

5   This exchange of foods went in both directions. The **explorers** also brought new foods back to their countries. They planted crops such as corn and potatoes, which became very important in the Old World.

Table 3.1 Foods of the Old World and New World

FOOD	AREA OF ORIGIN	BIGGEST PRODUCER TODAY
Cheese	Central Asia/Middle East	United States
Chili peppers	Central/South America	India
Chocolate	Mexico	Ivory Coast
Coffee	Yemen	Brazil
Pineapple	Brazil/Paraguay	Thailand
Potato	South America	China
Sugar cane	South/Southeast Asia	Brazil

Source: Wikipedia

Many New World crops are easy to grow even when the soil and weather are not good. New World crops like potatoes could also feed a lot of people. This increase in food helped the world's population grow quickly in the eighteenth and nineteenth centuries.

6   Some New World foods, like corn and potatoes, were available to almost everyone in the Old World. However, other foods from the New World, like chocolate and pineapples, were only for rich people. They did not grow in the Old World, so they were rare. Poor people could not pay for them. In the seventeenth century, pineapples were so valuable that people did not eat them. They put them on their tables, like **flowers**.

7   Many different foods are available all over the world today, so it is sometimes difficult to remember that this was not always true. Thirty percent of all food plants in the world today came from the New World. Think about ice cream. Three of the most popular flavors of ice cream are vanilla, chocolate, and strawberry. All three of these flavors are from plants. Five hundred years ago, these plants grew only in the New World. Next time you make dinner or a snack, think about how much of it has its origins in the New World.

WHILE YOU READ 4

What is the main idea of paragraph 6? Highlight it.

Main Idea Check

Here are the main ideas of paragraphs 2–6 in Reading 1. Match each paragraph to its main idea. Write the number of the paragraph on the blank line.

_5_ A Some New World crops were very successful in the Old World.

_3_ B Before explorers came to the New World, many familiar foods of today were not available in the New World.

_4_ C People from the Old World planted crops in the New World.

_2_ D Before explorers came to the New World, many familiar foods of today were not available in the Old World.

_6_ E Some New World crops were very expensive in the Old World.

A Closer Look

Look back at Reading 1 to answer the following questions.

1 Before the fifteenth century, many familiar foods were not available to everyone in the world. **True** or **False**? (Par. 2)

2 What kinds of animals did people in the New World raise for food? (Par. 3)
   a Sheep
   b Pigs
   c Chickens
   d None of these

3 What were some reasons for the success of potatoes in the Old World? Circle three answers. (Par. 5)
   a They are easy to grow.
   b They are not expensive.
   c They can grow in bad weather.
   d They can feed a lot of people.

4 What was one result of the success of these New World crops? (Par. 5)
   a No one was hungry.
   b The population increased.
   c Some foods became too expensive for poor people.
   d People stopped planting Old World crops.

5 Coffee is one New World food that was available only to rich people. **True or False?** (Par. 6)

6 Brazil is the largest producer of sugar cane. **True** or **False?** (Fig. 3.1)

7 According to the whole reading, were the following foods originally from the Old World or the New World? Write *O* (for *Old World*) or *N* (for *New World*) on the blank lines.

a __N__ corn

b __N__ chocolate

c __O__ bananas

d __O__ apples

e __N__ potatoes

f __O__ sugar cane

g __N__ tomatoes

Skill Review

In Skills and Strategies 5, you learned that some verbs and nouns frequently occur together. It is important to notice these verb + noun collocations as you read.

A There are many verb + noun collocations in Reading 1. The verbs from the reading are in the left-hand column of the chart, and the nouns are in the top row. Put a check (✓) in the columns to make collocations from the reading. Some of the verbs make collocations with more than one noun.

	breakfast	dinner	food	plants	crops	animals
eat	✓	✓	✓			✓
grow				✓	✓	
hunt						✓
make	✓	✓	✓			
plant			✓	✓	✓	
raise			✓		✓	✓

B Choose from the verbs in **A** to fill in the blanks below.

1 __raise__ pigs

2 __grow__ sugar cane

3 __plant__ bananas

4 __eat__ chickens

5 __eat__ tomatoes

6 __hunt__ elephants

Definitions

Find the words in Reading 1 that complete the following definitions.

1 To _occure_ is to happen. (v) Par. 2

2 To _explore_ is to travel to a new place and find out about it. (v) Par. 2

3 Animals that are _wild_ do not live with people. They live in their natural environment. (adj) Par. 3

4 _insects_ are small animals with six legs, such as an ant. (n) Par. 3

5 A/An _exchange_ is something you give someone in return for something else. (v) Par. 5

6 The _soil_ is dirt where plants grow. (n) Par. 5

7 A/An _population_ is all of the people who live in one place. (n) Par. 5

8 A/An _snack_ is a small amount of food that you eat between meals. (n) Par. 7

Words in Context

Complete the passages with words from Reading 1 in the box below.

available	crop	flavor	rare
chili	familiar	produce	valuable

1 The _chili_ᵃ is a kind of pepper that gives a hot and spicy _flavor_ᵇ to many foods. Some are so hot that they can burn your tongue. They first grew in South America where they were an important _crop_ᶜ more than 6,000 years ago. Today they are _available_ᵈ all over the world.

2 Most of us eat _familiar_ᵉ fruit such as apples and bananas. However, some fruits are very _rare_ᶠ, so they are also very _valuable_ᵍ. In 2011, the world's most expensive fruit was the Ruby Roman Grape. It cost $225 per grape! Farmers do not _produce_ʰ very many of them so they can charge a lot of money for them.

Critical Thinking

In Reading 1, you read that about 500 years ago, the New World and the Old World exchanged food products such as plants and animals. This has been called the *Columbian Exchange*, named after Christopher Columbus.

A Discuss the following questions with a small group of classmates.

1 How do you think these new plants and animals changed the lives of people in the Old and New World? Give some examples.

2 In the *Columbian Exchange*, plants and animals were exchanged. What other things were exchanged? Give some examples.

3 How would your world be different without the *Columbian Exchange*, that is, if the New World and the Old World were still separate? In what ways would it be better? In what ways would it be worse? Give some examples.

B Share your answers and examples with the rest of the class.

> **ANALYZING INFORMATION**
>
> Critical thinking involves thinking carefully about important topics that the writer has not completely explained.

Research

A Choose one of the foods from the list below and find out if it was originally from the Old World or the New World.

- Chilies
- Olives
- Popcorn
- Squash

B Then find the answer for some of your favorite foods.

Writing

Write a brief summary about the foods that you researched.

• Connecting to the Topic

Discuss the following questions with a partner.

1 Do you enjoy fast food?

2 Why do you think so many people like fast food?

3 How often do you eat fast food? Once a week? Once a month?

4 What is your favorite fast food restaurant? McDonald's? KFC?

Previewing and Predicting

> Reading the first sentence of each paragraph can help you predict what a reading will be about.

A **Quickly read the first sentence of each paragraph in Reading 2. Then put a check (✓) next to the topics that you think will be discussed in the reading**

_____ a The secret recipe for KFC's fried chicken

___✓___ b The spread of fast food around the world

___✓___ c The history of fast food

___✓___ d Differences in the fast-food business in different areas of the world

_____ e The most delicious fast food

___✓___ f Fast food and health

B **Compare your answers with a partner's.**

While You Read

As you read, stop at the end of each sentence that contains words in bold. Then follow the instructions in the box in the margin.

◀)) Fast Food

1   Fast food is global. People all over the world love to eat fast food. They like hamburgers, fried chicken, and pizza, and thousands of fast-food restaurants are on every continent. The **popularity** of fast food is increasing. There are several reasons for this popularity. Many people don't want to cook their own food, so fast food makes their lives easier. Fast food is not expensive. It tastes good, and it is also – fast!

WHILE YOU READ 1

Is *popularity* (a) a noun, (b) a verb, or (c) an adjective? Highlight the suffix.

2   Although the first fast-food restaurants were in the United States, the fast-food business is growing all over the world. Today, many fast-food companies make more money in other countries. For example, McDonald's has more than 33,000 restaurants in 119 countries. The majority of them are outside the United States. Many fast-food companies plan to open more restaurants in countries such as China and Brazil in the next 10 **years**.

WHILE YOU READ 2

Look back in paragraph 2 for a collocation with a verb and the noun *money*. Highlight the collocation.

3   Not all fast-food companies serve the same food all over the world. They serve different foods in different countries because they want to satisfy their customers. For example, in the United States, KFC restaurants serve white chicken meat and potatoes. In China, KFC serves dark chicken meat and rice instead of potatoes. Most Chinese customers prefer these choices. In India, most people do not eat beef, so McDonald's serves burgers made from chicken and vegetables. In Japan, some of the burgers are made from **shrimp**.

WHILE YOU READ 3

What is the main idea of paragraph 3? Highlight it.

4   Not all fast-food restaurants sell burgers and pizza, and not all fast-food companies are American. Many successful fast-food companies started in other countries. They sell food that is popular in those countries. Some of them have become popular in the United States. One example is the chicken restaurant, El Pollo Loco. A man in

Fast food is popular all over the world, including Kenya as shown here.

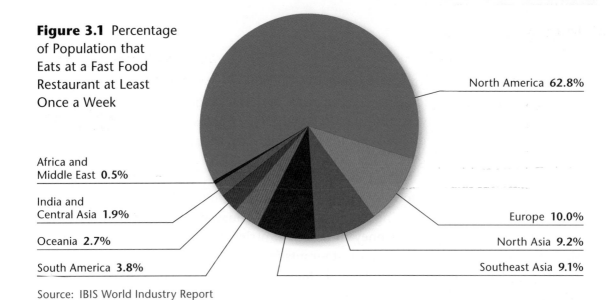

Figure 3.1 Percentage of Population that Eats at a Fast Food Restaurant at Least Once a Week

North America **62.8%**

Africa and Middle East **0.5%**

India and Central Asia **1.9%**

Oceania **2.7%**

South America **3.8%**

Europe **10.0%**

North Asia **9.2%**

Southeast Asia **9.1%**

Source: IBIS World Industry Report

a small town in Mexico made tasty chicken for his friends and family and decided to open a restaurant. It quickly became popular, and soon there were El Pollo Loco restaurants all over the country. In 1980, the first American El Pollo Loco opened in Los Angeles. On its first day, hundreds of people waited outside for it to open. Some of them were immigrants from Mexico, and they wanted a taste of food from home.

5   Fast food is convenient, inexpensive, and tastes good, but it may not be good for you. Many people worry about the effect of fast food on their health. Most fast food has a lot of fat, salt, and sugar in it. Some scientists and doctors believe there is a connection between fast food and health problems. Many doctors tell us not to eat fast food too often. People who eat a lot of fast food often **gain weight**; that is, they get heavier. As a result of these concerns, many fast-food restaurants now offer other choices, such as fruit, salad, and yogurt. These choices do not have so much fat, salt, and sugar. However, many customers still prefer the flavor of meals that have a lot of fat, salt, and sugar in them.

6   It is likely that the number of fast-food restaurants will continue to increase. American companies, such as McDonald's, will continue to expand. Fast food consumption across the world will also grow as more people eat at fast-food restaurants instead of at home. About half of all Americans eat in a fast-food restaurant once a week. The percentage is even higher in some Asian countries. In 2011, the global revenue for fast-food restaurants was about $675 billion. Although fast food may not be good for your health, people all over the world love it and will continue to eat it.

WHILE YOU READ ④

Find a clue in this sentence that signals a definition of *gain weight*. Highlight the definition.

Main Idea Check

Here are the main ideas of paragraphs 2–6 in Reading 2. Match each paragraph to its main idea. Write the number of the paragraph on the blank line.

___2___ **A** Fast-food companies make most of their money outside of the United States.

___6___ **B** More and more people will eat fast food in the future.

___5___ **C** Most fast food is not very good for your health.

___3___ **D** Some fast-food companies serve the same food everywhere; others serve different things in different countries.

___4___ **E** There are many popular fast-food restaurants that have started outside of the United States.

A Closer Look

Look back at Reading 2 to answer the following questions.

1 Why is fast food popular? Circle three answers. (Par. 1)

   (a) It tastes good.

   (b) It is inexpensive.

   c It is international.

   (d) It makes people's lives easier.

2 Almost all of the fast-food business is in the United States. **True or (False)? (**Par. 2)

3 Why are the burgers in India made from chicken? (Par. 3)

   a Most Indians do not like shrimp.

   b Most Indians prefer dark chicken meat.

   c Most Indians like rice, and chicken is better with rice.

   (d) Most Indians do not eat beef.

4 What one fact in paragraph 4 suggests that El Pollo Loco is popular?

   (a) Customers waited for hours.

   b Customers bought a lot of chicken.

   c Customers liked El Pollo Loco better than KFC.

   d Customers traveled a long way.

5 Why do doctors think most fast food is not good for your health? Circle two answers. (Par. 5)

   a Young people eat too much fast food.

   (b) It has a lot of fat, salt, and sugar.

   c Yogurt is not good for you.

   (d) Eating a lot of fast food can make you too heavy.

6 According to Figure 3.1 on page 78, where do fast-food companies make most of their money?

a Europe
b Asia
(c) North America
d The Middle East

Skill Review

> In Skills and Strategies 5, you learned about verb + noun collocations. You can use your knowledge of one collocation to create new verb + noun combinations. Frequently, nouns with similar meanings occur with the same verbs.

A Study the sentences below from Reading 2. Notice the verb + noun collocations in **bold**. Then put a check (✓) in the appropriate column in the chart if you think you can make a collocation with the verb in the left-hand column. The first one has been done for you.

- A man in a small town in Mexico **opened a restaurant**.
- Many people don't like to **cook food**.
- Not all fast-food restaurants **serve** the same **food**.
- People who eat a lot of fast food often **gain weight**.

	rice	soup	a business	5 pounds	ice cream	a kilo	salad	an office
open			✓					✓
cook	✓	✓						
serve	✓	✓			✓		✓	
gain				✓		✓		

B Compare your chart with a partner's.

Definitions

Find the words in Reading 2 that complete the following definitions.

1 Something that is in every part of the world is _____global_____. (adj) Par. 1

2 A/An _____continent_____ is a large piece of land with water all around it. (n) Par. 1

3 A/An _____majority_____ is more than half of something. (n) Par. 2

4 To _____serve_____ people is to give them what they want or need. (v) Par. 3

5 A/An _____effect_____ is the result of an influence. (n) Par. 5

6 To _____offer_____ something is to give or provide it. (v) Par. 5

7 Something that will probably happen is _____likely_____. (adj) Par. 6

8 _____Consumption_____ is eating or using something. (n) Par. 6

Words in Context

Complete the sentences with words or phrases from Reading 2 in the box below.

convenient	gain weight	percentage	tasty
expand	instead of	serves	worry

1 There is a higher _____percentage_____ of women than men in American universities.

2 If you eat a lot of candy, you will _____gain weight_____

3 She ate a salad _____instead of_____ a sandwich because she was not very hungry.

4 The restaurant _____serves_____ dinner between 5:30 and 9:00 p.m.

5 She liked her new apartment because it was so _____convenient_____ It was very close to her job.

6 The food at this restaurant is very _____tasty_____. I like it a lot.

7 Modern cities are growing, and they will continue to _____expand_____ in the twenty-first century.

8 Parents often _____worry_____ about their children when they are out with their friends. They want them to be safe.

Critical Thinking

Reading 2 gives several reasons why people like fast food. These include convenience, speed, and taste. The reading also states that fast food is usually not very healthy.

EXPLORING OPINIONS

Critical readers form their own opinions about important topics in a text.

A Discuss the following questions with a partner.

1 If fast food is bad for our health, why do you think it is still so popular?

2 Is it true that all fast food is bad for our health? Can you think of examples of healthy fast food?

3 Do you think in the future that more fast food will be available that will be good for our health?

4 Some people also believe that fast food is bad not only for our health, but it is also bad for our culture. Do you agree or disagree? Explain your answers.

B Share your answers with the rest of the class.

Research

Do some research in your class about fast food. Ask your classmates the following questions.

- How often do you eat in fast-food restaurants?
- How much money do you spend in fast-food restaurants every week?
- What is your favorite kind of fast food?

Writing

Use your class's results to create charts like the one below. Use answers to one of the questions above to create your chart. Then write a few sentences about the information in the chart.

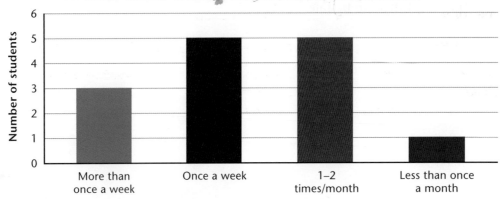

How often we eat at fast-food restaurants

Finding Supporting Details

As you learned in Skills and Strategies 4 on page 51, each paragraph has a main idea. The main idea tells you what the writer wants to say about the topic. A well-written paragraph also has *supporting details*. Supporting details are statements with specific information to support the main idea. Supporting details are usually facts, examples, or reasons. Finding supporting details will help you understand what you read.

Examples & Explanations

①At certain points in history, being overweight was a sign of good health. ②Now, research shows that too much food is not a good idea. ③For example, a study of people over 100 years old shows that they eat very little. ④Research also shows that people who eat too much often have health problems. ⑤They do not live as long as other people. ⑥Eating less helps people live long and healthy lives.

Sentence 2 contains the main idea of the paragraph: *too much food is not a good idea.*

Sentence 3 provides the first supporting detail: *people over 100 years old eat very little.*

Sentence 4 provides the second supporting detail: *people who eat too much often have health problems.*

Sentence 5 provides the third supporting detail: *people who eat too much do not live as long as other people.*

Sentence 6 is a conclusion sentence. It restates the main idea.

The Language of Supporting Details

Sometimes writers use words or phrases to signal a list of supporting details. Here are some common words and phrases that signal supporting details.

WORDS AND PHRASES THAT SIGNAL SUPPORTING DETAILS			
for example	first	one reason	research shows
for instance	next	one example	a study shows
	finally	one explanation	

Strategies

These strategies will help you find supporting details while you read.

- First, identify the main idea. Use the strategies you learned in Skills and Strategies 4 on page 52.
- Look for examples, facts, and reasons that support the main idea.
- Notice specific words or phrases that signal these supporting details.
- Number or underline supporting details as you read. Check that these details support the main idea by looking back and rereading the main idea.

Skill Practice 1

Read the following pairs of sentences. Write _M_ next to the sentence in each pair that is a main idea. Write _S_ next to the sentence that is a supporting detail.

1. _S_ A Research shows that people started to grow rice over 5,000 years ago.
   _M_ B Rice is one of the oldest crops in the world.

2. _S_ A Some people use it in soaps; some people use it for cooking.
   _M_ B The almond has many uses all over the world.

3. _S_ A It was the first place where people sat at tables and ordered from a menu.
   _M_ B The first restaurant started in 1765 in Paris.

4. _M_ A People all over the world celebrate the New Year by eating special types of food.
   _S_ B For example, in Spain and Portugal, people eat 12 grapes at midnight for good luck in each month of the new year.

5. _M_ A It is a good idea to eat fish at least twice a week.
   _S_ B Research shows that the type of fat in fish is good for your heart.

6. _M_ A Some restaurants in the past were "family style."
   _S_ B Guests helped themselves to food that the host put on a table.

Skill Practice 2

Read the following paragraphs. The main ideas are given to you. Find the supporting details in each paragraph, and write them on the blank lines.

1   A visitor from 1,000 years ago might not recognize many of today's fruits and vegetables. First, some of them are different colors. For example, carrots were once purple instead of orange. Second, some fruits and vegetables taste very different today. Many apples were very sour and not very good to eat. Finally, many fruits are much bigger today. Strawberries are a good example. In the seventeenth century, they were about the size of a grape. Fruits and vegetables have changed a lot in the last thousand years.

Main idea: Some fruits and vegetables are very different today than in the past.
Supporting detail: First, some of them are different colors
Supporting detail: 2nd some fruits and vegetables taste very different today
Supporting detail: finally many fruits are much bigger

2   Foods with certain colors or shapes have special meanings at New Year's celebrations. For example, in Peru, people eat gold-colored food on New Year's Day. In the Philippines, people eat food that is green. Another New Year's custom is to eat different types of beans that are shaped like coins. The idea of all these different customs is the same: At the beginning of the new year, eat food that is the color of money or that looks like money, and you will have enough money all during the year.

Main idea: People eat food of certain shapes or colors at New Year's celebrations.
Supporting detail: _____
Supporting detail: _____
Supporting detail: _____

3   Rice is one of the most important food crops in the world. Research shows that about half of the people in the world depend on rice for a major part of their diet. It takes a lot of work and a lot of water to grow rice, but one seed of rice produces about 3,000 grains of rice. Rice is the basis of the diet in Asia, but people grow it everywhere in the world except for Antarctica. Few crops are as important as rice.

Main idea: Rice is a very important crop.
Supporting detail: _____
Supporting detail: _____
Supporting detail: _____

Connecting to the Topic

Discuss the following questions with a partner.

→ Palillos

1 Do you usually use a fork, chopsticks, or your hands when you eat? *fork*

2 When you visit someone for dinner, how do you know when to begin eating? *when everyone is in the table*

3 How do you politely show that you have had enough to eat? *I tell to the person*

4 Is the way we act during meals important? Explain your answer.

Previewing and Predicting

When a reading is divided into sections, preview the headings and read the opening sentences of each section. This will help you predict what each section will be about and will help you understand the reading more easily.

A Read the section headings and the first sentence of each section of Reading 3. Then read the questions below. Write the number of the section (*I*, *II*, or *III*) next to the question or questions you think the section will answer.

SECTION	QUESTION
I	What are table manners?
III	How do table manners show that we enjoy food?
III	How do people show their appreciation of food in different ways in different cultures?
II	Why are table manners important?
II	What are some examples of how table manners keep us safe?
I	What are some different ways of eating food?

B Compare your answers with a partner's.

While You Read

As you read, stop at the end of each sentence that contains words in **bold**. Then follow the instructions in the box in the margin.

Table Manners

I. The Importance and History of Table Manners

1   Mealtimes are important in every culture. Meals give friends and family a chance to sit down, enjoy food, and talk together. When you visit a different country, mealtimes can help you learn about a new culture and its customs. However, it is important to know how to act at mealtimes. **Table manners**, that is, how people act at mealtimes, are different around the world.

2   Should you use your hands or a fork to pick up your food? Is it polite to make noise when you eat? Should you leave any food on your plate? If you make a mistake in your mealtime behavior, people may think you are impolite. In order to understand these customs, it is helpful to understand more about their origins. There are cultural and historical explanations for many of our table manners today.

3   Table manners have changed throughout **history**. We call them table manners, but long ago, people did not eat at tables. In ancient Rome, people lay down at meals. They leaned on one hand and ate with the other hand. In Europe, until about 1500, there were no plates and no forks. Instead of plates, people ate their food from a piece of old, dry bread. They ate with their fingers or used pieces of bread to bring food to their mouths.

II. Table Manners and Safety

4   One explanation for our table manners today is physical safety. Knives were the first things that people used to eat their food. In the past, men brought their own knives to the table. They used the same

> **WHILE YOU READ** ❶
>
> Find a clue in this sentence that signals a definition of *table manners*. Highlight the definition.

> **WHILE YOU READ** ❷
>
> Find three supporting details for this main idea. Highlight them.

Table manners have changed a lot in the last 500 years.

knives for hunting and protection. These knives were very useful, but they were also dangerous. There were often fights at mealtimes, and sometimes people died. As a result, the king of France issued an order that all table knives had to have round ends.

5   The danger of knives may explain table manners today in some countries such as Spain. In Spain, for example, men carried knives and also guns at meals. Sometimes they kept these **weapons** under the table in case there was a fight during the meal. However, it is difficult to hide a weapon in your hands if your hands are visible. In Spain and some other countries today, it is polite to keep your hands above the table where everyone can see them. Although most people are not worried about guns and knives at meals anymore, this custom remains.

WHILE YOU READ 3

Find clues in the previous sentence for the meaning of *weapon*. Highlight the clues.

6   **Another** explanation for our table manners is the safety of the food. Germs can spread easily at mealtime. Some table manners help stop germs from spreading, and this can keep people healthy. For instance, in most cultures, it is impolite to put your own fork, chopsticks, or your hands into a central dish because this can spread germs. Instead, you should use another fork or the other end of your chopsticks. In some countries, for example, India, many people eat their food with their hands. Hosts in India provide a place for people to wash their hands before and after the meal. These customs help prevent germs from spreading during meals.

WHILE YOU READ 4

What is the earlier idea that *another* refers to? Highlight it.

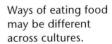

Ways of eating food may be different across cultures.

III. Showing Appreciation of Our Food

7   A final explanation for some table manners today is the way we show appreciation of the food we eat. We show this appreciation in different ways in different cultures. In Japan, for example, it is fine to make noises when you are eating soup or noodles. These noises show that you are enjoying your meal. However, in most western countries and some other Asian countries, it is impolite to make these **noises**.

WHILE YOU READ 5

Look in this sentence for a word with a prefix. Highlight the prefix.

8   Hosts like to know that their guests have enjoyed their food. However, even more important, they want to be sure their guests have had enough to eat. How can you show that you enjoyed the meal, but you do not want to eat more? In most western countries, you can show that you enjoyed your meal if you finish all the food on your plate.

9   In other countries, however, if you eat everything on your plate, you might offend the host. In these countries, you should leave a little bit of food on your plate. This shows that you are satisfied. It also shows that you are finished. If you finish everything on your plate, this says that you are still hungry. Your hosts may try to give you more food. Guests who misunderstand these customs about food may eat too much, or they may go home **hungry**!

WHILE YOU READ 6

What is the main idea of paragraph 9? Highlight it.

10   Mealtimes are a good time to observe another culture. You can learn more than just good table manners. You can learn what is important in other cultures, too. For example, you may observe that the oldest member of a family receives food first. This can show you how important older members are in some cultures. Observe carefully at mealtimes, and you will not embarrass yourself or offend other people. You can also learn a lot about another culture.

Learning table manners in a new culture can be an important thing to do.

Main Idea Check

Match the main ideas below to five of the paragraphs in Reading 3. Write the number of the paragraph on the blank line.

_9_ A In some cultures, it is polite to leave some food on your plate.

_2_ B We show our appreciation of food in different ways.

_3_ C There are historical explanations for today's table manners.

_6_ D Some table manners can stop germs from spreading.

_8_ E In some cultures, you should finish everything on your plate.

A Closer Look

Look back at Reading 3 to answer the following questions.

1 What might happen if you make a mistake in your table manners? (Par. 2)
   a It will be hard to understand the culture.
   b You will use the wrong fork.
   c People will think you are impolite.
   d It will be more difficult to learn the language.

2 The ancient Romans did not sit at a table for meals. **True or False?** (Par. 3)

3 Before 1500, Europeans used bread for plates. **True or False?** (Par. 3)

4 According to paragraph 5, what was the origin of the Spanish custom of keeping your hands on the table?
   a People could not take food and hide it under the table.
   b People could hide their dirty hands.
   c People could keep their knives under the table.
   d People could not hide weapons under the table.

5 What might happen if people put their fork or chopsticks in the central dish after they have used them? (Par. 6)
   a People will think they are dirty.
   b The host will ask them to wash their hands.
   c Everyone will feel comfortable.
   d Germs may spread to other people.

6 What are some ways to show appreciation of food in different cultures? Circle three answers. (Pars. 7–9)
   a Make noises.
   b Finish everything.
   c Don't finish everything.
   d Leave your fork on your plate.

7 In some cultures, if you finish everything on your plate, this may offend your host. Why? (Par. 9)

    a It shows appreciation of your food.
    b Your host will want you to eat more food.
    c Your host will not know what to say.
    d It tells the host you are still hungry.

Skill Review

> In Skills and Strategies 6, you learned that supporting details are statements with specific information, such as facts, examples, or reasons. Finding supporting details will help you understand what you read.

A You are given the main idea of paragraphs in Reading 3 listed below. Find the supporting details for these paragraphs in the reading. Write them on the blank lines.

1 Main idea of paragraphs 4 and 5: *Physical safety can explain some of today's customs and manners.*

    a For example, men carried knives and also guns at meals

    b As a result, the king of France issued an order that all table knives had to have round ends

2 Main idea of paragraphs 7 and 8: *We show appreciation of food in different ways in different cultures.*

    a For example, it is fine to make noise when you are . . . ,

    b However, in most western countries and some other . . . ,

    c However, even more important, they want to be . . .

B Compare your answers with a partner's.

Definitions

Find the words in Reading 3 that complete the following definitions.

1 A/An _____ is a very strong request or demand. (*n*) Par. 4

2 A/An _____ is an object for fighting, such as a knife or a gun. (*n*) Par. 5

3 To _____ something is to put it where no one can see it. (*v*) Par. 5

4 Something that you can see is _____. (*adj*) Par. 5

5 _____ are small living things that can cause disease. (*n*) Par. 6

6 If things _____, they move across a bigger area and have a stronger effect. (*v*) Par. 6

7 _____ are people who invite you to their homes. (*n pl*) Par. 6

8 The _____ thing is the last thing. (*adj*) Par. 7

Word Families

A The words in bold in the chart are from Reading 3. The words next to them are from the same word family. Study and learn these words.

NOUN	VERB
appreciation	appreciate
behavior	behave
observation	**observe**
offense	**offend**
protection	protect

B Choose the correct form of the words from the chart to complete the following sentences. Use the correct verb tenses and subject-verb agreement. Use the correct singular and plural noun forms.

1 Her _____ at the party made everyone angry.

2 The soldiers _____ the people during the war.

3 They showed their _____ by bringing gifts to their hosts.

4 The scientists _____ the animals in the forest. They wanted to know what they eat and where they sleep.

5 The president said some things that _____ the visitors. He said bad things about their country.

6 The teacher told the children to _____ nicely while they were visiting the museum.

7 The people in the village asked the police for their _____.

8 I thanked everyone and told them how much I _____ their help.

9 If you do not eat all of the food on your plate, your hosts may take

_____ .

10 In their science class, the students had to make careful _____ every day
for two weeks.

Academic Word List

**The following are Academic Word List words from all the readings in Unit 3. Use
these words to complete the sentences. (For more on the Academic Word List, see
page 260.)**

appreciation (n)	consumption (n)	final (adj)	majority (n)	percentage (n)
available (adj)	expanding (v)	global (adj)	occurred (v)	visible (adj)

1 He used a/an _____ of the money to pay for his education.

2 The _____ of the class passed the test, but a few did not.

3 The _____ of chocolate around the world increased in the
nineteenth century.

4 He gave two reasons for his decision to sell his house, but the third and

_____ one was the most important.

5 The sun was still _____ between the clouds.

6 Many businesses today are _____. They have offices all over the world.

7 The fast-food business is _____ quickly. New restaurants are opening
every month.

8 The children and their parents showed their _____ by bringing gifts to
the teacher.

9 This coat is _____ in three different colors.

10 World War I _____ at the beginning of the twentieth century.

Critical Thinking

In Reading 3, you learned that different cultures have different customs relating to table manners.

PERSONALIZING

Thinking about how new information applies to your own life can help your understand a text better.

A Make a list of table manners that are important in your culture.

B Share your list with your classmates, and discuss the following questions with the whole class.

1 Have you ever eaten with people from another culture, but you did not understand their customs? Describe what happened.

2 Has a person from another culture ever eaten with you, and he or she broke the rules for eating in your culture? Describe what happened.

Research

Interview a classmate or someone from outside of your classroom about table manners. Find answers to the following questions.

- What are two table manners that you think are the most important?
- Why do you think they are important?

Writing

Write a short description of your research on table manners.

Improving Your Reading Speed

Good readers read quickly and still understand most of what they read.

A Read the instructions and strategies for Improving Your Reading Speed in Appendix 3 on page 273.

B Choose one of the readings in this unit. Read it without stopping. Time how long it takes you to finish the text in minutes and seconds. Enter the time in the chart on page 274. Then calculate your reading speed in number of words per minute.

> ## EXAMPLE CONNECTORS
>
> In Making Connections on page 63, you learned that writers use words, such as *another*, *other*, and *also*, to add new information to an earlier idea, person, or thing.
>
> Writers can also add information by using *transition* words or phrases. They may use these connectors when they add a specific example or fact to support a main idea. Such transition words or phrases include *for example*, *for instance*, or *in addition*. You learned some of these transition words and phrases in Skills and Strategies 6 on page 83.

Exercise 1

Read the following groups of sentences. Highlight any transition words or phrases that signal additional facts or examples. Underline the original idea, person, or thing in the first sentence. Underline the additional fact or example. The first one has been done for you.

1 Many young people gain weight when they go to college. For instance, many students gain about fifteen pounds in their freshman year of college.

2 Today, tourists can find familiar food anywhere they go. For example, there are many KFC restaurants in China.

3 A research study in France found that consumption of tea has health benefits for women. For instance, it may protect them from heart attacks.

4 We waited for 20 minutes before the waiter offered to take our order. In addition, he was impolite when we complained.

5 Shoppers can find food from all over the world in grocery stores now. For example, in Japan, you can buy apples from the United States and cookies from France.

6 The cold weather killed a large percentage of the crops. In addition, the price of seeds increased. Farmers had a very bad year.

Exercise 2

Make a clear paragraph by putting sentences A, B, and C into the best order after the numbered sentence. Look for pronouns and words or phrases that signal additional facts and examples to help you. Write the letters in the correct order on the blank lines.

1 Government health officials sometimes warn people not to eat a certain kind of food. ____ ____ ____

A This usually occurs because of germs in the food.	B If the germs spread, many people get sick.	C In addition, they tell grocery stores to stop selling the food.

2 Customs for tipping are different all over the world. ____ ____ ____

A For example, in most Asian countries, no one leaves a tip for the waiter or waitress.	B This is not the custom in the United States, where waiters and waitresses depend on tips for most of their salary.	C If you get good service in a restaurant in the United States or Canada, pay a tip of 20 percent.

3 The word *tea* usually refers to something you drink. ____ ____ ____

A In Britain, it also refers to a meal.	B Other British people make tea the main meal of the day instead of a light meal.	C For example, it can mean a light meal in the late afternoon.

4 Consumption of sugar is very high in the United States. ____ ____ ____

A For example, many people get a disease called *diabetes* because they eat too much sugar.	B This has a bad effect on people's health.	C Studies show that each person in the United States consumes about 140 pounds of sugar every year.

5 All over the world, there are different customs for eating rice. ____ ____ ____

A It's important to learn these customs before you travel.	B For example, in some countries it is impolite to pick up a bowl of rice and eat from it.	C In other countries, it is polite to do this.

4 TRANSPORTATION

SKILLS AND STRATEGIES

- Phrases
- Finding Contrasts

Phrases

test #4

> As you learned in Skills and Strategies 5, on page 66, some verbs and nouns often go together. These are collocations. Another group of words that go together are *phrases*, for example, *on the whole* and *all of a sudden*. These phrases are fixed, that is, they don't change any of their parts. Good readers notice fixed phrases and learn them. If you can find fixed phrases in a reading, it can help you understand a reading better and read more quickly.

Examples & Explanations

In general, the bus system works well.

The passengers got on the train **one by one**.

Fixed phrases are very common in English.

in general = usually

You can't change anything in a fixed phrase. For example, in this sentence, you can't change *by* to *after*. You can't say, "one after one."

one by one = separately, one after the other

The Language of Fixed Phrases

Here are some common fixed phrases and their meanings.

FIXED PHRASES	MEANINGS
all in all	*thinking about everything*
all of a sudden	*something happens quickly without warning*
as a result	*consequently; therefore; for this reason*
at first	*in the beginning*
for the time being	*for the present time only*
in general	*usually*
in fact	*actually; even more than that*
in the end	*finally*
in the long run	*in the future after other things have happened*
on the whole	*in most cases*
on time	*at the expected time*
once in a while	*sometimes; occasionally*
one by one	*separately, one after the other*
so far	*until now*

Strategies

These strategies will help you identify and learn fixed phrases.

- When you read, look for words that often go together.
- When you make a list of new vocabulary to study, write words that go together, not just the single words.
- When you look up a word in a dictionary, notice any fixed phrases that are listed with the word.

Skill Practice 1

Read the following paragraphs. Fill in the blank lines with fixed phrases from the box above each paragraph. If you need help, use the Language of Fixed Phrases chart on page 98. One has been done for you.

all in all	as a result	on time
all of a sudden	in general	once in a while

1   In the past, public transportation was not popular in my city. Buses were never
On time , so people were often late to work. _All in all_ ,
     a   b
it was not a great way to get to work. Then, _all of a sudden_ , gas prices
                                                  c
became very high. _As a result_ , people began to appreciate public
                                            d
transportation. They decided to leave their cars at home and take the bus
once in a while . _in general_ , people are happier with the public
    e   f
transportation system now.

at first	in fact	one by one
for the time being	in the long run	so far

2   Last month, the city started to build a new subway. _So far_ , it has
                                                a
caused a lot of problems. The city has closed many streets _one by one_
                                                  b
while they work on the subway. So, _for the time being_ , everything is very
                                               c
confusing. _at first_ , people didn't want a new subway.
                       d
in fact , they hated the idea. _in the long run_ , however,
    e   f
people will enjoy the convenience.

Skill Practice 2

Here are some other common fixed phrases. Read them. Then read the paragraph that follows the phrases. Look at the words in parentheses in each paragraph. Try to guess which of the fixed phrases in the box above the paragraph they match. Write them on the blank lines. The first one has been done for you.

according to	all over the world	day by day
a great deal of	as much as	in the meantime

1. Cities (everywhere) __all over the world__ have traffic problems, but few cities in
   a
   the world have more problems than São Paolo, Brazil. There are too many cars in the
   city. People spend (a lot of) _a great deal of_ time trying to get places. Some
   b
   people spend (up to) _as much as_ 3 hours a day getting to work and
   c
   home again. This situation is getting worse (every day) _day by day_. (As
   d
   we read in) _according to_ *Time Magazine*, people in Brazil buy almost 7,000
   e
   new cars each week. City leaders need to act soon to solve this problem. (Until
   something else happens) _in the meantime_, drivers have to sit in their cars
   f
   and wait.

[handwritten margin note: I have informat to someone else]

as a matter of fact	by plane	more and more
before too long	instead of	these days

2. It is not very far from Paris to London (in the air) _by plane_. (The
   a
   truth is) _as a matter of fact_, it only takes about 1 hour. Unfortunately, (now)
   b
   these days it takes (a larger amount of) _more and more_ time to
   c d
   get to the airport and go through security. A lot of people are now taking the train
   (not) _instead of_ a plane. (Soon) _before too long_, airlines may
   e f
   stop flying between cities that are this close to each other.

Connecting to the Topic

post #4

Discuss the following questions with a partner.

1 What do you think people used before public transportation?

2 What were some of the earliest forms of public transportation?

3 What are some advantages of public transportation?

4 Do you often use public transportation where you live? Why or why not?

Previewing and Predicting

> Even just quickly reading the beginnings of the first sentences in each paragraph can help you predict what a reading will be about.

A The following are the beginnings of the first sentences of each paragraph in Reading 1. Read these beginnings.

1 In the past, most people lived far from cities . . . (Par. 1) *in small groups or on farms*

2 The first modern form of public transportation was . . . (Par. 2) *the electric street car*

3 At the end of the nineteenth century, a new form of transportation appeared in cities . . . (Par. 3) *electric trains*

4 In the early twentieth century, although elevated trains and subway systems were . . . (Par. 4) *very popular in major cities*

5 In older cities, especially in Europe and Asia, driving a car was . . . (Par. 5) *not always easy*

6 The U.S. government also built big roads between . . . (Par. 6) *major cities*

7 Public transportation systems in other parts of the world . . . (Par. 7) *specially subways*

B The following are the topics of each paragraph. Put the numbers 1–7 on the blank lines to match the beginnings in **A** with the topics. The first one has been done for you.

__7__ a Public transportation in different parts of the world

__1__ b Earliest forms of public transportation

__5__ c Driving in older cities with small streets

__3__ d New forms of public transportation at the end of the nineteenth century

__2__ e The first modern public transportation

__6__ f The U.S. highway system and its effects

__4__ g Competition for elevated trains and subways

While You Read

As you read, stop at the end of each sentence that contains words in bold. Then follow the instructions in the box in the margin.

🔊 A Short History of Public Transportation

1   In the past, most people lived far from cities in small groups or on farms. When they went from place to place, they walked or rode **animals**. Then people began to move to towns and cities, where there were a lot more people. They needed to get to work, to school, to shops, or to the doctor. Because many people were going to the same places, it was easier for them to travel together. This was the beginning of public transportation.

WHILE YOU READ 1

Look back in this sentence for a fixed phrase. Highlight it.

2   The first modern form of public transportation was the electric streetcar in the early nineteenth century. These streetcars operated along rails in the street. They were the major form of public transportation for many years. Streetcars were faster than horses. However, they had one big problem. They operated in the street where there were also many horses, carts, and bicycles. The streets were crowded, so the streetcars could not move very quickly.

3   At the end of the nineteenth century, a new form of transportation appeared in cities – electric trains. Some electric trains operated

Streetcars were a common form of transportation in the nineteenth century.

Elevated trains first appeared at the end of the nineteenth century.

above the streets. These are called elevated trains. Others ran through tunnels under the ground. These underground trains are sometimes called **subways**. The first major subway system was the London Underground. Soon, other cities, including Budapest, Paris, Berlin, and New York, built subway systems.

4   In the early twentieth century, although elevated trains and subway systems were very popular in major cities, soon they had competition from a new form of transportation – cars. Cars used gasoline instead of electricity. Public buses also became more available at this time, but with a car, people could go anywhere they wanted. They could come and go at any **time**. They did not have to wait for a streetcar, a train, or a bus. Everyone wanted a car. However, they were very expensive. At first, only rich people could buy them. Soon, cars became much cheaper. As a result, more and more people began to buy cars.

5   In older cities, especially in Europe and Asia, driving a car was not always easy. The streets were narrow and crowded. There were no streetlights. Many newer

WHILE YOU READ 2

Look back in the last sentence for a word that signals additional information. Highlight the word. Then highlight the earlier word it connects to.

WHILE YOU READ 3

Look back in this sentence for a fixed phrase. Highlight it.

cities, especially in North America, were different. They were built for cars. They had wide roads and streetlights. In the United States, the government spent lots of money to build these roads, especially in locations like California.

6   The U.S. government also built big roads between major cities. All these roads encouraged more people to buy cars. Cities like Los Angeles had public transportation, but people preferred to drive their own cars. People with cars moved to homes far outside of the cities. The public transportation system did not reach these homes, so people needed cars to go everywhere. Because more people chose to drive, public transportation systems in cities like Los Angeles began to lose money. Today, these cities still have public transportation systems, but on the whole, they are not very successful. All over the country, public transportation systems began to decline.

7   Public transportation systems in other parts of the world, especially subways, have been very successful. (See Figure 4.1.) Moscow and Tokyo for example, have very large systems, which they have had for a long time. China has greatly expanded its use of subways in recent years. Now, four of the twelve largest subway systems in the world are in China. Millions of people use them. In many countries, the governments spend a lot of money on public transportation. They understand that it is more efficient than cars. Public transportation also uses less energy, and it produces less **pollution**.

WHILE YOU READ 4

What is the main idea of paragraph 7? Highlight the sentence that contains the main idea.

Figure 4.1 Top Twelve Subway Systems Rides per Year (in billions) 2011

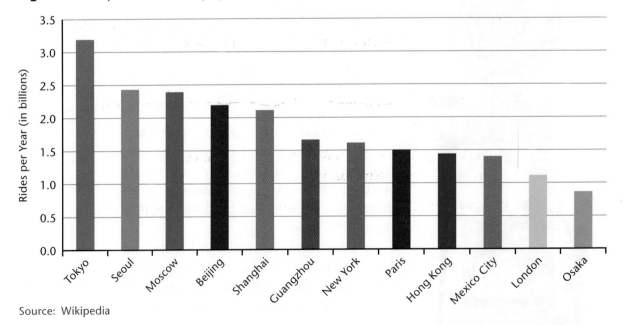

Source: Wikipedia

Main Idea Check

Here are the main ideas of paragraphs 2–6 in Reading 1. Match each paragraph to its main idea. Write the number of the paragraph on the blank line.

_2_ A Electric streetcars were fast, but they also had some problems.

_6_ B Some American public transportation systems lost lots of money when more people chose to drive cars.

_5_ C It is often easier to drive cars in new cities than it is in old cities.

_4_ D Cars began to be a popular form of transportation.

_3_ E Electric railways worked better because they ran above or below the street.

A Closer Look

Look back at Reading 1 to answer the following questions.

1 How did people get to places far from their homes before public transportation? Circle two answers. (Par. 1)
   (a) They walked.   (c) They rode animals.
   b They did not go anywhere.   d They rode bicycles.

2 What was the problem with electric streetcars? (Par. 2)
   a They often broke.
   (b) The streets were crowded, so they could not move quickly.
   c Electricity made them very expensive.
   d They were very noisy and dirty, so they were not popular.

3 New York built the first subway system in the world. **True or (False?)** (Par. 3)

4 Why did public transportation systems in many U.S. cities begin to decline? Put sentences A–D in the correct order of events. Write the correct letter in each box.

   [B] → [C] → [A] → [D]

   A Many people bought cars to get to their new homes and stopped using public transportation.
   B The government built lots of roads to places far from the city.
   C People moved far from the city where there was no public transportation
   D Public transportation systems lost money.

5 What are some advantages of public transportation over cars? Circle two answers. (Par. 7)
   a It is less expensive.   (c) It uses less energy.
   (b) It causes less pollution.   d It is faster.

6 According to Figure 4.1 on page 104, which subway system has more than three billion rides per year?

   a New York
   b Moscow
   c (Tokyo)
   d Shanghai

7 Number the different forms of transportation in the correct order in which they first appeared. Write the correct numbers on the blank lines. Put *1* next to the earliest form and *4* next to the most recent form.

   a __4__ Cars
   b __1__ Horses
   c __3__ Electric trains
   d __2__ Streetcars

Skill Review

> In Skills and Strategies 7, you learned that fixed phrases should be learned as units. Knowing many fixed phrases will allow you to understand a reading better and read more quickly.

A Fill in each blank line in the sentences below with one word to make a complete fixed phrase from Reading 1. The words in **bold** are part of the complete fixed phrase

1 This song is very popular. People **all** __over__ **the** __country__ are listening to it. (Par. 6)

2 The soil varies **from** __place__ **to** __place__, so some crops do not grow well everywhere. (Par. 1)

3 I occasionally drink tea in the morning, but __on__ **the** __whole__ I prefer coffee. (Par. 6)

4 Today people do not have to wait to watch the news on television. They can find it on the Internet __at__ **any** __time__. (Par. 4)

5 The students must finish their work by **the** __end__ __of__ **the** week. (Par. 3)

6 Travel is becoming more difficult because **more** __and__ **more** countries are requiring visitors to get a visa. (Par. 4)

B With a partner, review Reading 1. Go back to the paragraphs that contain the fixed phrases, and check to see if your answers are correct.

Definitions

Find the words in Reading 1 that complete the following definitions.

1 A place that is full of people and things is _crowded_. (adj) Par. 2

2 _tunnels_ are long roads that run under the ground. (n pl) Par. 3

3 A/An _system_ is a group of connected things that work together. (n) Par. 3

4 Something that has a short distance between one side and the other is _narrow_. (adj) Par. 5

5 Something that has a long distance between one side and the other is _wide_. (adj) Par. 5

6 _location_ are places. (n pl) Par. 5

7 Something that works well without waste is _efficient_. (adj) Par. 7

8 _Energy_ is the power from something like oil or electricity, which brings light, heat, and transportation. (n) Par. 7

Word Families

A The words in **bold** in the chart are from Reading 1. The words next to them are from the same word family. Study and learn these words.

NOUN	VERB
competition	compete
decline	*decline*
encouragement	*encourage*
operation	*operate*
pollution	pollute

B Choose the correct form of the words from the chart to complete the following sentences. Use the correct verb tenses and subject-verb agreement. Use the correct singular and plural noun forms.

1 The teachers _encourage_ their students to write a lot.

2 The factories near the town _pollute_ its air and water.

3 There was a / an _decline_ in bicycle production in the United States in the 1970s.

4 A central computer controls the _operation_ of the trains across the city.

5 Air _pollution_ can make it difficult for some people to breathe.

6 The child did not get very much _encouragement_ from his parents or teachers, so he did not do well in school.

7 At the end of the year, the 10 best runners will _compete_ for a prize.

8 Elevated trains _operate_ on rails above the street.

9 Production of radios _decline_ in the twentieth century.

10 There is a lot of _competition_ among the students for the best grades.

Critical Thinking

In paragraphs, 5, 6, and 7 of Reading 1, the writer contrasts public transportation in the United States with other countries around the world.

> **UNDERSTANDING POINT OF VIEW**
>
> Critical readers notice when a writer has a point of view. They are aware that a writer's point of view may affect how the writer reports facts.

A Work with a partner and decide what the writer's point of view is by answering the following questions. As you explain your answers, point to places in Reading 1 that support them.

1 Does the writer think the increase in cars in the United States is good? Explain your answer.

2 Does the writer think the decline of public transportation in the United States is good? Explain your answer.

3 Does the writer have a positive view of the public transportation in other parts of the world? Explain your answer.

B Share your answers with the rest of the class.

Research

Find out about public transportation in your city or a city you know well. Find answers to the following questions.

- What are the main forms of transportation in the city?
- How much does a single ride cost?
- Does public transportation go outside of the city?
- How many people in the city use public transportation every day or every year?

Writing

Write a short description of the public transportation system you researched.

Connecting to the Topic

Discuss the following questions with a partner.

1 Do you have a bicycle? How often do you ride it?

2 Do a lot of people in your city or town ride bicycles to school or to work?

3 Does your town or city have special roads for bicycles?

4 What are the advantages and disadvantages of bicycles as a form of transportation?

Previewing and Predicting

> Previewing art, graphic material, and the first sentence of each paragraph can help you predict what a reading will be about.

A Read the title and the first sentence of each paragraph in Reading 2. Then look at the photographs and Figure 4.2 on pages 110–112. Put a check (✓) next to the topics you think will be discussed in the reading.

_____✓_ a Bicycles and pollution

_____✓_ b Improving bicycle safety

_____✓_ c Bicycle-sharing programs

_____✓_ d Comparison of bicycles and cars

_____ e Car accidents

_____ f Bicycle racing

_____✓_ g Bicycle use around the world

B Compare your answers with a partner's.

While You Read

As you read, stop at the end of each sentence that contains words in **bold**. Then follow the instructions in the box in the margin.

Bicycles for City Transportation

1   All over the world, more and more people are buying cars. An increase in cars means more roads, more traffic, and more pollution. One solution to these problems is more bicycle use. **Bicycles have many advantages.** They do not pollute, they are inexpensive, and they can improve health. Of course, bicycles also have disadvantages compared to cars. They are slower than cars. Cars can also carry more people and more things. However, some city leaders believe bicycles have more advantages than disadvantages. As a result, these cities are trying to increase the use of bicycles.

2   Bicycles are already popular in many countries. There are more than a billion bicycles around the world, and the number is increasing every year. Experts predict that annual sales for bicycles will soon be $80 billion. Bicycle production has gone up significantly since the middle of the twentieth century. In 1960, the rate of production was 20 million bicycles every year. In 2007, it was more than 130 million. (See Figure 4.2.) China makes more bicycles than any other country. Two of every three bicycles sold in the world today are made in **China**.

3   In many cities around the world, traffic and pollution are serious concerns. Bicycles can help cities with some of these problems. So,

WHILE YOU READ 1

As you read, look for supporting details for this main idea. Highlight them.

WHILE YOU READ 2

What is the main idea of paragraph 2? Highlight it.

Bicycles are a popular form of transportation in many countries.

Figure 4.2 Bicycle Production (in millions)

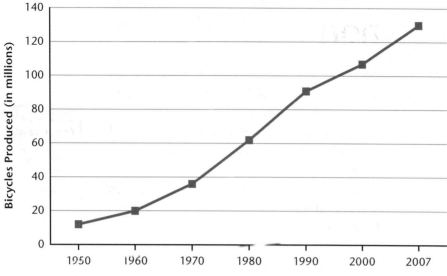

Source: Worldometers

some cities have started bicycle-sharing programs. These cities hope they will help reduce traffic and pollution. These programs encourage people to leave their cars at home and use bicycles instead. The programs provide hundreds or thousands of bicycles across the city. Everyone shares them. People can get a bicycle in one place, ride it for a short time, and leave it in another place. Then someone else can use it.

4   The popularity of bicycle sharing is growing. In 2010, there were about 200 bicycle-sharing programs in cities all over the world, including Barcelona, Mexico City, Paris, and Rio de Janeiro. That is almost double the number of programs in 2008. The biggest bicycle-sharing program is in Hangzhou, China. It has more than 60,000 bicycles. Many of these programs are very successful. However, they also have problems. Every year, many bicycles are stolen or damaged.

5   More people are riding bicycles, so bicycle safety is becoming an important issue. Most bicycle accidents occur with cars. As a result, many cities and towns try to separate bicycles and cars. They decided to create paths for bicycles that are not on the street. The introduction of special paths encourages people to take their bicycles instead of cars. Studies in Denmark and Canada showed increases of almost 20 percent in the number of people on bicycles after special paths were built. However, research shows that these paths do not always decrease the number of bicycle accidents. The research shows

WHILE YOU READ ③

Look back in this sentence for a fixed phrase. Highlight it.

Bicycle safety is very important.

that bicycle riders think they are safer on these paths. Therefore, they sometimes ride less carefully on paths than they do on roads with cars.

6   Bicycle riders can also do some things to stay safe. All bicycle riders should wear a helmet. A helmet protects a rider's head in an accident. Most people who die in bicycle accidents were not wearing helmets. Of course, it is more important to avoid an accident. Many accidents occur because riders do not follow the traffic rules. Riders should follow the same rules as cars. In addition, riders should make sure they are visible. They should wear something bright. At night, they should always have a light on their bicycle. With these simple steps, riding a bicycle can be a safe way to get **around**.

7   Bicycles and bicycle-sharing programs are good for riders. Riding a bicycle is less expensive than driving a car. Bicycles also give people exercise. **This** can improve their health. Bicycles are good for cities, too. New bicycle-sharing programs are cheaper than new buses or trains. Bicycle use also reduces the number of cars, so the streets are less crowded. Perhaps the most important thing is their effect on pollution. When more people use bicycles instead of cars, air pollution decreases. However, they are only beneficial if riders use them safely.

WHILE YOU READ ④

Look back in paragraph 6 for a collocation with the verb *follow* and a noun. Highlight the collocation.

WHILE YOU READ ⑤

What earlier idea does *this* refer to? Highlight it.

Main Idea Check

Here are the main ideas of paragraphs 2–6 in Reading 2. Match each paragraph to its main idea. Write the number of the paragraph on the blank line.

___4___ A Bicycle-sharing programs are becoming more popular.

___2___ B The number of bicycles in the world is growing.

___3___ C Bicycle-sharing programs can reduce pollution and traffic.

___6___ D Bicycle riders can do things to stay safe.

___5___ E Cities and towns are trying to improve bicycle safety.

A Closer Look

Look back at Reading 2 to answer the following questions.

1 What are the disadvantages of bicycles? Circle two answers. (Par. 1)
   a They are heavy.
   b They are slow.
   c They cannot carry a lot.
   d They are too expensive for poor people.

2 The people of China ride their bicycles more than people in other countries. True or False? (Par. 4)

3 According to Figure 4.2 on page 111, which statement was true about bicycle production in 2007?
   a It was double the production of 1990.
   b It was less that the production 10 years before.
   c It was more than three times the production of 1970.
   d It is only a little higher than the production in 1980.

4 Which statements are true about bicycle-sharing programs? Circle three answers. (Par. 3)
   a People can use the bicycles for a few weeks or months.
   b Riders can pick up a bicycle in one place and leave it in another place.
   c The number of these programs is increasing.
   d The programs can help reduce pollution.

5 What is one problem bicycle-sharing programs have? (Par. 4)
   a People prefer to drive.
   b They lose a lot of money.
   c Not enough people use the shared-bicycles
   d Many bicycles are stolen.

6 What are some of the consequences of separate bicycle paths? Circle two answers. (Par. 5)

a The number of accidents goes down.
(b) The number of bicycles goes up.
(c) Riders are often less careful.
d Riders stop wearing their helmets.

Skill Review

In Skills and Strategies 6, you learned that supporting details are statements with specific information, such as facts, examples, or reasons. They support the claim the writer is making. Finding supporting details will help you understand what you read.

A Reread paragraphs 4, 6, and 7 in Reading 2. You are given the main ideas for each of these paragraphs below. Find the supporting details, and write them on the blank lines.

1 **Main idea of paragraph 4:** *Bicycle-sharing programs are becoming more popular.*

a there were about 200 bicycle programs all over the world
b the biggest bicycle program is in China
c every year many bicicles are stolen or damaged

2 **Main idea of paragraph 6:** *Bicycle riders can do things to stay safe.*

a there are more than a billion bycicles around the world
b In 1960 the rate of production was 20 million
c I 2007 it was more than 130 million

3 **Main idea of paragraph 7:** *Bicycles are good for both individuals and cities.*

a bycicles improves their health
b bycicles are cheaper than buses or trams
c " also reduce the number of cars
d Air pollution decreases
e is beneficial if riders use them safely

B Compare your answers with a partner's.

Definitions

Find the words in Reading 2 that complete the following definitions.

1 _traffic_ is all of the cars, buses, and trucks on the road. (n) Par. 1

2 A/An _solution_ is an answer to a problem. (n) Par. 1

3 _rate_ is the speed at which something happens. (n) Par. 2

4 To _separate_ things or people is to keep them apart. (v) Par. 5

5 To _create_ is to make something new. (v) Par. 5

6 If things _decrease_, they go down. (v) Par. 5

7 A/An _helmets_ is a strong, hard hat that protects the head. (n) Par. 6

8 Something that is _beneficial_ is useful and helpful. (adj) Par. 7

Words in Context

Complete the sentences with words from Reading 2 in the box below.

annual ✓	contrast ✓	issue ✓	predict ✓
concerns ✓	expert ✓	path ✓	significantly ✓

1 She had a lot of _concerns_ about the house, so she decided not to buy it.

2 They walked along the _path_ by the river.

3 This week's warm weather is in _contrast_ to last week's cold rain.

4 It is important to ask for advice from a medical _expert_ when your child is sick.

5 Many people believe that the most important _issue_ in the country today is the economy.

6 Every January, the company publishes its _annual_ report.

7 The number of cars in China has increased _significantly_ in the last 10 years.

8 Our ability to _predict_ the weather has improved. We know when to expect a storm.

Critical Thinking

In Readings 1 and 2, you read about forms of transportation that can reduce traffic and pollution.

SYNTHESIZING

Critical thinking includes connecting new information to information you learned in previous readings.

A **Discuss the following questions with a partner. Support your answers with arguments from the readings and your own opinions or ideas.**

1 Do you agree that governments should try to control the number of cars on the road?

2 How can governments encourage the use of public transportation?

3 How can governments encourage the use of bicycles?

4 What else can governments do to reduce the number of cars on the road?

B **Share your answers with the rest of the class.**

Research

Choose a city. Find out how much it helps bicycle riders. Find answers to the following questions.

- Are there separate paths for bicycles?
- Is there a bicycle-sharing program?
- Can riders take their bicycles on public transportation?
- Do many people ride bicycles?

Writing

Write a short description of your research.

Finding Contrasts

As you learned in Skills and Strategies 6 on page 83, writers use words or phrases to signal supporting details. Writers can also use words or phrases to signal the relationships between ideas, such as a contrast. A *contrast* is the difference between two or more ideas. Often the contrast shows the reader something unexpected or surprising. *However* and *but* are two common words that signal a contrast. Good readers notice these kinds of words or phrases. They help readers find contrasts and understand what a writer is trying to say.

Examples & Explanations

①Major car companies introduce new cars every year, **but** some new cars come from very small companies. ②In the late 1970s, a man named John DeLorean started a company to produce an unusual sports car. ③**However**, he did not sell enough cars, so he closed the company after only two years. ④**Although** the company only built 9,000 cars, you can sometimes see a DeLorean sports car on the road.

The main idea in this reading is introduced by the word *but*. But introduces a contrast between major car companies and very small companies.

However shows another contrast. In sentence 2, DeLorean started a company. In sentence 3, he closed the company.

Although shows an unexpected contrast: The company built very few cars, but some are still on the road.

The Language of Contrasts

Here are some common words and phrases that signal contrast.

WORDS AND PHRASES THAT SIGNAL CONTRASTS			
but	instead	although	on the one hand
however	in contrast	nevertheless	on the other hand

Strategies

These strategies will help you find contrasts while you read.

- Look for words and phrases that signal contrasts.
- When you see a contrast word or phrase, notice the meaning of the next idea. Ask yourself: *What idea is it different from?*
- If the reading is contrasting things, make a list of the differences.

Skill Practice 1

Read the following paragraphs. Highlight five words or phrases in each paragraph that signal contrasts. Then answer the questions below. The first one has been done for you.

1   Starting a company is always difficult, but starting a car manufacturing company is very difficult. It requires a great deal of money and knowledge. Nevertheless, some people start new companies to build cars. Malcolm Bricklin is one of those people. He started a company in Canada to build cars in 1971. However, he did not know a lot about building cars. He had problems with the design, and it was expensive to make the cars. He sold his first cars in 1974, but the company ran out of money less than two years later. Although the company failed, the cars still win prizes at car shows.

   a Is starting a company to manufacture cars easier than starting other companies?
      It's more difficult.

      What word or phrase signaled this contrast? *but*

   b Why is it surprising that people start companies to make cars? _____
      What word or phrase signaled this contrast? _____

   c The company started selling cars in 1974. When did it close? _____
      What word or phrase signaled this contrast? _____

   d The company failed. What is surprising? _____
      What word or phrase signaled this contrast? _____

2   Henry Ford's first car was very similar to other cars in the early 1900s. However, he tried to make his cars more cheaply. Ford's ideas about making cars were unique. First, Ford did not design cars for rich people. Instead, he wanted average people to own cars. To make his cars less expensive, he found a new way to make cars. Other car designers made cars one by one. A few workers did all the work to finish one car before they started work on the next car. At Ford's company, on the other hand, the cars moved down a line past workers. Each worker completed one

part of a car as it moved down the line. In this way, Ford made more cars quickly, and sold them for less money. Ford also cared about his workers. Although other carmakers paid their workers less than $3 a day, Ford paid his workers $5 a day. He even started an English language school for his workers. Ford sold a lot of cars and became very rich, but he never forgot the people who made the cars.

a How were Ford's cars different from other cars in the early 1900s? _____

What word or phrase signaled this contrast? _____

b Most carmakers in the past designed cars for rich people. Who did Ford design cars for? _____

What word or phrase signaled this contrast? _____

c Most manufacturers made cars one by one. What was different about the way Ford's company made cars? _____

What word or phrase signaled this contrast? _____

d Did Ford pay his workers the same amount as other carmakers? _____

What word or phrase signaled this contrast? _____

Skill Practice 2

Read the following paragraph. Highlight the words or phrases that signal a contrast. Write the differences between the two types of cars in the chart. The first one has been done for you.

When you want to buy a car, should you buy a new car or a used car? On the one hand, new cars are clean and beautiful. Old cars don't look as nice. New cars have all the newest technology. In contrast, used cars have older technology. New cars usually don't have problems, but used cars may need repairs. On the other hand, new cars are more expensive. You don't have to pay as much for a used car.

NEW CARS	USED CARS
are clean and beautiful	don't look as nice

Connecting to the Topic

Discuss the following questions with a partner.

1 Do you think it is safe to eat or drink while you are driving?
2 Do you think it is safe to use the phone while you are driving?
3 Do you always wear a seat belt when you drive or ride in a car?
4 Are there laws about these activities in your country?

Previewing and Predicting

> Reading the title, section headings, and first sentences of each paragraph can help you predict what the different sections of a reading will be about.

A Read the title, the section headings, and the first sentence of each paragraph in Reading 3. Look at the photographs and captions on pages 121–123. Then read the questions below. Write the number of the section (*I, II, III,* or *IV*) next to the question or questions you think the section will answer.

SECTION	QUESTION
IV	How does technology improve car safety?
II	Does cell phone use cause accidents?
III	What are other distractions for drivers?
I	Do a lot of people die in car accidents?
IV	What can people do to make travel by car safer?
III	Is eating while driving dangerous?
II	How do cell phones distract drivers?

B Compare your answers with a partner's.

While You Read

As you read, stop at the end of each sentence that contains words in **bold**. Then follow the instructions in the box in the margin.

The Dangers of Driving

I. Driving Safely

1   Cars can help us in many ways, but they can also be dangerous. Car accidents cause between 20 and 50 million injuries every year around the world. More than a million people die in car accidents every year; in other words, about 3,500 people every day. Every year more and more people drive cars, so this number will probably increase. By 2020, the number of deaths from car accidents will probably rise to almost two million every year.

2   What can drivers do to reduce the number of deaths and injuries in accidents? There is one thing, and it is very easy to do. Drivers should always wear a seat belt. Research shows that 50 percent of deaths in car accidents could be prevented by the use of seat belts. Many countries have laws that require drivers to wear seat belts, but not everyone obeys these laws. Many people don't wear their seat belts because they think they will not have an accident. They think, "I am not driving very far" or "I am not driving very fast." However, most accidents happen when people are driving less than 37 miles per hour (60 kilometers per hour) and when they are near their **homes**.

3   There is one other serious danger for drivers – **distractions**. These are the things that can take a driver's attention away from driving: other cars, people on the street, the weather. It is therefore difficult and dangerous for them to do other things while they are driving. There are many distractions for drivers, such as the radio, passengers in the car, or even a cup of coffee. All of these distractions can cause accidents.

WHILE YOU READ 1

Look back in paragraph 2 for words that signal a contrast. Highlight the signals.

WHILE YOU READ 2

Look in the next sentence for a definition of *distraction*. Highlight it.

Wearing a seat belt helps prevent serious injury in a car accident.

It is really dangerous to write and read text messages while driving.

II. Cell Phones

4   One recent cause of distraction is cell phones. The number of cell phones has increased significantly. Drivers are much more likely to have an accident if they are talking on the phone. Many places now have laws against holding a phone while you are driving. However, research shows that the problem is not just the phone. The problem is the conversation. Phones that do not require hands are just as dangerous as phones that drivers must hold in their hands.

5   Texting, that is, reading or writing on your phone, while driving is even more dangerous than talking. When drivers text, they are not looking at the road. Instead, they are looking at their phone for four or five seconds. Teenagers are the most likely to use their phones while they are driving. A study of U.S. teenagers showed that half of them say they text while they drive. This can lead to an accident. In the United States, more than 3,000 deaths were caused by distractions while driving in 2010. Some experts recommend that cell phone use in cars should be **banned**.

6   According to a recent study, drivers know texting or talking while driving is dangerous. Why do they still do it? Some people want to stay connected to their friends and family. Other people want to stay connected to their office. They do not want to miss an important call. They feel they need to continue working while they are driving. Finally, sometimes people are just bored when they are driving and they want something to do.

III. Other Distractions for Drivers

7   There are other dangerous distractions for drivers. Research shows that eating or drinking while driving is also very dangerous. Eating and drinking means that drivers must take their hands off the wheel. When drivers are doing two things at the same time, it is difficult for them to pay attention. Nevertheless, driving and eating or drinking is

WHILE YOU READ 3

Look back in paragraph 5 for a word that signals a contrast. Highlight the signal.

very common. One study found that 70 percent of drivers sometimes eat when they drive, and 83 percent sometimes drink when they drive. It may be surprising, but eating and drinking while driving is even more dangerous than texting or talking on the phone while driving. One study estimates that it can increase the chance of an accident by 80 percent!

8   One final distraction may be surprising. Some people shave or put on makeup while they are driving. Of course, this is dangerous because drivers must take one or both of their hands off the wheel. Also, they have to look away from the road for a few seconds. In 2009, a driver in Chicago was putting on nail polish when she hit and killed a motorcycle rider. She is now in jail. A study of women drivers in England in 2009 shows that 20 percent of them sometimes put on their makeup while they are driving.

IV. New Safety Technology

9   Scientists and engineers are finding ways to improve safety and decrease the number of accidents. They are using new technology to do this. There are new cell phones that turn off when the car is moving. Some "smart" cars also have new technology that tells drivers if they are too close to another car or if they are not in the center of the road. These cars can also tell when a driver is starting to fall asleep. If a smart car senses it may hit another car, it can stop very quickly – before the driver touches the **brakes**.

10   Driving can be dangerous, but people and technology can make it safer. If people drive carefully, wear a seat belt, and avoid distractions such as cell phones, food, and makeup, they will be safer. They will also make the roads safer for other people.

WHILE YOU READ 4

What is the main idea of paragraph 9? Highlight it.

What makes this man such a dangerous driver?

Main Idea Check

Match the main ideas below to five of the paragraphs in Reading 3. Write the number of the paragraph on the blank line.

__6__ A Although drivers know some things are dangerous, they still do them.

__9__ B New technology can decrease distractions and accidents.

__3__ C Many things can distract drivers.

__5__ D Texting is a serious distraction.

__2__ E Seat belts are the best way to prevent death and injury.

A Closer Look

Look back at Reading 3 to answer the following questions.

1 The number of people who die every year in car accidents continues to increase.
True or False? (Par. 1)

2 What is the most important thing that drivers can do to prevent deaths or injuries in accidents? (Par. 2)
   a They should pay attention to traffic.
   b They should wear their seat belts.
   c They should not talk while they are driving.
   d They should drive more slowly.

3 What is *not* mentioned as a distraction for drivers? (Par. 3)
   a The radio
   b A cup of coffee
   c The weather
   d Traffic signals
   e Other passengers

4 Phones that do not require hands are safer than phones that require hands.
True or False? (Par. 4)

5 Distractions cause many accidents. Some experts believe in banning cell phone use while driving, to decrease the number of accidents. **True or False?** (Par. 5)

6 What are some dangerous distractions for drivers? Circle three answers.
   (Pars. 7 and 8)
   a Shaving
   b Eating
   c Singing
   d Talking
   e Putting on makeup

7 Which activity increases the chance of accidents the most? (Par. 7)
   a Using a cell phone
   b Putting on makeup
   c Eating or drinking
   d Listening to the radio

8 How will new technology prevent accidents? Circle three answers. (Par. 9)

a Cell phones will signal that a driver is starting to fall asleep.

b Cars will signal that the driver is not driving in a straight line.

c Cars will not let drivers operate the radio.

d Cell phones will not operate in moving cars.

e Cars will signal that the driver is starting to fall asleep.

9 How do all of the activities described in Reading 3 distract drivers?

a They are all against the law.

b They all take drivers attention away from driving.

c They all use new technology.

d They all make drivers go too fast.

Skill Review

In Skills and Strategies 8, you learned that writers use word and phrases to signal that they are contrasting ideas. Noticing these words and phrases will help you see the relationships between ideas in a reading.

A **Read these sentences from Reading 3. Find and highlight the words that signal contrast.**

1 Many countries have laws that require drivers to wear seat belts, but not everyone obeys these laws.

2 They think, "I am not driving very far" or "I am not driving very fast." However, most accidents happen when people are driving less than 37 miles per hour (60 kilometers per hour) and when they are near their homes.

3 Many places now have laws against holding a phone while you are driving. However, research shows that the problem is not just the phone. The problem is the conversation. Phones that do not require hands are just as dangerous as phones that drivers must hold in their hands.

4 When drivers text, they are not looking at the road. Instead, they are looking at their phone for four or five seconds.

5 Research shows that eating or drinking while driving is also very dangerous. Eating and drinking means that drivers must take their hands off the wheel. When drivers are doing two things at the same time, it is difficult for them to pay attention. Nevertheless, driving and eating or drinking is very common.

B **Work with a partner, and discuss what the writer is contrasting in each case.**

Vocabulary Development

Definitions

Find the words in Reading 3 that complete the following definitions.

1 _seat belt_ go across your body while you are driving. They protect you in an accident. (n pl) Par. 2

2 An _distraction_ is something that stops you from paying attention. (n) Par. 3

3 _passengers_ are people in a car, train, bus, or plane who are not driving. (n pl) Par. 3

4 _teenagers_ are people older than twelve but younger than twenty. (n pl) Par. 5

5 To _recommend_ something is to give a good idea. (v) Par. 5

6 To _shave_ is to cut hair from the face or body. (v) Par. 8

7 _makeup_ is something women put on their faces, especially their eyes and mouth, to make them look prettier. (n) Par. 8

8 _brakes_ are the part of the car that you touch with your foot to stop the car from moving. (n pl) Par. 9

Synonyms

Complete the sentences with words from Reading 3 in the box below. These words replace the words or phrases in parentheses, which are similar in meaning.

avoid	conversation	injuries	missed
banned	estimated	lead to	obeyed

1 The children (followed) _obeyed_ the teacher's instructions.

2 They had a long (talk) _conversation_ about their plans for the future.

3 The government (guessed) _estimated_ that about 200 people died in the fire.

4 The accident caused (physical harm) _injuries_. The bike riders had broken legs and arms.

5 She tries to (stay away from) _avoid_ food with a lot of fat and sugar.

6 The government has (stopped) _banned_ texting while driving.

7 Texting while driving can (result in) _lead to_ an accident.

8 I (did not receive) _missed_ your phone call because I was not at home.

Academic Word List

The following are Academic Word List words from all the readings in Unit 4. Use these words to complete the sentences. (For more on the Academic Word List, see page 260.)

annual (adj)	create (v)	estimated (v)	injuries (n)	location (n)
beneficial (adj)	decline (n)	experts (n)	issues (n)	significantly (adv)

1 The company hired several computer _experts_ to improve the company's technology.

2 The government must _create_ more jobs so that more people can work.

3 We get a/an _annual_ card from our cousins every New Year's Day.

4 The store has moved to a new _location_ on the other side of the city.

5 Good food and exercise are _beneficial_ for your health.

6 The child's health has improved _significantly_. He is feeling much better this week.

7 There was a/an _decline_ in the president's popularity after the election.

8 He _estimated_ that it would cost about $1,000 to repair the car.

9 The government committee discussed two very important _issues_ – air and water pollution.

10 Some of the soldiers died, and others had serious _injuries_.

Critical Thinking

Reading 3 discusses many different activities that are dangerous for drivers. It also discusses laws that limit some of these activities.

PERSONALIZING

Thinking about how new information applies to your own life can help you understand a text better. The new information can also make you think about whether you should change your own behavior and values.

A Discuss the following questions with a group of your classmates.

1 Have you or people you know ever done the following when driving?

   a Eat or drink   d Shave or put on makeup

   b Talk on the phone   e Listen to music

   c Text

2 Have you ever done or seen another person do something else that was dangerous while driving? What was it?

3 Should there be a punishment for people who do these things while driving? What should it be?

B Share your answers with the rest of your classmates.

Research

Do some research in the city or town where you live. Find answers to the following questions.

- Are there laws that require seat belts?
- Are there laws that require special seats for babies and children?
- Are there laws against talking on the phone while driving?
- Are there laws against texting while driving?

Writing

Write a brief summary of the driving laws that you found.

Improving Your Reading Speed

Good readers read quickly and still understand most of what they read.

A Read the instructions and strategies for Improving Your Reading Speed in Appendix 3 on page 273.

B Choose one of the readings in this unit. Read it without stopping. Time how long it takes you to finish the text in minutes and seconds. Enter the time in the chart on page 274. Then calculate your reading speed in number of words per minute.

CONTRAST CONNECTORS

Writers often connect ideas by showing a contrast between them. A contrast explains how one idea is different from another idea. Writers can use transition words or phrases such as *however, on the one hand, on the other hand, in contrast,* or *nevertheless* to make these connections. You learned these words and phrases in Skills and Strategies 8 on page 117.

Exercise 1

Read the following paragraphs. Highlight any words or phrases that signal contrast. Underline any words or phrases that signal additional information (see page 63) or facts and examples (see page 95). The first one has been done for you.

1   When visiting another country, driving a car is a good way to see the countryside. However, this may be dangerous, because driving in another country may be very different. For instance, in Canada and the United States, people drive on the right side of the road. In contrast, in England and Japan, people drive on the left.

2   In many countries all over the world, teenagers can start to drive at 18. However, in some countries, for example in New Zealand, they can get their driver's license at 15. On the other hand, in other locations teenagers cannot drive by themselves for the first year of their license.

3   Many places have special rules for teenage drivers. For example, the rules may require teenager drivers to have an older driver in the car, or they may limit the number of passengers in the car. Teenagers may not like these rules. Nevertheless, these rules help to make the roads safe for all drivers.

4   Motorcycles are more energy efficient than cars. Research shows that motorcycles use half the fuel that cars use. On the other hand, they are also more dangerous. Eighty percent of motorcycle accidents result in injury or death. In contrast, only 20 percent of automobile accidents result in injury or death.

5   At one time, Los Angeles had a fast and efficient public transportation system. However, the city took away the streetcars and built more highways. Now, Los Angeles has the worst traffic in the United States. It also has very bad pollution.

Exercise 2

Make a clear paragraph by putting sentences A, B, and C into the best order after the numbered sentence. Look for pronouns and words or phrases that signal contrast or addition to help you. Write the letters in the correct order on the blank lines.

1 Companies have several choices about how to transport their products. ___ ___ ___

| **A** They are also cheaper because they need fewer workers to operate them. | **B** However, they are often not as convenient as trucks. | **C** For instance, trains use less energy than trucks. |

2 Bicycles with electric motors are becoming more popular. ___ ___ ___

| **A** This is because they go faster than other bicycles on the road and cannot stop as quickly. | **B** However, this has become a concern in some places. | **C** For example, in China they have caused a lot of injuries. |

3 People used to get good exercise when they rode their bicycles to work. ___ ___ ___

| **A** Now, however, more and more people ride bicycles with electric motors. | **B** However, the only exercise they get is starting the motor. | **C** These make it easier for people to get to work. |

4 Many parents encourage their children to obey all safety laws. ___ ___ ___

| **A** They also make them wear helmets when they ride their bicycles. | **B** For example, they make sure that their children wear seat belts in the car. | **C** These actions will help children avoid injuries. |

5 Roundabouts are traffic circles where roads meet. ___ ___ ___

| **A** This is because some drivers don't know which direction to drive in. | **B** On the other hand, studies suggest that they reduce the number of injuries. | **C** They are sometimes confusing for drivers. |

5

SLEEP

SKILLS AND STRATEGIES

- Finding the Meanings of Words
- Finding Causes and Effects

Finding the Meanings of Words

As you learned in Skills and Strategies 1 on page 2, writers sometimes give definitions to explain words that readers may not know. Sometimes, however, writers do not give exact definitions. Instead, they give additional information such as examples or contrasts. Examples and contrasts can help show the meaning of the word. You learned about some words and phrases that signal examples in Skills and Strategies 6 on page 83. You learned about some words and phrases that signal contrast in Skills and Strategies 8 on page 117. Good readers look for definitions as they read, but they also look for words and phrases that signal additional information. This helps them find the meanings of words.

Examples & Explanations

Sleepwalking may be **genetic**. For example, a person who sleepwalks is likely to have a family member who also walks in his or her sleep.

Sometimes writers give examples that show the meaning of a word. They sometimes introduce the examples with phrases, such as *for example, for instance,* or *such as.*

genetic = common among family members

I used to have **insomnia**, but now I have no difficulty sleeping at all.

Sometimes you can figure out a word because the writer gives a contrast or an opposite meaning. Here, the writer says that she had *insomnia* in the past. She signals a contrast with the word *but* and says that now she has no difficulty sleeping.

insomnia = difficulty sleeping

Strategies

These strategies will help you find the meanings of words while you read.

- When you read a word you do not know, do not stop reading. Continue to the end of the sentence that contains the difficult word, and then read the next sentence.
- Look for definitions of difficult words. See Skills and Strategies 1 on page 2.
- Search for words and phrases that signal examples or contrasts. Use this information to guess the meaning of a word.

Skill Practice 1

Read the following sentences. What kind of additional information in each sentence can help you figure out the meaning of the words in bold? Is the information an example, a contrast, or a definition? Circle the type of information. Then highlight the clues that helped you. The first one has been done for you.

1 I had to sleep on the floor last night, but today I bought a **mattress** for my bed. I was much more comfortable.

   a example   **b** contrast   c definition

2 **Snoring** can be very loud. For example, when someone in a family snores, it may wake up other people sleeping nearby.

   a example   b contrast   c definition

3 People often have **nightmares**. However, when they wake up, they often can't remember what scared them.

   a example   b contrast   c definition

4 Animals such as bears **hibernate**; that is, they go to sleep for the winter.

   a example   b contrast   c definition

5 Small, flat beds such as **futons** are very useful in small apartments.

   a example   b contrast   c definition

6 Some people take a **sleeping pill** at night, but many people have hot milk instead of medicine when they can't sleep.

   a example   b contrast   c definition

7 On cold nights I sleep with two **blankets**. However, on warm nights I don't use anything to cover myself.

   a example   b contrast   c definition

8 Although a lot of people avoid **caffeine** at night, I don't have any trouble sleeping when I have coffee or tea after dinner.

   a example   b contrast   c definition

Skill Practice 2

Read the sentences in Skill Practice 1 again to figure out the meaning of each word in bold. Circle the correct meaning. The first one has been done for you.

1 I had to sleep on the floor last night, but today I bought a **mattress** for my bed. I was much more comfortable.

   a the thing that goes under your head when you sleep

   (b) the part of a bed that you put your whole body on when you sleep

2 **Snoring** can be very loud. For example, when someone in a family snores, it may wake up other people sleeping nearby.

   a walking while you sleep

   b making noise while you sleep

3 People often have **nightmares**. However, when they wake up, they often can't remember what scared them.

   a something that scares you while you sleep

   b something good that happens to you while you sleep

4 Animals such as bears **hibernate**; that is, they go to sleep for the winter.

   a go to sleep for the winter

   b go to a warmer area to live in the winter

5 Small, flat beds such as **futons** are very useful in small apartments.

   a small beds

   b small apartments

6 Some people take a **sleeping pill** at night, but many people have hot milk instead of medicine when they can't sleep.

   a medicine that helps you wake up in the morning

   b medicine that helps you sleep

7 On cold nights I sleep with two **blankets**. However, on warm nights I don't use anything to cover myself.

   a something to put under your head when you sleep

   b a warm cover

8 Although a lot of people avoid **caffeine** at night, I don't have any trouble sleeping when I have coffee or tea after dinner.

   a a chemical in things such as coffee and tea that makes people feel more awake

   b a special strong coffee that people drink in very small cups after dinner

Connecting to the Topic

Discuss the following questions with a partner.

1 How many hours do you sleep every night? _10 hours_

2 Do you sleep more or less than you did when you were younger? Explain your answer.

3 How do you feel if you don't get enough sleep? Explain your answer.

4 Do you dream every night? Do you remember your dreams?

Previewing and Predicting

Preview any graphic material in a text before you start reading it. This can help prepare you for some of the information that you will read about.

A Look at Figures 5.1 and 5.2 on pages 136 and 137. Then write *T* on the blank lines if the following statements are true and *F* if they are false.

_T_ a Human adults sleep 8–9 hours every day.

_F_ b Cows and pigs sleep more than human adults.

_T_ c Cows and sheep sleep less than human adults.

_F_ d The amount of sleep that adults need increases as they grow older.

_T_ e Little babies are asleep more than they are awake.

_T_ f After the age of 50, most adults sleep less than 7 hours a day.

B Compare you answers with a partner's. Then discuss what information you will probably read in the text.

While You Read

As you read, stop at the end of each sentence that contains words in **bold**. Then follow the instructions in the box in the margin.

◀)) The Importance of Sleep

1   For about one third of your life, your eyes will be closed. You will not move very much. You will breathe very slowly. You will be quiet. In other words, for about one third of your life, you will be asleep.

2   Why do we sleep so much? What is the **purpose**? Scientists do not have a complete answer. They believe that sleep restores your energy and helps your brain work better. If you do not sleep enough, you cannot concentrate on your work, and you feel tired all day. Without enough sleep, you are also more likely to get sick.

3   Sleep is important for normal development. This means that children need a lot of sleep in order to grow up strong and healthy. During the first two weeks of life, babies sleep for about 16 hours every day. This changes as they grow and need less sleep. Teenagers still need about 9 hours of sleep every night, but most adults need less – only about 8 hours. After about the age of 70, most adults only sleep for about 6 hours every night. (See Figure 5.1.)

4   All animals need sleep, but there is great variation in how much they sleep. (See Figure 5.2.) For example, some big snakes sleep for more than 18 hours a day. Sheep only sleep for about 4 hours, and giraffes sleep less than 2 hours a day! Pigs sleep for 8 hours a day just like adult **humans**.

> **WHILE YOU READ** 1
>
> As you read paragraphs 2 and 3, look for four supporting details for the purpose of sleep. Highlight them.

> **WHILE YOU READ** 2
>
> What is the main idea of paragraph 4? Highlight it.

Figure 5.1 Number of Hours of Sleep We Need as We Grow

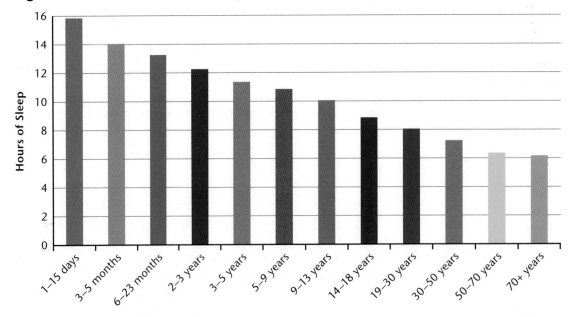

Source: www.faculty.washington.edu

Figure 5.2 Hours of Sleep per Day

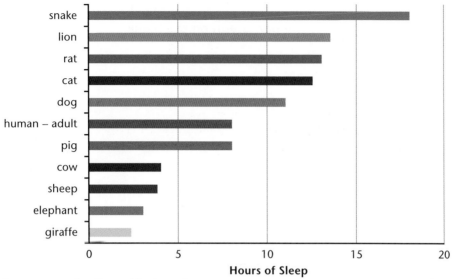

Source: www.faculty.washington.edu

5   Adult humans usually sleep for a long period and then are awake for a long period. In contrast, most animals do not sleep for one long period. Instead, they sleep for shorter periods during the day and night. Human babies and animals have similar sleep patterns. They sleep for a few hours, and then they stay awake for a few hours.

6   Scientists are also learning more about how people sleep. They know there are five different stages of sleep. Brain activity changes during these stages. During the last stage of sleep, something strange happens. Many of the muscles in your body are paralyzed; in contrast, your brain becomes very active. While your body is inactive, your eyes move rapidly, and you breathe more quickly, **too**. This stage is called Rapid Eye Movement (REM) sleep. Adults usually go through about five periods of REM sleep every night.

7   REM sleep is when people have most of their dreams. If a person has one dream in each of these REM periods, that is about 2,000 dreams every year. Humans and many animals have dreams, but scientists are not sure of the purpose of dreams. Some scientists believe dreams help people understand things that happen during the day. Other scientists think dreams help us remember **things**.

8   There are still many things we do not understand about sleep. However, one thing we do know is that all animals, including humans, need to sleep. They need to sleep in order to grow and to keep their brains and bodies active and healthy. They need to sleep or they will get sick and die.

WHILE YOU READ 3

Look in this sentence for a word with a prefix. Highlight the prefix.

WHILE YOU READ 4

Look back in paragraph 7 for a collocation with a verb and the noun *dream*. Highlight the collocation.

Main Idea Check

Here are the main ideas of paragraphs 2–7 in Reading 1. Match each paragraph to its main idea. Write the number of the paragraph on the blank line.

_7_ A Dreams occur during REM sleep.

_2_ B Scientists believe sleep may have several purposes.

_3_ C Sleep is very important for healthy growth.

_6_ D The REM stage of sleep is when the brain is most active.

_5_ E Some animals sleep for one long period every day; others sleep for several shorter periods.

_4_ F Not all animals need the same amount of sleep.

A Closer Look

Look back at Reading 1 to answer the following questions.

1 You sleep for about half of your life. **True or False?** (Par. 1)

2 Which of the following is *not* stated as a purpose of sleep? (Pars. 2 and 3)
   a Sleep restores our energy.
   b Sleep keeps us healthy.
   c Sleep helps us think better.
   d Sleep makes us more intelligent.
   e Sleep helps children grow up healthy.

3 Our need for sleep changes as we grow older. About how many hours do we need at each age? Fill in the chart with the number of hours we need at each age. (Par. 3)

AGES	HOURS OF SLEEP
Babies	16
Teenagers	9
Adults	8
People over 70 years old	6

4 What is similar about the sleep patterns of human babies and many animals? (Par. 5)
   a They sleep for 16 hours a day.
   b They need less sleep as they grow older.
   c They sleep for short periods and then are awake for short periods.
   d They cannot concentrate if they do not sleep enough.

5 What does *not* happen during the REM stage of sleep? (Pars. 6 and 7)
   a You breathe more quickly.
   b You save energy.
   c You dream.
   d Your body does not move.
   e Your eyes move.

6 Some scientists believe that dreams help people understand what happens to them during the day. **True or False?** (Par. 7)

Skill Review

In Skills and Strategies 9, you learned that writers sometimes give additional information in the form of examples or contrasts. Noticing this information can sometimes help you figure out the meaning of some unfamiliar words in a text.

A Read the sentences below from Reading 1. Decide if the writer is using *contrast* or *examples* to explain the words in **bold**. Write *C* (for *contrast*) or *E* (for *example*) on the blank lines, and highlight the part of each text that contains either the contrast or the example.

1 ___C___ Sleep is important for **normal development**. This means that children need a lot of sleep in order to grow up strong and healthy.

2 ___C___ Teenagers still need about 9 hours of sleep every night, but most **adults** need less – only about 8 hours.

3 ___E___ All animals need sleep, but there is great **variation** in how much they sleep. For example, some big snakes sleep for more than 18 hours a day. Sheep only sleep for about 4 hours, and giraffes sleep less than 2 hours a day!

4 ___C___ Human babies and animals have similar sleep **patterns**. They sleep for a few hours, and then they stay awake for a few hours.

5 ___C___ Many of the muscles in your body are **paralyzed**; in contrast, your brain becomes very active.

B Read the sentences below. They each include an example or contrast that helps explain a word that you have learned in earlier units. Choose the word in **bold** that fits the meaning of the sentence best.

1 Today there are many choices for **production** / **protection** / **transportation**, for example, buses, trains, subways and cars.

2 The first speaker was very **loud** / **brief** / **distracted**, but the second speaker continued for more than 2 hours.

3 In the middle of the day, stores are often very **crowded** / **familiar** / **quiet**; in contrast, there are very few people early in the morning.

4 Computers have many **features** / **advantages** / **differences** compared to paper and pencil. You can write faster and make changes and save them easily.

5 The students were very **childish** / **embarrassed** / **serious**. They were throwing food and drawing funny pictures of their teachers.

Definitions

Find the words in Reading 1 that complete the following definitions.

1 To _____ something is to make it the way it was earlier. (*v*) Par. 2

2 Something that is usual and expected is _____. (*adj*) Par. 3

3 A / An _____ is a person who is 18 years or older. (*n pl*) Par. 3

4 _____ are the particular way that things occur. They occur in these same ways over and over. (*n pl*) Par. 5

5 _____ are specific periods during an activity. (*n pl*) Par. 6

6 Something that is very unusual is _____. (*adj*) Par. 6

7 _____ are the parts of the body that make you move. (*n pl*) Par. 6

8 Someone or something that cannot move is _____. (*adj*) Par. 6

Words in Context

A Use context clues to match the first part of each sentence to its correct second part and to understand the meaning of the words in **bold**.

_____ 1 The **development** of the brain begins

_____ 2 There is a lot of **variation** in

_____ 3 Many people are **inactive** during the cold weather,

_____ 4 I cannot **concentrate**

_____ 5 **Snakes** often eat

_____ 6 People often speak **rapidly**

_____ 7 Many people do not remember their **dreams**

_____ 8 People **breathe** more quickly

a when they wake up in the morning.

b when they are nervous.

c how English is spoken around the world.

d long before birth.

e when they run or swim.

f but they do more exercise when it gets warmer.

g animals that are quite large.

h when there is a lot of noise in the room.

B Compare your answers with a partner's. Discuss what clues helped you match the parts of the sentences and helped you understand what the words in **bold** mean.

Critical Thinking

In Reading 1, you learned about sleep patterns that seem familiar or ordinary to most people today. However, you may be surprised to know that these sleep patterns are not ordinary to many people who live outside of the modern western world. They were also not ordinary to people in the western world until about 200 years ago.

> **ANALYZING INFORMATION**
>
> Critical thinking means thinking carefully about important topics that the writer has not completely explained.

A Discuss the following questions with a partner.

1 What might some other sleep patterns be?

2 Why do you think other cultures have different sleep patterns?

3 Why do you think the familiar sleep patterns in Reading 1 are so recent – only about 200 years old?

B Share your ideas with the rest of the class.

Research

Do some research on sleep. Ask 10 people of different ages the following questions.

- How many hours do you usually sleep at night?
- How much sleep do you think you need?

Do their answers to your questions match the descriptions in paragraph 3 of Reading 1?

Writing

Write a brief summary comparing your class results with Figure 5.1 on page 136.

Connecting to the Topic

Discuss the following questions with a partner.

1 Is it difficult for you to fall asleep at night?

2 Do you use a clock to wake up in the morning, or do you wake up without help?

3 Do you ever sleep during the day? Explain your answer.

4 Has anything bad ever happened to you when you didn't get enough sleep? Explain your answer.

Previewing and Predicting

> Reading the first paragraph and looking at any art can help you predict what a reading will be about.

A Read the first paragraph of Reading 2, and look at the photographs on pages 143 and 144. Then put a check (✓) next to the topics you think will be discussed in the reading.

____✓ a The importance of sleep for learning

_____ b The science of dreams

_____ c Sleeping on airplanes

_____ d The importance of sleep for making good decisions

____✓ e What happens when people do not get enough sleep

____✓ f Medications that can help you sleep

____✓ g Sleep and accidents

B Compare your answer with a partner's. Discuss where you got the information for each answer – the text or the photographs.

While You Read

As you read, stop at the end of each sentence that contains words in bold. Then follow the instructions in the box in the margin.

◀)) Getting Enough Sleep

1   Sleep is important for our physical health. Without sleep, people would be too tired to work or play. **However**, sleep may be even more important for our mental health. Sleep helps our brains work when we are awake. It improves our ability to remember, learn, and make good decisions. It also helps us respond to things around us. If people don't get enough sleep, there can be serious **consequences**.

2   Sleep is necessary for memory and learning. People do not learn and remember as well when they are tired. One study compared two groups of students. The first group studied for a test for a few hours and then went to sleep for 8 hours. The second group studied for most of the night and slept for only a few hours. The students in the first group did much better on the test the next day.

3   Good decisions and good judgment also require sleep. To make a good decision, it is useful to consider different aspects of a problem or situation. Research shows that people who have not slept enough cannot do this very well. As a result, they sometimes make bad decisions. Sleepy people often do not realize that there is a problem with their behavior. They believe that they are acting and thinking normally.

4   Scientists have found that you respond more slowly if you have not had enough sleep. Many times every day, you respond to everything around you, such as a hot plate, a bright light, or a loud noise. It is often essential to respond quickly. Response time is especially important if you are driving or using a machine. For example, if a person walks into the street in front of your car, you must stop quickly. If

Getting enough sleep is very important for people who drive or operate machines.

WHILE YOU READ ❶

Highlight the two ideas in paragraph 1 that are in contrast.

WHILE YOU READ ❷

Look back in paragraph 1 for a collocation with a verb and the noun *decisions*. Highlight the collocation.

you are sleepy, you may respond too slowly. Many car accidents occur because drivers are tired. One recent study showed that even small reductions of sleep make a big difference. In other words, if you get 7 hours of sleep – just 1 hour less than the 8 hours that doctors recommend – your response time will get **worse**.

5   Although the importance of sleep is clear, many people do not get enough sleep. Many adults have sleep problems, or insomnia. They cannot fall asleep easily, or they wake up and cannot go back to sleep. There are many reasons for this. Some people have health problems that prevent them from sleeping well. Other people eat or drink something, such as coffee, that keeps them awake. However, the most important reason for insomnia is stress. People often feel **stress**, for instance, when they work too hard or if they are worried about something.

6   There are some things you can do if you do not get enough sleep during the night. One solution is a nap – a short sleep during the day. A short nap of about 10 to 20 minutes can help restore your energy and improve your response time. Many famous people in history liked to take naps. Albert Einstein, Winston Churchill, and Ronald Reagan often took naps. They believed that naps helped them work **better**.

7   Sleep is important for health and safety, so it is unfortunate that so many people do not get sufficient sleep. If you cannot fall asleep or stay asleep, here are some ideas that may help you:

- Try to go to sleep and wake up at about the same time every day.
- Don't eat just before you go to bed.
- Don't drink alcohol or coffee before you go to bed.
- Don't work just before you go to bed.
- Do something that is low stress for at least 30 minutes before you go to bed. Read a book, listen to quiet music, or watch television.
- Make sure your room is not too hot or too cold.
- Make sure your bed is comfortable.

WHILE YOU READ ❸

What is the main idea of paragraph 4? Highlight it.

WHILE YOU READ ❹

Find a clue in this sentence that signals the definition of *stress*. Highlight the definition.

WHILE YOU READ ❺

Look back in paragraph 6 for a collocation with a verb and the noun *nap*. Highlight the collocation.

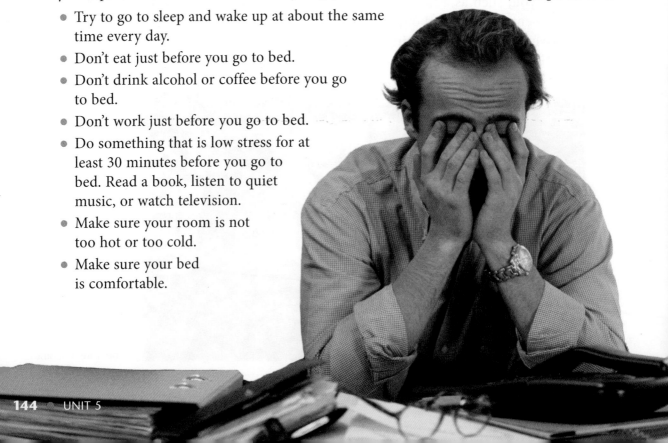

Main Idea Check

Here are the main ideas of paragraphs 2–7 in Reading 2. Match each paragraph to its main idea. Write the number of the paragraph on the blank line.

_3_ A You need a good night's sleep to have good judgment.

_2_ B Sleep helps you learn and remember.

_7_ C There are things you can do to help you fall asleep.

_5_ D Many people do not sleep enough.

_6_ E A nap can help if you do not sleep enough at night.

_4_ F Sleep influences response time.

A Closer Look

Look back at Reading 2 to answer the following questions.

1 One study showed that students who study all night do well on tests. **True or False?** (Par. 2)

2 What happens to people's judgment if they do not sleep enough? Circle two answers. (Par. 3)

    a People who do not sleep enough cannot think about different sides of a question or problem.

    b People who do not sleep enough often make decisions too quickly.

    c People who do not sleep enough do not know they are making bad decisions.

    d People who do not sleep enough sometimes get angry.

3 Why is response time important? Circle two answers. (Par. 4)

    a If you don't respond quickly, you will not get enough work done.

    b If you don't respond quickly in a dangerous situation, you could injure yourself.

    c If you don't respond quickly, you may forget important information.

    d If you don't respond quickly in a dangerous situation, you may injure someone else.

4 A small reduction in the amount of time you sleep will not have much effect on your response time. **True or False?** (Par. 4)

5 Why do people have trouble falling asleep? Circle three answers. (Par. 5)

    a They eat or drink something that keeps them awake.

    b They have a lot of stress in their lives.

    c They nap during the day.

    d They take too much medicine.

    e They have health problems

6 According to paragraph 3, which of the following statements are true about naps? Circle two answers. (Par. 6)

(a) Many famous people have liked to take naps.

b It can be dangerous to nap when you are at work.

c They make it difficult to sleep at night.

(d) They can restore your energy.

7 Look at the list at the end of the reading. What are some ideas for people who cannot fall asleep at night? Circle three answers.

a Eat something small just before you go to bed.

(b) Do something that is low stress for 30 minutes before you go to bed.

c Run for 30 minutes just before you go to bed.

d Make sure your room is warm.

(e) Go to bed and wake up at about the same time every day.

(f) Don't drink coffee at night.

Skill Review

In Skills and Strategies 1, you learned that writers sometimes signal that they are providing a definition of a word or phrase. In Skills and Strategies 9, on the other hand, you learned that writers sometimes provide examples that can help you figure out the meaning of words. Looking for these signals can help you understand unfamiliar vocabulary.

A Read the sentences below from Reading 2 to find definitions and examples of the words in **bold**. Highlight the words and signals that help you understand the meaning of the words in **bold**.

1 **Response time** is especially important if you are driving or using a machine. For example, if a person walks into the street in front of your car, you must stop quickly. If you are sleepy, you may respond too slowly.

2 There are some things you can do if you do not get enough sleep during the night. One solution is a **nap** – a short sleep during the day.

3 One recent study showed that even small **reductions** of sleep make a difference. In other words, if you get 7 hours of sleep – just 1 hour less than the 8 hours that doctors recommend – your response time will get worse.

4 Although the importance of sleep is clear, many people do not get enough sleep. Many adults have sleep problems, or **insomnia**.

B Compare your answers with a partner's.

Definitions

Find the words in Reading 2 that complete the following definitions.

1 _____ issues are related to thinking and to the brain. (*adj*) Par. 1

2 People who have good _____ can make good decisions. (*n*) Par. 3

3 A/An _____ is a particular feature of something, especially of something that is complicated. (*n*) Par. 3

4 To _____ something is to come to understand it, often quickly. (*v*) Par. 3

5 Something that is very, very important is _____. (*adj*) Par. 4

6 _____ is great concern and worry about a difficult situation. (*n*) Par. 5

7 A/An _____ is a short sleep during the day. (*n*) Par. 6

8 _____ is a liquid that is in wine and beer that makes people behave differently. (*n*) Par. 7

Words in Context

Complete the sentences with words or phrases from Reading 2 in the box below.

ability	comfortable	fell asleep	sufficient
at least	consequences	memory	unfortunate

1 Small babies do not have the _____ to speak or walk.

2 His family did not have _____ money to buy an expensive car, so they chose a smaller, less expensive one.

3 You must be _____ 18 years old to vote for the president.

4 The new student had an excellent _____. He never forgot anything.

5 It was _____ that there was bad weather during the football game.

6 She was very tired, so she _____ soon after dinner.

7 The _____ of insomnia include problems with remembering and making decisions.

8 This bed was very _____. I slept very well last night.

Critical Thinking

In Reading 2, you read that *sleep deprivation* **occurs when you don't get enough sleep for several nights. Two important facts that have come from studies of sleep deprivation are:**

APPLYING INFORMATION

You use critical thinking when you apply information you have just learned to new situations.

- Even a small amount of sleep deprivation, for example, 6 hours a night for 2 nights, causes problems with thinking, responding, and making decisions.
- People with sleep deprivation don't know that they are having these problems. They think they are thinking and responding normally.

A **With a partner, make a list of what could happen if the following people suffered from serious sleep deprivation.**

a Pilots
b Students
c Soldiers
d Doctors
e Truck drivers
f Professional athletes

B **Compare your ideas with the rest of your class.**

Research

Do some research on sleep with your classmates. Find answers to the following questions.

- What do you do just before you go to bed?
- What do you do if you cannot fall asleep?
- What do you do if you wake up in the middle of the night?

Writing

Based on your classmates' responses, write a list of suggestions like the ones at the end of Reading 2. Include suggestions for the following.

- What to do if you want to fall asleep
- What to do if you wake up in the middle of the night and can't fall asleep again

Finding Causes and Effects

As you learned in Skills and Strategies 8 on page 117, writers use words or phrases to signal the relationship between ideas, such as a contrast. Writers can also use words or phrases to signal causes and effects. A *cause* gives reasons for an *effect* or a result. It explains why something happens. Common words or phrases that signal causes and effects are *because, for this reason, so,* and *as a result.* Good readers notice these kinds of words or phrases. They help readers find causes and effects and understand what a writer is trying to say.

Examples & Explanations

①Although we think it is normal to sleep at night in our own separate rooms, this was not always normal. ②In early human history, many people slept together in one place. ③They did this **because** it was safer. ④A large group could fight together against dangerous animals or enemies. ⑤Some people had to stay awake to watch for danger. ⑥**As a result**, some people slept at night, and others slept in the daytime. ⑦Now, people don't sleep in large groups, and most people sleep at night.

The main idea in this reading is in sentence 1: *People did not always sleep the way we do now.*

Sentence 2 gives the first supporting detail: *In early human history, many people slept together in one place.*

Sentence 3 explains why. The word *because* introduces the reason: *It was safer.*

Sentence 4 explains why it was safer: *A large group could fight together.*

Sentence 5 gives another supporting detail: *Some people had to stay awake to watch for danger.*

In sentence 6, *as a result* introduces the effect: *Some people did not sleep at night.*

Sentence 7 is the conclusion.

The Language of Cause or Effect

Here are some common words and phrases that signal cause and effect.

WORDS AND PHRASES THAT SIGNAL CAUSES OR REASONS	WORDS AND PHRASES THAT SIGNAL EFFECTS
because	so
since	therefore
one reason is	because of this
one of the causes is	as a result

Strategies

These strategies will help you find causes and effects while you read.

- Look for words and phrases that signal causes and effects.
- When you see a cause or effect word, notice the meaning of the ideas before and after the word. Ask yourself: *Which idea is the cause? Which idea is the effect?*
- If the reading has a lot of causes and effects, it is a good idea to make a list of them as you read.

Skill Practice 1

Read the following paragraphs. Highlight four words or phrases in each paragraph that signal causes and effects. Then answer the questions. The first one has been done for you.

1   Some people have trouble falling asleep. One reason may be the food they eat at night. Some foods help you sleep because they create a chemical in your body called *serotonin*. Rice, pasta, and bread are good to eat at dinner, since they create serotonin, which will make you sleepy. On the other hand, foods such as ham, cheese, and chocolate create the opposite effect from serotonin. As a result, these foods will keep you awake at night.

    a Why do some people have trouble falling asleep? *The food they eat.*

       What words or phrases signaled this cause? *one reason*

    b Why do some foods help you sleep? _____

       What words or phrases signaled this effect? _____

    c Why are rice, pasta, and bread good to eat at dinner? _____

       What words or phrases signaled this effect? _____

    d What happens if you have foods such as ham or cheese at night? _____

       What words or phrases signaled this effect? _____

2   Recent studies show that children are sleeping less than they used to. One of the causes is that young people often have cell phones or computers in their bedrooms. Instead of going to sleep, they get on the computer or on the phone. For this reason, doctors don't think it is a good idea for children to have computers, televisions, or phones in their bedrooms. Children who get less sleep are also more likely to gain weight than other children. This happens because too little sleep makes people hungrier. Children who don't get enough sleep are tired during the daytime, so they don't want to exercise.

a What is a reason that young people are sleeping less now? _____

What words or phrases signaled this cause? _____

b Why do doctors think that children should not have computers, television, or phones in their bedrooms? _____

What words or phrases signaled this cause? _____

c Why do children who sleep less gain weight? _____

What words or phrases signaled this cause? _____

d What happens because children are tired when they don't get enough sleep?

_____

What words or phrases signaled this effect? _____

Skill Practice 2

Read the following paragraph. Highlight the words that signal causes and effects. Then fill in the charts. Find two effects for the cause in Chart 1. Find two causes for the effect in Chart 2.

Where do young babies sleep? This depends on the culture. In most cultures, parents think that newborn babies cannot be alone, since they are so tiny. Therefore, the babies sleep with their mothers or in their parents' bed. In other cultures, mothers put their babies in separate beds and even separate rooms. Some mothers do this because they worry that they will roll over on their babies if they sleep in the same bed. Other mothers do this simply because it's a cultural custom.

Chart 1

CAUSE	EFFECTS
newborn babies are tiny	_____ _____

Chart 2

CAUSES	EFFECT
_____ _____	babies put in separate beds

Connecting to the Topic

Discuss the following questions with a partner.

1 When do you like to wake up?

2 When do you like to go to bed?

3 At what time of day do you have the most energy?

4 Have you always woken up and gone to bed at the same time? Have these times changed as you have grown older?

Previewing and Predicting

> Reading the title, section headings, and first sentences of each section can help you predict what a reading will be about.

A Read the title, the section headings, and the first sentence of each section of Reading 3. Then read the questions below. Write the number of the section (*I*, *II*, or *III*) next to the question or questions you think the section will answer.

SECTION	QUESTION
III	Does everyone have the same body clock?
I	What is the body clock?
III	What happens when people have different body clocks?
II	Why do blind people have problems with their body clock?
II	What situations cause problems for the body clock?
II	What happens to people who work at night?

B Compare your answers with a partner's.

While You Read

As you read, stop at the end of each sentence that contains words in **bold**. Then follow the instructions in the box in the margin.

◀)) Your Body Clock

I. How the Body Clock Works

1   Your body has a clock. It is a place in your brain that tells you when to sleep and when to be awake. This body clock responds to changes in light. Light signals you to wake up. Other things, like noise and stress, can also affect your body clock, but they cannot alter it very much. It is generally difficult to change your body clock.

2   Some situations can cause confusion for your body clock. If you travel a long distance across time zones, for example, from New York to Paris, your body clock loses 6 hours. You may arrive at night in Paris when everyone is going to bed. However, your body clock thinks you are still in New **York**. It tells you that it is time for lunch. The next morning, the alarm clock rings. It wakes you up, but your body clock thinks it is the middle of the night. As a result, you probably feel exhausted. This confusion is called *jet lag*. Gradually, your body clock will change to Paris time because it will begin to respond to the light and darkness in Paris. It usually takes several days for your body clock to adjust to a new time **zone**.

WHILE YOU READ ❶

Look back to find the word that signals contrast. Highlight the two ideas that are in contrast.

WHILE YOU READ ❷

What is the main idea of paragraph 2? Highlight it.

Flying long distances to different time zones causes jet lag.

II. Problems for the Body Clock

3   Blind people have problems with their body clocks because they cannot see the light that tells their bodies to wake up. Without this light, many blind people have trouble with sleep. They have a sort of permanent jet lag.

4   Some people have jobs that cause problems for their body clocks. Electric light allows people to work at any time of day or night. People who work at night must be awake when it is dark outside. This is the time when their body clocks tell them to sleep. When they get home, it is bright, and their body clock tells them to stay awake. As a result, they may have trouble falling asleep.

5   Night jobs can sometimes be dangerous. People who work at night sometimes get sleepy, and then they make mistakes. Injuries and accidents in factories often occur at night because of this problem. On April 26, 1986, just after one o'clock in the morning, there was an accident in a nuclear power[1] plant in Chernobyl, Ukraine. It was the worst nuclear accident in history. Some scientists believe that the cause was a sleepy worker who made a mistake.

People who work at night may have problems with their body clocks.

III. Different Body Clocks

6   Most people sleep at night and stay awake during the day. However, not every body clock is the same. Some people like to wake up very early. They have a lot of physical and mental energy in the morning, but by evening, their energy is gone. They are sleepy and they want to go to bed early. These people are "early birds." Other people do not like to get out of bed in the morning, but they have a lot of energy in the evening. Sometimes they stay awake until one or two o'clock in the morning. These people are "night owls." *Owls* are birds that are awake at **night**.

7   When night owls are married to early birds, they may have problems. An early bird may complain about his wife. For example, he may say that his wife goes to sleep too late, and she keeps him awake. A night owl may complain about her husband. She may say he is too noisy in the morning, and he disturbs her while she is still sleeping.

8   Research shows that older people are usually early birds, and teenagers are usually night owls. Many teenagers cannot fall asleep

WHILE YOU READ ❸

What is the main idea of paragraph 6? Highlight it.

---

[1] *Nuclear power:* energy from atoms

until late at night. They are not very alert in the morning. In most countries, however, the school day begins early, between 7:00 and 8:30 in the morning. **This** means that many teenagers do not get enough sleep. They are not ready to learn when they get to school. For this reason, some schools now start later in the day.

WHILE YOU READ 4
What idea does *this* refer to? Highlight it.

9   Scientists have studied people with different body clocks. Many scientists believe that we cannot control our preferences. They think that this preference for morning or evening may be genetic, like eye color. In one study, scientists researched the **habits** of early birds and night owls. For example, they asked them how they felt and what they did at different times every day. The chart below shows some typical answers that they gave.

WHILE YOU READ 5
As you read, find the words that help you understand the meaning of *habits*. Highlight them.

10   The body clock has a powerful effect on our daily activities and how we feel. Modern life, with airplane travel, night jobs, and electric lights, can cause problems for our body clocks. Most people would like to change their lives to fit their body clocks. However, this is usually not possible, so most people have to adjust their body clocks to fit their jobs, their studies, and their family life.

Table 5.1 Early Birds and Night Owls

	EARLY BIRDS	NIGHT OWLS
Do you use an alarm clock to wake up?	No	Yes
Do you eat breakfast?	Yes, I have coffee and read the newspaper.	No I don't have time for breakfast. I am always late in the morning.
What is your favorite meal?	Breakfast	Dinner
Do you sleep well most of the time?	Yes	No
How does your mood change during the day?	I wake up in a good mood, but I am often in a bad mood at the end of the day.	I sometimes wake up in a bad mood, but my mood improves during the day.
Do you take naps?	Rarely	Sometimes
When do you like to exercise?	Morning	Evening

WHILE YOU READ 6
Look for a fixed phrase in the fifth row of the table. Highlight it.

Main Idea Check

Match the main ideas below to five of the paragraphs in Reading 3. Write the number of the paragraph on the blank line.

_____ A Husbands and wives with different body clocks may have problems.

_____ B People who work at night often have problems with their body clocks.

_____ C Different people have different sleep patterns.

_____ D Traveling to different time zones can cause confusion for your body clock.

_____ E Most teenagers are night owls.

A Closer Look

Look back at Reading 3 to answer the following questions.

1 What is the most important signal for your body clock? (Par. 1)
   a Time
   b Noise
   c Light
   d Night

2 How does the body clock adjust after jet lag? (Par. 2)
   a The body clock knows when your body changes to a new time zone.
   b The light in the new time zone signals the body clock.
   c An alarm clock in the new city tells the body clock to change.
   d The body clock responds to rapid travel across time zones.

3 Why are night jobs sometimes dangerous? (Par. 5)
   a Machines often break during the night.
   b There is not as much light at night, so workers get sleepy.
   c Workers who are tired can make serious mistakes.
   d Injuries are more common at night.

4 Which of the following statements about night owls and early birds are true? Circle two answers (Pars. 7–8)
   a They sometimes complain about each other.
   b Night owls are often noisy.
   c Early birds do not like to exercise.
   d As people get older, they often change from night owls to early birds.

5 Why do some schools start later in the day? (Par. 8)
   a It is too dark to start school early in the morning.
   b Teenage students are not ready to learn early in the morning.
   c It saves energy to start school later in the day.
   d Students have too much homework, so they have to work late at night.

6 Scientists think that our body clocks are genetic. **True or False?** (Par. 9)

7 Complete the chart below. Put a check (✓) next to the statements that are true for early birds. Put a check (✓) next to the statements that are true for night owls. (Par. 9)

STATEMENT	EARLY BIRD	NIGHT OWL
They wake up early.	✓	
They have no energy at night.	✓	
They like to stay up late.		✓
They don't like to wake up in the morning.		✓
They go to bed early.	✓	

Skill Review

In Skills and Strategies 10, you learned that writers use words and phrases that signal cause and effect relationships between ideas.

A Read the sentences below from Reading 3. Highlight the words or phrases that signal cause or effect.

1 The next morning, the alarm clock rings. It wakes you up, but your body clock thinks it is the middle of the night. As a result, you probably feel exhausted.

2 Blind people have problems with their body clocks because they cannot see the light that tells their bodies to wake up.

3 When they get home, it is bright, and their body clock tells them to stay awake. As a result, they may have trouble falling asleep.

4 It was the worst nuclear accident in history. Some scientists believe that the cause was a sleepy worker who made a mistake.

5 They are not ready to learn when they get to school. For this reason, some schools now start later in the day.

6 Most people would like to change their lives to fit their body clocks. However, this is usually not possible, so most people have to adjust their body clocks to fit their jobs, their studies, and their family life.

B Read the sentences again. Write C above the cause and E above the effect in the sentences.

Vocabulary Development

Definitions

Find the words in Reading 3 that complete the following definitions.

1 To _____effect_____ is to have an influence on someone or something (v) Par. 1

2 If you are _____excausted_____ you are very tired. (adj) Par. 2

3 Something that goes on forever is _____. (adj) Par. 3

4 A/An _____Plans_____ is a kind of factory. (n) Par. 5

5 If you are _____alert_____, you are awake and have enough energy to understand and learn. (adj) Par. 8

6 _____ are actions you do over and over again, often without really thinking about them. (n pl) Par. 9

7 A/An _____mood_____ is the way you feel at a certain time. (n) (Table 5.1)

8 If something is _____tipical_____, it has the characteristics of a particular person or thing. (adj) Par. 9

Word Families

A The words in **bold** in the chart are from Reading 3. The words next to them are from the same word family. Study and learn these words.

NOUN	VERB
adjustment	**adjust**
alteration	**alter**
complaint	**complain**
confusion	confuse
disturbance	**disturb**

B Choose the correct form of the words from the chart to complete the following sentences. Use the correct verb tenses and subject-verb agreement. Use the correct singular and plural noun forms.

1 Light and noise _____disturb_____ her. They prevent her from sleeping.

2 He tried to _____alter_____ his answers after the test was over.

3 When she returned to her hometown, many things had changed. All of the new streets and buildings _____confuse_____ her.

4 Because the flights are always late, there are many _____complaint_____ about the airline.

5 My neighbors had a party, so the next day, they said they were sorry for the _____disturbance_____.

6 When we left the dark building, it took a while for our eyes to _____adjust_____ to the bright light.

7 There have been many _____altevation_____ to these rooms in the last 250 years.

8 Several people _____complain_____ about the food. They said the soup was cold.

9 Too little sleep can cause _alteration_ and strange behavior.

10 Living in a new country requires many _adjusment_. You have to learn new customs and, often, a new language.

Academic Word List

The following are Academic Word List words from all the readings in Unit 5. Use these words to complete the sentences. (For more on the Academic Word List, see page 260.)

adjust (v)	aspects (n)	mental (adj)	restored (v)	sufficient (adj)
affects (v)	concentrate (v)	normal (adj)	stress (n)	variation (n)

1 There is a lot of _____ in people's sleep patterns. Some people need more sleep than others.

2 She was worried about others things, so she could not _____ on her schoolwork.

3 It is important to consider all _____ of a situation before you make a decision.

4 If you move to a different country, it may take some time to _____ to the new culture.

5 There is a lot of _____ in his new job. He works 12 hours a day, and he worries a lot.

6 Competition in the Olympic Games requires both physical and _____ energy.

7 It is _____ to be nervous before an important event. Most people feel this way.

8 Two weeks of vacation _____ her health and energy. She felt much better when she returned to her job.

9 The food we eat _____ how we feel and how we behave.

10 If you do not get _____ sleep, you may get sick. Adults should get about 8 hours of sleep a night.

Critical Thinking

In Reading 3, you read how some people are early birds and others are night owls. Early birds like to get up early but do not like to stay up late. Night owls are the opposite. They hate to get up early and like to stay up late.

PERSONALIZING

Thinking about how new information applies to your own life can help you understand a text better.

A Reread the last section of Reading 3, and decide if you are an early bird or a night owl. Explain to a partner which you think you are and why.

B With your partner, discuss the effects of being a night owl or an early bird. Discuss how it can make a difference in the following situations.

a Personal life, for example, your relationships with others
b School life, for example, how you perform in your classes
c Work life, for example, how you perform in your job

C Share what you have discussed with the rest of the class.

Research

Do a survey on early birds and night owls.

- Use the questions in Table 5.1 on page 155.
- Choose 3 of them and ask 10 people to answer your questions.
- Ask people of different ages.

Writing

Write a short summary of your survey research.

Improving Your Reading Speed

Good readers read quickly and still understand most of what they read.

A Read the instructions and strategies for Improving Your Reading Speed in Appendix 3 on page 273.

B Choose one of the readings in this unit. Read it without stopping. Time how long it takes you to finish the text in minutes and seconds. Enter the time in the chart on page 274. Then calculate your reading speed in number of words per minute.

CAUSE-AND-EFFECT CONNECTORS

Writers often connect ideas by showing how one event (the cause) causes another event (the effect) to happen. Sometimes writers emphasize the cause and sometimes the effect. Writers use words or phrases such as *because, because of this, for this reason, as a result,* or *therefore* to show these connections. You learned these words and phrases in Skills and Strategies 10 on page 149.

Exercise 1

Read the following paragraphs. Circle any words or phrases that signal cause and effect. Highlight each cause and effect. Mark each cause with *C*, and mark each effect with an *E*. The first one has been done for you.

1   A lot of the research about sleep has concentrated on western cultures. Because of this, some people wonder if it is accurate. There are many variations in sleeping patterns around the world. For example, in some cultures, adults sleep twice a day. They sleep in the afternoon for a couple of hours and again at night for about 6 hours.

2   Thomas Edison invented the lightbulb, but did he ever imagine the consequences? Before the invention of the lightbulb, people went to sleep early because they did not have very much they could do after dark. As a result, they got plenty of sleep. The development of electricity let people stay awake easily and comfortably.

3   When people don't get enough sleep, they can't concentrate very well. Because of this, there are sometimes terrible accidents. For example, a huge ship ran into rocks in Alaska. The reason for this unfortunate accident was too little sleep.

4   Everyone knows that sleep is essential. It affects memory and mood. However, many people don't realize that it is also essential for life. In one study, researchers prevented rats from sleeping for 5 days. As a result, the rats died.

5   Sometimes people complain when they wake up. They say that they didn't sleep all night. It is possible they were asleep part of the night, but they thought they were awake the whole night. Because of this, they feel tired even when they get enough sleep.

Exercise 2

Make a clear paragraph by putting sentences A, B, and C into the best order after the numbered sentence. Look for pronouns and words or phrases that signal addition, contrast, or cause and effect to help you. Write the letters in the correct order on the blank lines.

1 Not sleeping can affect your work. ____ ____ ____

| **A** Because they are exhausted, they sometimes do not have good judgment. | **B** For example, doctors in training at hospitals sometimes work for 3 days without sleep. | **C** However, some jobs require people to work long hours with no time off. |

2 Whales and dolphins have to think about breathing because they do not have the ability to breathe automatically. ____ ____ ____

| **A** Therefore, they cannot go completely to sleep. | **B** The other half stays awake. | **C** Instead, they sleep with half of their brain. |

3 The typical sleep pattern for most people in western cultures today is about 8 hours of sleep during the night. ____ ____ ____

| **A** As result of the invention of electric light, this sleep pattern began to change. | **B** People used to go to sleep early in the evening, wake up for a few hours, and sleep again. | **C** However, sleeping through the entire night is a recent habit. |

4 Doctors understand that some babies die because of how they sleep. ____ ____ ____

| **A** They fall asleep on their stomachs, and then they cannot breathe very well. | **B** However, they are not strong enough to turn onto their backs. | **C** Therefore, doctors now tell parents to put tiny babies on their backs to sleep. |

5 Babies sometimes have a flat area on the back of their heads because they spend a lot of time on their backs. ____ ____ ____

| **A** However, this is not a permanent change, so parents should not worry. | **B** This happens because their heads are quite soft. | **C** As a result, their heads can change shape when they are on the bed. |

6

MUSIC

SKILLS AND STRATEGIES

- Noticing Parts of Words
- Organizing Notes in Timelines

Noticing Parts of Words

As you learned in Skills and Strategies 3 on page 34, one way to understand the meaning of a word is to notice the parts of the word, such as prefixes and suffixes. Sometimes, understanding the *root* of a word may also help you. A root is the basic part of a word. Many roots come from Greek or Latin, and you can often find the same root in several different words. For example, the root *port* means *to carry*. You see it in words such as *export* and *passport*. Roots don't usually give you the exact meaning of a word, but they can give you a clue to the meaning. Good readers notice roots. They use their knowledge of these roots as well as prefixes and suffixes to figure out a word's meaning.

Examples & Explanations

Many people prefer laptop computers because they are **portable**.

A root can give you a clue to the meaning of a word. For example, the root *port* means *to carry*.

The suffix *-able* means *to be able to do something*.

portable = able to be carried

His music is **popular** in China, and the **population** of China is so large that his music sells a lot of copies.

Common roots can give you a clue about the meaning of a word, but they can't always tell you the specific meaning.

For example, the root *pop* means *people*. This is a clue that the words *popular* and *population* are related to people, even though they have different specific meanings.

popular = liked by many people
population = the number of people living in an area

Many people today use cell phones instead of home or office **telephones**. One advantage of cell phones is that you can use them anywhere.

Sometimes words have two roots in them, for example, *telephone*. The root *tele* means *distant*, and the root *phon* means *sound*.

telephone = a piece of equipment used to talk to someone in a distant place

The Language of Word Roots

Here are some common roots and their meanings.

ROOTS	MEANINGS
aud	hearing
auto	self
cogn	know
graph	write
mem	remember
mov, mob, mot	move
multi	many
nect	join

ROOTS	MEANINGS
phon	sound
pop	people
port	carry
tech	skill
tele	distant
uni	one
vid, vis	seeing
vit, viv	live

Strategies

These strategies will help you notice word roots. They may help you understand the meanings of words while you read.

- Study and remember the meanings of the roots in the chart.
- To learn more roots, find a dictionary or a source on the Internet that lists roots.
- Notice if a word you don't know has a familiar root. Ask yourself questions: *What other words have the same root as this word? What other words are related to this word?*
- Look at the whole sentence and the sentences around it. Notice how the meaning of the root connects to the other words and the general meaning of the sentence.

Skill Practice 1

Read the following sentences, and notice the different parts of the words in bold. Highlight any roots you see in the words. The first one has been done for you.

move
1 The **motion** of the sea makes some people feel sick.

one
2 The singers came from all over the country to make a CD together. They **united** to raise money for poor children.

skill
3 A **technician** in the recording studio made a lot of changes to the recording. It sounds much better now.

seeing
4 The schoolchildren have a **vision** test every year to find out if they need glasses.

5 I have many happy **memories** of my childhood.

6 There are some sounds that are only **audible** to dogs, not humans.

self 7 She bought an automatic coffeemaker. It turns on by itself, so the coffee is ready
when she wakes up.

people 8 People started to call **popular** music "pop" in the early 1900s.

Skill Practice 2

Read the sentences in Skill Practice 1 again. Look at the roots you highlighted in each sentence. Then figure out the definitions for the words in bold. Write the definitions on the blank lines. The first one has been done for you.

1 The **motion** of the sea makes some people feel sick.

   motion = <u>movement</u>

2 The singers came from all over the country to make a CD together. They **united** to raise money for poor children.

   unite = _____

3 A **technician** in the recording studio made a lot of changes to the recording. It sounds much better now.

   technician = _____

4 The schoolchildren have a **vision** test every year to find out if they need glasses.

   vision = _____

5 I have many happy **memories** of my childhood.

   memories = _____

6 There are some sounds that are only **audible** to dogs, not humans.

   audible = _____

7 She bought an **automatic** coffeemaker. It turns on by itself, so the coffee is ready when she wakes up.

   automatic = _____

8 People started to call **popular** music "pop" in the early 1900s.

   popular = _____

Connecting to the Topic

Discuss the following questions with a partner.

1 Do you like listening to music? What type of music do you listen to? Explain your answer.

2 How does music affect your mood? Does it make you feel happy? Sad?

3 What are some ways that music comes into our daily lives? Make a list.

Previewing and Predicting

> Looking at art and reading the first sentence of each paragraph before you read can help you predict what a reading will be about.

A Read the first sentence in each paragraph of Reading 1, and look at the photographs on pages 168 and 169. Then put a check (✓) next to the topics you think will be discussed in the reading.

_____ a How businesses use music

___✓__ b How music can help you to get to sleep

___✓__ c The emotional effects of music

___✓__ d Learning to play an instrument

___✓__ e The effect of music on memory

_____ f The most popular styles of music

B Compare your answers with a partner's. Then discuss what you expect to learn about those topics.

While You Read

As you read, stop at the end of each sentence that contains words in bold. Then follow the instructions in the box in the margin.

The Power of Music

1 There are only a few things that make human beings different from all other animals. The ability to create music is one of the things that makes us unique. Our connection with music begins early in life. Small babies respond to music. Mothers all over the world sing to their babies to comfort them and to help them sleep. All cultures create some kind of music.

2 Why is music important in the lives of humans? Some scientists believe that music plays a role in brain **development**. Research shows that children who learn to play musical instruments can often solve problems more quickly and easily than children who do not. Scientists

WHILE YOU READ 1

Look back in this sentence for a noun + verb collocation. Highlight it.

Children who study music may have an advantage at school.

believe that learning to play music is different from learning about other things like history or science. It can change the way cells are connected in your brain. These new connections may improve how the brain works. It is possible that long ago, music helped people think better and solve problems. **This** ability helped people survive.

3 Music continues to help people today. **Many doctors use music to help their patients.** They use music to relieve pain and stress. Music is especially useful for patients with brain diseases or brain injuries.

WHILE YOU READ 2

Look in this sentence for a word with a root that means *live*. Highlight the word.

WHILE YOU READ 3

Highlight two supporting details for this idea.

It can help people who have problems speaking. Patients who can no longer speak well may listen to familiar songs. When they hear the songs, they can recognize the words. Sometimes they can sing these familiar songs before they can speak again.

4   Music also has a powerful effect on memory. Music can help people **remember** the words in a message. For example, songs can help children memorize important information, such as the letters of the alphabet. Research shows that the repetition and rhythm in music help people remember words.

WHILE YOU READ 4

Look in the last sentence for a word with a root that means *remember*. Highlight the word.

5   Companies that want people to remember their products know the effect of music on memory. Therefore, they often use music in their advertisements. One study of advertisements compared listeners' memories. One group of advertisements had just words; another group had words and music. Listeners remembered the messages with words and music better than they remembered the messages with only **words**.

Music can help children memorize words in a song.

WHILE YOU READ 5

Look back in paragraph 5 for a word that signals cause and effect. Highlight the effect.

6   Businesses use the power of music in other ways, too. Department stores and supermarkets often use music to try to influence how much money their customers spend. They choose music they think will make their customers feel happy. They want customers to feel good, stay longer, and spend more money. Restaurant owners use music in the same way. Some may choose soft, slow music. They believe this music makes people relax and spend more money. Other restaurant owners may choose something faster with a strong rhythm. With fast music, customers may feel energetic and finish more quickly. This lets the restaurant serve more customers.

7   Music influences our emotions in many ways. You may have noticed that some songs make you relax and feel happy, and other songs make you feel sad. When you listen to music, your brain releases chemicals that affect your emotions. This is why you may choose one kind of music for a party and another kind of music for a quiet **dinner**.

WHILE YOU READ 6

What is the main idea of Paragraph 7? Highlight it.

8   Music has a powerful influence on our feelings, behavior, decisions, and learning. Teachers use it to help children learn. Doctors use it to help their patients recover. Businesses use it to encourage people to relax, shop, and buy their products. If you understand the power of music, you can make it work for you.

Main Idea Check

Here are the main ideas of paragraph 2–7 in Reading 1. Match each paragraph to its main idea. Write the number of the paragraph on the blank line.

___6___ A Businesses use music to control how long customers stay.

___4___ B Music improves memory.

___2___ C Music helps brain development.

___5___ D Advertisers use music to encourage people to remember their products.

___3___ E Doctors use music to help sick people.

___7___ F Music can make you feel happy or sad.

A Closer Look

Look back at Reading 1 to answer the following questions.

1 The ability to create music is unique to humans. **True** or False? (Par. 1)

2 What makes scientists believe that music helps brain development? (Par. 2)
   a Children who listen to music do better in school.
   b People who play musical instruments remember things better.
   c Learning songs helps children learn to read quickly.
   d Children who play musical instruments solve problems quickly.

3 How do doctors use music to treat patients? Circle three answers. (Par. 3)
   a To relieve stress
   b To help people learn to speak again
   c To help people learn new songs
   d To relieve pain
   e To help people play music again

4 Why do advertisers use songs? (Par. 5)
   a People prefer to hear advertisements with music.
   b Music helps people remember the product in the advertisement.
   c Songs make people remember things from their past.
   d Music makes people relax.

5 Put the events (A–D) in the correct order in which they happen. Write the correct letter in each box. (Par. 6)

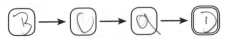

B → C → A → D

   A Customers eat quickly.
   B Restaurant owners play fast music with a strong rhythm.
   C Customers feel energetic when they hear the music.
   D The restaurant serves more customers.

6 What parts of our lives does music influence, according to the reading? Circle three answers.
  a Emotions
  b Development of the brain
  c Memory
  d Personality
  e Relationships with other people

Skill Review

In Skills and Strategies 11, you learned that understanding the *root* of a word may help you understand its meaning. Knowing word roots can expand your vocabulary and help you understand what you read.

A Work with a partner. Underline the roots in the words below, and write the meaning of the roots on the blank line. Four of the words are from Reading 1.

1 autograph *A signature*

2 connection *A relationship with a person or something*

3 memorize *Commit to memory; learn by heart* *remember*

4 microphone *An instrument for converting sound waves*

5 recognize *identify*

6 revive *restore to life*

7 telescope *instrument to see distant objects* *distant*

8 unique *being the only one of its kind* *one*

B Complete the sentences below with the words in **A**. When completed, the sentences give definitions of the words.

1 A / An _Microphone_ is a small machine that makes sounds louder.

2 A / An _telescope_ is a machine that lets you see objects that are very far away, such as stars.

3 If something is _Unique_, it is the only one of its kind.

4 If you realize you have seen something before, you _recognize_ it.

5 When two or more things are joined together, they have a _connection_.

6 To _revive_ someone or something is to make it live again.

7 A / An _Autograph_ is a signature – a person's name in writing.

8 If you _memorize_ something, you learn it so well that you will not forget it.

Vocabulary Development

Definitions

Find the words in Reading 1 that complete the following definitions.

1 _____cells_____ are the smallest units of living things. Skin, muscles, and your brain are all made of them. (*n pl*) Par. 2

2 To _____survive_____ is to continue to exist, especially after a dangerous situation. (*v*) Par. 2

3 To _____realize_____ is to make pain or a bad feeling less. (*v*) Par. 3

4 To _____recognize_____ is to realize you have seen someone or something before. (*v*) Par. 3

5 A/An _____words_____ is a set of letters that are used to write a language. (*n*) Par. 4

6 _____repetition_____ is doing something again and again. (*n*) Par. 4

7 _____Departments store_____ are places that sell many different things, such as clothing and furniture. (*n pl*) Par. 6

8 To _____releases_____ something is to let it go. (*v*) Par. 7

Words in Context

Complete the passages with words from Reading 1 in the box below.

comfort	instruments	recover	rhythm
energetic	patients	relax	role

1 Experts say that music can play a/an _____role_____ in good health. Some
   (a)
   doctors believe that their _____patients_____ who play musical _____instruments_____ or
   (b)   (c)
   listen to music a lot _____recover_____ more quickly after an illness.
   (d)

2 People enjoy music for different reasons. Some people like music with a strong
   _____rhythm_____ because it makes them feel _____energetic_____ and ready to work
   (e)   (f)
   or study. Other people prefer soft music because it helps them _____relax_____
   (g)
   and go to sleep. Finally, some music can _____comfort_____ people when they feel
   (h)
   sad or lonely.

Critical Thinking

Reading 1 claims that music plays an important role in our lives. It affects our behavior, learning, memory, and emotions.

PERSONALIZING

Thinking about how new information applies to your own life can help you understand a text better.

A Discuss the following questions with a partner.

in my feelings, when I'm sad make me happy / *music*

1 In what ways has music been important in your life?

2 Think of an example of how music has affected you in at least two of the areas that are discussed in the reading.

and for learning

3 Do you think the importance of music changes as you grow older?

yes,

B Share your ideas with the rest of the class.

Research

Do some research on music and advertising. Ask several of your classmates to think of one product that uses music in its advertisement. Then find answers to the following questions.

- What is the product?
- What do you remember about the music in its advertisement?
- Were there words as well as music? If so, do you remember the words?
- Did the advertisement make you want to buy the product? Explain your answer.

Writing

Based on your research, write a short summary on what you think makes a musical advertisement effective.

Connecting to the Topic

Discuss the following questions with a partner.

1 Did you study a musical instrument when you were younger? Was it difficult? Describe your experience.

2 Have you ever tried *karaoke*? Describe the experience.

3 Have you ever tried to play music on a cell phone?

Previewing and Predicting

> Reading the title and looking at photographs before you read can help you predict what a reading will be about.

A **Read the title of Reading 2, and look at the photographs on pages 175 and 176. Then put a check (✓) next to the topics you think will be discussed in the reading.**

_____ a The popularity of karaoke

_____ b The role of technology in music

_____ c Learning to play the piano

_____ d Playing music on a smart phone

_____ e Musical education in schools

B **Compare your answers with a partner's.**

While You Read

As you read, stop at the end of each sentence that contains words in bold. Then follow the instructions in the box in the margin.

◀)) Can Anyone Be a Musician?

1   Long ago, people made music by singing and playing simple instruments like drums. Music was an activity for everyone, and anyone could participate. In modern times, musical instruments became more complicated, so it took a lot of time and practice to learn to play them. As a result, not many people could learn to play musical instruments. So, making music became a job for professionals. People had to pay to hear music created and produced by professionals.

2   Music became an industry. Producing music became too complicated and expensive for ordinary people. Professional musicians needed special equipment and musical instruments to create music. They also needed special equipment to record and store music. All of this technology increased the distance between musicians and consumers.

3   In the second half of the twentieth century, this began to change. Technology, which had prevented ordinary people from producing music, was moving in a new direction. One important change was that music was becoming portable. If ordinary people wanted to sing with a band, all they needed was a small machine to play recorded music. This was the beginning of karaoke, which soon became very popular, especially in Japan. Karaoke allows anyone to sing along with recorded music: at a party, at a restaurant, or even at home. By the end of the century, the popularity of karaoke had spread all over the world.

Karaoke is very popular in Japan.

4   **The** next important development was the smart phone, for example, the iPhone or Blackberry. Although their first function was to make telephone calls, soon there were hundreds of "apps," or small programs for smart phones. With these apps, people can play games, watch the news, or find a restaurant. They can also make music with **mobile** music apps.

WHILE YOU READ **1**

As your read paragraph 4, find verb + noun collocations for *games* and *music*. Highlight the collocations.

5   Mobile music apps allow ordinary people without any musical education to create their own music. Some apps turn a smart phone into a tiny piano; others allow you to blow into the microphone to make music. There are also apps that allow you to play an instrument along with a famous song. For example, as the song plays, you place your fingers on the picture of an instrument on the smart phone. The app changes your finger movements into musical notes. You can learn to play music on apps much faster than you can learn to play a musical **instrument**.

WHILE YOU READ **2**

Highlight the root of the word *mobile*.

6   There has also been a change in karaoke. In karaoke, you sing along with recorded music. Now it is possible to do the opposite. New smart phone apps can record your voice and create the rest of the music – the piano, the drums and other instruments – to go with it. There are also apps that can make your voice sound much better than it really is. If you sing an incorrect note, there is an app that changes the note **automatically** so it sounds perfect. As a result, you can sound professional without a lot of work or a lot of talent. All of these new apps make it easy to create music. Anyone with access to new technology can do it.

WHILE YOU READ **3**

What is the main idea of paragraph 5? Highlight it.

WHILE YOU READ **4**

Highlight the root of the word *automatically*.

7   New apps for mobile music make it fun and easy to create music. However, some people complain that this is not serious music. They say that serious music takes many years of practice and education. They also say it requires talent. You cannot get talent from a mobile music app. So, can anyone be a musician? The people who create music apps think so. They believe in the power of technology to unlock everyone's musical ability. Others believe that creating music is only for professionals, and apps are just games.

Mobile music apps can help everyone make music.

Main Idea Check

Here are the main ideas of paragraphs 2–6 in Reading 2. Match each paragraph to its main idea. Write the number of the paragraph on the blank line.

_5_ A Mobile music apps allow ordinary people to create music.

_3_ B Karaoke was the first big development in helping people make their own music.

_6_ C New technology can make your voice sound better than it really is.

_2_ D At first, technology separated people into music producers and music consumers.

_4_ E Smart phone apps can help people create music.

A Closer Look

Look back at Reading 2 to answer the following questions.

1 Why did many ordinary people stop producing music? (Par. 2)
   a They did not like modern music.
   b They were not professional.
   c They did not want to practice all the time.
   d Making music became too complicated.

2 What features of karaoke made it so popular? Circle two answers. (Par. 3)
   a People could enjoy it anywhere.
   b People could enjoy singing with other people.
   c People used it to learn to play music quickly.
   d People did not need other musicians to perform.

3 What are "apps"? (Par. 4)
   a Small smart phones
   b Small computer programs for smart phones
   c Musical computer programs
   d Electronic musical instruments

4 Making music with a music app is easier than making music with traditional instruments. True or False? (Par. 5)

5 There is a music app that can correct notes that you sing incorrectly. True or False? (Par. 6)

6 Put the events (A–D) in the correct order in which they happen. Write the correct letter in each box.

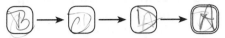

A Ordinary people could produce music.
B Everyone participated in music.
C Technology divided music producers and ordinary people.
D Mobile music apps were developed.

Skill Review

> In Skills and Strategies 10, you learned that writers use words and phrases to signal the relationship between ideas such as causes and effects.

A Reread paragraph 1 from Reading 2 below. Highlight the transition words that signal *cause* and *effect*. Then create a "chain," with five events that shows how one event led to the next one. The first event has been done for you.

Long ago, people made music by singing and playing simple instruments like drums. Music was an activity for everyone, and anyone could participate. In modern times, musical instruments became more complicated, so it took a lot of time and practice to learn to play them. As a result, not many people could learn to play musical instruments. So, making music became a job for professionals. People had to pay to hear music created and produced by professionals.

1 Musical instruments became more complicated
  ↓
2 It took a lot of time to learn
  ↓
3 Not many people play musical instrument
  ↓
4 Only professionals make music
  ↓
5 People had to pay to hear music

B Compare your cause-and-effect chain with a partner's.

Vocabulary Development

Definitions

Find the words in Reading 2 that complete the following definitions.

1 To _participate_ is to take part in or become involved in something. (v) Par. 1

2 A/An _industry_ is a business that produces or sells something. (n) Par. 2

3 Something that is _complicate_ is difficult to understand. (adj) Par. 2

4 A/An _consumer_ is someone who buys things for his or her own use. (n) Par. 2

5 If something is _portable_, you can move or carry it easily. (adj) Par. 3

6 If something is _mouel_, it moves easily, and does not need to be connected to electricity. (adj) Par. 4

7 A/An _talent_ is a special, natural ability. (n) Par. 6

8 To have _access_ to something is to be able to get into it and use it. (n) Par. 6

Words in Context

Complete the sentences with words from Reading 2 in the box below.

band	equipment	practice	the rest
distance	notes	recorded	unlock

1 The _distance_ between Beijing and Shanghai is about 665 miles (1070 km).

2 You can write a simple song with just a few _notes_.

3 There are four people in the _band_: One person plays the piano, one person plays the drums, and two people play guitars.

4 I could not _unlock_ the door so I had to wait outside.

5 If you want to be a professional musician, you need to _practice_ many hours every day.

6 The doctor needed lot of special medical _equipment_ to care for her patients.

7 Some of the government officials took the train to the meeting, but _the rest_ went by plane.

8 I was not in school last week so my friend _recorded_ my class lectures for me. I listened to them when I returned.

Critical Thinking

A designer of some of the popular mobile music apps described in Reading 2 says he has always believed that "everyone is musical, but they are too embarrassed to do anything about it."

> **AGREEING AND DISAGREEING**
>
> When the writer or someone in a text expresses an opinion, ask yourself if you agree or disagree with the opinion.

A Discuss the opinion above with a small group.

1 Do you agree or disagree with the statement? Explain and provide support for your answer.

2 Find out which members of your group are musical. Do the people who are musical tend to have the same opinion about the statement?

B Share your answers with the rest of the class. Find out how many agree with the statement and how many disagree. Find out if the people who are musical all have the same opinion.

Research

Find at least two classmates or friends who sing or play a musical instrument. Find answers to the following questions.

- Do you sing or play an instrument? What instrument do you play?
- How long have you been doing this?
- How many hours a day or week do you practice?
- Why do you continue to sing or play?

Writing

Write a short summary of why people play music.

Organizing Notes in Timelines

Sometimes you need to understand a reading and remember the most important information for a test. Good readers take notes to help them study for tests. Sometimes a reading gives important information about when different events happened. The best way to understand and remember these events is to organize your notes into a timeline. A timeline lists the events in the order in which they happened. To make a timeline, look for dates, numbers, and words like *before*, *until*, and *then*. These will help you understand the *time sequence*, that is, the order in which things happened.

Examples & Explanations

①An Italian named Bartolemeo Cristofori invented the first piano **in the early 1700s**. ②Few musicians knew about this musical instrument **until 1747** when Johann Sebastian Bach wrote some music for the piano. ③The first pianos had a soft sound and were very small, but **by 1860**, the piano looked and sounded like modern pianos.

The topic of this paragraph is the history of the piano. The time phrases *in the early 1700s*, *until 1747*, and *by 1860* give you information about when things happened.

There are two possible ways to make a timeline of this paragraph.

1. You can write a list of dates like this:

   • *early 1700s – Cristofori – first piano*

   • *1747 – Bach wrote music for piano, people learned about it*

   • *1860 – piano looked, sounded like modern pianos*

2. You can draw a line with the earliest event on the left and the most recent event on the right like this:

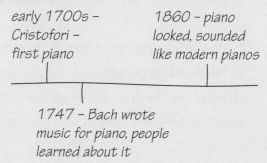

early 1700s –
Cristofori –
first piano

1860 – piano
looked, sounded
like modern pianos

1747 – Bach wrote
music for piano, people
learned about it

Note that you don't have to use complete sentences in a timeline. Just write the important words.

The Language of Time Sequence

Here are some common words or phrases that signal time sequence.

in (year)	after	by	earlier
on (date)	before	since	later
	then	until	now

Strategies

These strategies will help you understand when events in a reading happened.

- As you read a paragraph, look for words or phrases that signal when something happened.
- As you read, ask yourself questions: *When did this happen? Was it before or after other events in the reading?*
- Underline important dates, and number events to show the order.
- Take notes in a timeline to understand and remember the sequence of events.

Skill Practice 1

Read the following paragraphs. Highlight four words or phrases in each paragraph that signal when something happened. Then answer the questions. The first one has been done for you.

1   In the early 1970s, a German professor started work on a project to send music over telephone lines. This was the beginning of the development of MP3 music players. It took more than 20 years to develop the technology. In 1995, researchers gave the name MP3 to this technology. Three years later, the first MP3 portable music players became available in the United States and in South Korea. Ten years after that, yearly sales of MP3 players were about 300 million.

a When did the work begin that led to the development of MP3 music players?
   in the early 1970s

b How many years did it take to develop the technology? _____

c When did researchers first use the name MP3? _____

d When did the first MP3 players become available? _____

e When did yearly sales of MP3 players reach 300 million? _____

2   Wolfgang Amadeus Mozart was born in 1756 in Salzburg, Austria. His father
was a well-known musician and violin teacher. Mozart started writing music when
he was only five years old. By 1764, he was writing symphonies (long pieces of
music for many instruments). Before he died in 1791, Mozart wrote almost 1,000
pieces of music.

a When was Mozart born? _____

b How old was he when he started writing music? _____

c When did he start to write symphonies? _____

d When did he die? _____

Skill Practice 2

**Read the following paragraph. Highlight the words or phrases that signal a time
sequence. Then make a timeline in the space below the paragraph. You can
choose to make a list with the earliest date and event first, or make a line with
the earliest date and event on the left side of the line.**

Rock music began in the United States. It started in Memphis, Tennessee, in
1951, with the first rock and roll record, "Rocket 88." Some of the early rock and
roll singers were Chuck Berry and Elvis Presley. In the 1960s, new styles of rock
and roll music began with soul music from Detroit, Michigan, and surfing music
from California. Things changed in 1964 when the Beatles came to the United
States from England. This was the beginning of the "British Invasion," when many
rock bands came from the United Kingdom. Now, rock is international, with
musicians from all over the world.

Connecting to the Topic

Discuss the following questions with a partner.

1 How do you listen to music? On your computer? On the radio? Another way?

2 Has the way that you listen to music changed in the last 10 years? Explain your answer.

3 When you buy music, do you buy one song at a time? Do you buy many songs from the same musician?

4 Do you like to share your favorite music with your friends? Explain your answer.

Previewing and Predicting

Reading section headings and the first few sentences of each section can help you predict what a reading will be about.

A Read the title, the section headings, and the first two sentences of each section in Reading 3. Then read the questions below. Write the number of the section (*I*, *II*, or *III*) next to the question or questions you think the section will answer.

SECTION	QUESTION
II	How did the Internet change the music business?
I	How did people listen to music before CDs?
III	What have been some recent changes in the music business?
III	Why have many people stopped downloading music?
I	When did people first begin to store music so they could listen to it any time they wanted to?
II	What is the difference between music on CDs and music on the Internet?

B Compare your answers with a partner's.

While You Read

As you read, stop at the end of each sentence that contains words in **bold**. Then follow the instructions in the box in the margin.

The Music Industry

I. Early Forms of Music Technology

1   Technology in the music industry has changed a lot in the past 100 years. In the early 1900s, it became possible to store music so that people could listen to it over and over again. They could listen to this music on the radio. However, most people wanted to buy the music that they listened to on the radio. They wanted to be able to listen to it whenever they wanted.

2   In the 1920s, new technology made this possible. People could buy music on records. Your parents or grandparents probably bought their music on these records. In the 1970s, the music business began to produce music on special tape. These tapes were much smaller than records. They were also less **fragile**. In other words, they did not break or scratch as often as records. The popularity of tapes increased in 1979, when *Sony* began to sell the Walkman, a portable tape player. With the Walkman, people could carry their music with them anywhere. During the 1990s, CDs (compact discs) became more popular. CDs are stronger than tapes, and the sound of the music is clearer.

WHILE YOU READ 1

Look ahead for the definition of *fragile*. Highlight it.

A cassette tape

A record

A compact disc

II. Music on the Internet

3   By about the year 2000, CD sales began to fall, and the sale of music in electronic form on the Internet began to rise. With the Internet, people could listen to songs on their computers. They could also download them to an MP3 player. This change had two important consequences for the music business. First, with records, tapes, or CDs, customers had to buy an **album**, which is a whole collection

WHILE YOU READ 2

Look in the rest of this sentence for a definition of *album*. Highlight it.

of songs. The whole collection usually lasts about an hour. With the Internet, customers can buy only the songs they like. They don't have to buy songs they don't like. They can create their own collections of songs.

4   There is a second and more important consequence. With electronic forms of music, it is easy to make copies and share them. When listeners download electronic copies, they can share them with all of their friends. The friends do not have to pay for their copies. It is very hard to prevent people from sharing their music. This is a challenge for musicians and music companies, because listeners do not pay for these copies.

5   Music companies have tried many ways to stop people from sharing their music. They have made changes in the electronic form of music. The changes make it harder for listeners to make copies and share their music. Music companies want the government to punish people who share music. However, none of these efforts have been very effective. People can always find the music they want easily, and they often do not have to pay for **it**.

WHILE YOU READ ❸

What is the main idea of paragraph 5? Highlight it.

6   The Internet has also had some positive effects for musicians. In general, it is very difficult to be a successful musician. It is hard for most musicians to sell their songs. However, the Internet makes it easier for musicians to bring their music to a large number of people quickly and easily. They do not have to pay a music company to record and distribute their music. They can sell their music directly to consumers. They can put it on a website, where people can listen to it and download it if they want to buy it.

Technology makes it possible to listen to music anywhere at anytime.

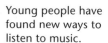
Young people have found new ways to listen to music.

III. Recent Changes in the Music Business

7   The music business is changing again. Many customers have stopped downloading music because now they can find it in a new way. In the past, customers wanted to own their music. They wanted all of their songs on their own computer or music player. Now, customers can play music directly from many different Internet music sites. They can find the music they want and play it on their computer, cell phones, or MP3 players. They can play it anywhere they want and at anytime they want. They don't need to own it.

8   **The music companies and musicians still want to make a profit, however.** They are trying two new methods. First, they ask other companies to pay for advertisements on the music sites. These companies hope that people will see their advertisements while they are listening to the music and then buy the products in the advertisements. Second, some music sites require customers to pay for access. For example, a customer might pay $10 a month for access to a large collection of songs. Some of these music sites are connected to other sites, like Facebook. This allows people to find out what their friends are listening to. They may want to listen to the same music.

9   Music companies, musicians, and customers are still trying to find the best solutions for everyone. Music companies and musicians need money for their products. Customers want to listen to music anywhere and anytime. One thing is certain – the music business will continue to change with new **technology**.

WHILE YOU READ 4
Find two supporting details for this idea. Highlight them.

WHILE YOU READ 5
Look back in paragraph 9 for a collocation with a verb and the noun *solutions*. Highlight the collocation.

Main Idea Check

Match the main ideas below to five of the paragraphs in Reading 3. Write the number of the paragraph on the blank line.

_4_ A People share their music and sometimes do not pay for it.

_1_ B Music companies are finding new ways to make money.

_3_ C At the beginning of the twenty-first century, people began to download their music from the Internet.

_2_ D Between 1920 and 2000, recorded music went from records to tapes to CDs.

_6_ E The Internet allows musicians to sell their music directly to customers.

A Closer Look

Look back at Reading 3 to answer the following questions.

1 In what ways are tapes better than records? Circle three answers. (Par. 2)

  (a) They are less fragile than records.
  b They are less expensive than records.
  (c) They are smaller than records.
  d They can be portable.
  (e) They sound better than records.

2 What was the importance of the Walkman? (Par. 2)

  a It made music less expensive to record.
  b It could hold more music than records.
  (c) It made music portable.
  d It made it possible to share music.

3 In what ways are CDs better than tapes? Circle two answers. (Par. 2)

  (a) They are stronger than tapes.
  b They are less expensive than tapes.
  (c) They sound better than tapes.
  d They are more popular than tapes.

4 By about 2000, the sales of CDs began to increase. **True or False?** (Par. 3)

5 What has been done to try to stop listeners from sharing their music? Circle two answers. (Par. 5)

  a The government has punished some people who copy and share music.
  b Some musicians will not sell their songs on the Internet because people copy them.
  c People can only listen to downloaded songs a few times.
  (d) Technical changes in music recordings have made them harder to copy.

6 The Internet has had a positive and negative effect on musicians. (Section II). Mark
each item with *P* (positive) or *N* (negative).

    a _N_ Customers don't have to buy a whole album. They may buy only one song.

    b _P_ Musicians can reach more people quickly.

    c _P_ Musicians can distribute their music directly to the public.

    d _N_ Customers often share their music so many people don't pay for songs.

7 What are some new ways that music companies hope to make a profit? Circle two
answers. (Par. 8)

    a Listeners will pay to share their music

    b Customers will pay for whole collections of music.

    c Other companies will pay to put advertisements on music websites.

    d Customers will pay for access to Internet music sites.

Skill Review

In Skills and Strategies 12, you learned that creating a timeline is a good way
to understand and remember when different events happened.

A **Look back at Reading 3, then put the different forms of music (A–E) in the correct
order on the timeline. Put the earliest form on the left of the line and the most
recent form on the right of the line. Write the correct letters on the blank lines.**

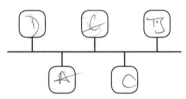

A Tapes
B Music websites where you can listen to songs without owning them
C Downloading from the Internet
D Records
E CDs

B **Using your timeline only, prepare a short presentation about changes in the way
consumers get access to music. Give your presentation to a partner or your class.**

Definitions

Find the words in Reading 3 that complete the following definitions.

1 ___*records*___ are large, flat circles of plastic on which music is stored. (*n pl*) Par. 2

2 If something is ___*fragile*___, it can break easily. (*adj*) Par. 2

3 To _____ is to make a small cut with something sharp. (*v*) Par. 2

4 To ___*download*___ something (for example, a document, photo, or song) is to take it from the Internet and put it on your own computer. (*v*) Par. 3

5 To ___*share*___ is to give someone else what you have or part of what you have. (*v*) Par. 4

6 A/An ___*challenge*___ is a very difficult situation or problem. (*n*) Par. 4

7 Something that is ___*positive*___ is happy and hopeful. (*adj*) Par. 6

8 A/An _____ is a way of doing something. (*n*) Par. 8

Word Families

A The words in **bold** in the chart are from Reading 3. The words next to them are from the same word family. Study and learn these words.

NOUN	VERB
collection	collect
copy	copy
distribution	distribute
profit	profit
punishment	punish

B Choose the correct form of the words from the chart to complete the following sentences. Use the correct verb tenses and subject-verb agreement. Use the correct singular and plural noun forms.

1 The manager will _____ the documents to everyone in the office tomorrow.

2 The company was very successful and quickly made a big _____ last year.

3 The children stole some candy from the store so their mother decided to _____ them.

4 I made a _____ of my passport before I left on my trip.

5 The government controls the _____ of expensive medicine so that everyone has access to it.

6 He had a _____ of old photographs in his desk.

7 After class, I always _____ new vocabulary words into a notebook.

8 When he was young, he liked to _____ rocks and seashells.

9 Many new businesses hope to ___*profit*___ from advertisements on the Internet.

10 Two students got into a fight in school. As a ___*punishment*___, they were not allowed to play sports for two weeks.

Academic Word List

The following are Academic Word List words from all the readings in Unit 6. Use these words to complete the sentences. (For more on the Academic Word List, see page 260.)

access (n)	consumers (n)	participates (v)	recover (v)	role (n)
challenge (n)	equipment (n)	positive (adj)	relax (v)	survived (v)

1 At school, she _____ in many different sports.

2 Climbing mountains requires a lot of special _____.

3 It took almost a month to _____ from her injury.

4 After a hard week of work, we all wanted to _____.

5 Children in many schools around the world do not have _____ to the Internet.

6 Exercise had a very ___*positive*___ effect on his health. He became thinner and felt much better.

7 Math class was always a/an _____ for him. He found the subject very difficult.

8 Education plays an important _____ in a person's ability to get a good job.

9 Businesses think a lot about what _____ want when they create new products.

10 Only a few families in the village _____ the terrible fire. Most of the people there died.

Critical Thinking

The music industry is trying to figure out its future. Reading 3 discusses what might happen in the future. What do you think will happen in the next 20 years?

ANALYZING INFORMATION

Critical thinking involves thinking carefully about important topics that the writer has not completely explained.

A Discuss the following questions with a small group.

1 What do you think will be the most common way to find and listen to music in the future? Why do you think so?

2 How will the music industry make money?

3 How do you think artists will be paid for their music?

A Share your answers with the rest of the class, and continue your discussion by answering the following question.

Who or what do you think has the strongest influence on music sales?

Research

Do a survey of your classmates about how they find new music. Find answers to the following questions.

- Do you listen to the radio?
- Do your friends recommend musicians and songs?
- Do you find out about music through social media sites like Facebook?
- Do you visit websites for your music?

Writing

Write a short summary of your research. Describe the most popular ways to find music. Explain why you think they are popular.

Improving Your Reading Speed

Good readers read quickly and still understand most of what they read.

A Read the instructions and strategies for Improving Your Reading Speed in Appendix 3 on page 273.

B Choose one of the readings in this unit. Read it without stopping. Time how long it takes you to finish the text in minutes and seconds. Enter the time in the chart on page 275. Then calculate your reading speed in number of words per minute.

> ### TIME SEQUENCE CONNECTORS
>
> When writers are describing a sequence of events, they often use words or phrases to help make the time sequence clear. They use words or phrases such as *then*, *after that*, *before that*, or *since then* to show how one event connects to another in time. You also learned words and phrases of time sequence in Skills and Strategies 12 on page 181.

Exercise 1

Read the following sentences. Highlight any words or phrases that signal time. Write *1* by the first event and *2* by the second event. The first one has been done for you.

1 The manager at the department store started to play classical music last summer. Before that, shoppers did not stay very long or buy very much.

2 In the early 1980s, CD players were very expensive. After a few years, the price dropped.

3 The rhythm of the music was slow at first. Then the music got much faster, and people started to dance.

4 In the 1950s, people could buy the first portable radios. Before that, people could only listen to large radios that were very heavy.

5 The website requires you to pay money. Then you can download the music or a movie.

6 She did not have access to music lessons as a child. Later, as an adult, she took piano lessons.

7 Last year all of the children participated in the music program. Before that, only the children with a lot of talent took part.

8 The director made them do a lot of repetitions of the same piece. Later, they performed the piece perfectly.

Exercise 2

Make a clear paragraph by putting sentences A, B, and C into the best order after the numbered sentence. Look for pronouns and words or phrases that signal time, addition, contrast, or cause and effect to help you. Write the letters in the correct order on the blank lines.

1 Two companies, Philips of the Netherlands and Sony of Japan, worked together to develop compact discs (CDs). ____ ____ ____

A It held songs from Abba, a Swedish pop group.	**B** They produced the first CD in 1982.	**C** Three years later, in 1985, a CD by Dire Straits was the first to sell one million copies.

2 A phonograph is a machine that uses a needle to play records. ____ ____ ____

A At first, his company rented phonographs to businesses for a small amount of money.	**B** Thomas Edison invented the first one in 1877.	**C** After 10 years, Edison started to sell phonographs to people for home use.

3 The doctor decided to try music as a way to relieve his patients' headaches. ____ ____ ____

A However, some said their headaches did not last as long when they played music.	**B** Many of them said it was not effective.	**C** Six months later, he asked his patients if the music relieved their headaches.

4 New equipment for playing music always gets people's attention. ____ ____ ____

A However, when prices dropped, people replaced their old record players with CD players.	**B** For example, people were very excited when CD players came out.	**C** At first, these were very expensive.

5 The Rolling Stones rock band started to play together in 1962. ____ ____ ____

A Over the next 50 years, they released more than 40 albums or CDs.	**B** Ten of these were recordings from live concerts.	**C** Who ever imagined in 1962 that this rock band would survive until the twenty-first century?

7

NATURAL DISASTERS

SKILLS AND STRATEGIES

- Collocations
- Organizing Notes in Outlines

Collocations

As you learned in Skills and Strategies 5 on page 66, when two or more words often appear together, we call this a *collocation*. You learned that some collocations have a verb and a noun. Another type of collocation has an adjective and a noun. Good readers know these collocations. This helps them read more quickly.

Examples & Explanations

The **heavy rain** caused floods.

Light snow fell all day in the mountains.

There are many collocations that we use to describe the weather. For example, we often use the adjectives *heavy* and *light* with the nouns *rain* and *snow*, such as **heavy rain, light rain, heavy snow,** or **light snow.**

The **high temperatures** this afternoon will fall by nighttime.

We often use the adjectives *high* and *low* with the noun *temperature*.

Everyone stayed home today because of the **severe** winter **weather**.

Sometimes the adjective and noun are not next to each other. In this example, an additional adjective, *winter*, is in the collocation **severe weather**.

The Language of Collocation

Here are a few common collocations with adjectives and nouns.

ADJECTIVE + NOUN			
heavy / light	*high / low*	*severe*	*strong*
• *rain*	• *pressure*	• *damage*	• *chance*
• *snow*	• *risk*	• *injuries*	• *impact*
• *traffic*	• *temperatures*	• *weather*	• *winds*

Strategies

These strategies will help you learn collocations.

- When you are reading, try to notice adjectives and nouns that often go together. These may be useful collocations. Be careful. Sometimes other words are between the adjective and noun. These words may not be part of the collocation.
- When you look up a word in a dictionary, notice words that go together with it.
- When you make a list of new vocabulary to study, write the collocations. Learn the words that go together, not just the single words.

Skill Practice 1

Read the following paragraphs. Choose words from the box above each paragraph to complete the collocations. Write the words on the blank lines. The first one has been done for you.

heavy	high	severe

1   In most of the world, there is some risk of _____*severe*_____ weather. In the
                                                          a

   mountains, winter storms bring _____ snow. In other places, storms
                                                                    b

   bring too much rain. If you don't like wet weather, perhaps the desert is the best

   place to live. There, you only have to worry about _____ temperatures.
                                                                               c

high	low	severe

2   Southern California has dry and sunny weather much of the year. However, there

   is a _____ risk of forest fires at certain times of the year because it is very
                            a

   dry. These fires often cause _____ damage. Signs at the entrance to a
                                                      b

   forest usually tell people whether the risk for fire is high or _____.
                                                                                          c

heavy	low	strong

3   Air pressure affects the weather. High air pressure usually creates cool, dry

   weather and clear skies. On the other hand, _____ air pressure creates
                                                                           a

   warm weather. With this type of pressure, there is a _____ chance of
                                                                                  b

   storms with _____ rain.
                              c

Skill Practice 2

Read the following paragraphs. Highlight any adjective and noun collocations you see. Then write the collocations on the blank lines next to their meanings. The first one has been done for you.

1   The new bridge was beautiful. The builders used advanced technology to build it. The bridge was only two years old, so it was a complete surprise to everyone when it fell. A huge number of drivers now have to find other ways to get across the river. For the next few months, drivers will have to use other bridges, either 10 miles south or 8 miles north of the city. There will be heavy traffic on the roads to those bridges.

a a lot _____

b something very unexpected _____

c the latest computers and equipment *advanced technology* _____

d a lot of cars _____

2   City officials are going to hold a public meeting to discuss building a new sea wall. The sea wall has strong support from people who live near the water. They think it will prevent severe flooding in a storm. Other people say there is a very low risk of flooding and that the new sea wall will be very expensive.

a problems with water coming over the land _____

b an event for people to talk to city leaders _____

c many positive opinions _____

d a small chance _____

3   It is difficult to get help to people after a natural disaster. At first, help usually goes to people in large urban areas. It takes much longer to get help to people in smaller rural areas. There may be no easy access to people if roads are blocked.

a direct and fast way to get close to or to enter an area _____

b places far away from a city or urban area _____

c an event of nature that causes serious damage _____

d cities _____

Connecting to the Topic

Read the definition of *natural disaster*, and then discuss the following questions with a partner.

> **natural disaster** (*n*) any event or force of nature that has terrible consequences, such as an earthquake, flood, forest fire, or hurricane

1 What are some recent examples of the natural disasters listed above? Describe them.

2 What other examples of natural disasters can you think of? Describe them.

3 Have you or someone you know experienced a natural disaster? Describe what happened.

Previewing and Predicting

> Reading the beginning of each paragraph can help you predict what the topics and main ideas in a reading will be.

A Read the beginnings of paragraphs 2–6 from Reading 1 in the chart below. With a partner, discuss what you think the paragraphs will be about.

B Then complete the chart. If you think a paragraph will be about weather, write *W* in the chart. If you think it will be about earthquakes, write *E*.

BEGINNINGS OF PARAGRAPHS	WEATHER OR EARTHQUAKES?
Violent storms bring heavy rain and strong winds. All of the rain can cause . . . (Par. 2)	
When floods occur in the mountains, sometimes the water mixes with earth . . . (Par. 3)	
Movement under the earth can also cause . . . (Par. 4)	
The most severe damage is usually at the center of an earthquake, but . . . (Par. 5)	
Although most earthquakes are caused by the natural movement of the earth, sometimes . . . (Par. 6)	

While You Read

As you read, stop at the end of each sentence that contains words in **bold**. Then follow the instructions in the box in the margin.

The Dark Side of Nature

1   Nature usually plays a positive role in our lives. Sometimes, however, nature can turn wild and dangerous. Some natural events can cause serious injuries, death, and significant damage. These events are called *natural disasters*. There are two main types of natural disasters. First, there are extreme weather events, such as violent storms. Second, some natural disasters are the result of movements under the earth. These movements can cause **earthquakes**.

WHILE YOU READ 1

Look back in the paragraph to find words that signal cause and effect. Highlight the effects.

2   Violent storms bring heavy rain and strong wind. All of the rain can cause floods. The most serious violent storms begin over oceans. These are called *hurricanes*, *cyclones*, or *typhoons*. Their names depend on their locations. A hurricane is a massive storm in the Atlantic Ocean or the eastern Pacific Ocean. A cyclone is a severe storm that starts in the Indian Ocean or in the southwestern Pacific Ocean near Australia or Africa. A typhoon is a storm in the northwestern Pacific Ocean near Asia. In 2009, a typhoon hit Taiwan. Eighty inches (two meters) of rain fell in two days. Heavy floods destroyed bridges and roads and caused widespread damage.

3   When floods occur in the mountains, sometimes the water mixes with earth to make **mud**. This heavy mud moves down the side of a mountain in a *mudslide*. Mudslides can destroy homes and injure people. In 1998, Hurricane Mitch resulted in about 10,000 deaths across the Caribbean. Many of the people died in the floods and mudslides when the water and mud washed their homes down the mountains.

WHILE YOU READ 2

Look back to find the definition of *mud*. Highlight it.

A mudslide washes through the streets after Hurricane Mitch.

Tsunami coming ashore in Japan in 2011

4   Movement under the earth can also cause natural disasters. Massive earthquakes are not frequent, but they can be deadly. In 2010, there was a major earthquake in Haiti. No one knows how many people died as a result. Estimates are between 50,000 and 300,000. It nearly destroyed or completely destroyed almost 300,000 buildings. A million people lost their homes.

5   The most severe damage is usually at the center of an earthquake, but an earthquake can also cause disaster far away. For example, in 2004, there was a major earthquake in the Indian Ocean near Indonesia. No people live in the ocean, so the earthquake did not hurt anyone. However, it caused a huge tsunami that hit 12 countries. A *tsunami* is a massive wall of water that hits the shore **suddenly**. This tsunami was 100 feet (30 meters) high. It destroyed many communities along the shore and killed about 230,000 people. More than one and a half million people had to leave their homes.

WHILE YOU READ ❸

Look back to find the definition of *tsunami*. Highlight it.

6   Although most earthquakes are caused by the natural movement of the earth, sometimes human activity contributes to natural disasters. Mines can increase the pressure under the earth. Dams, which store large amounts of water, can also cause an increase in pressure. This increase in pressure can lead to an **earthquake**.

WHILE YOU READ ❹

What is the main idea of paragraph 6? Highlight it.

People examine the damage after an earthquake.

7   Natural disasters occur when a community is vulnerable to natural events such as violent weather and movements under the earth. Perhaps homes are on land that is very low, or they are near a river. Perhaps the buildings are not very strong. These situations can make places vulnerable to storms, floods, or earthquakes. After disasters, communities often rebuild in ways that will help them to be less vulnerable to these events.

Table 7.1 The Ten Most Deadly Natural Disasters

EVENT	LOCATION	YEAR	NUMBER OF DEATHS
Flood	China	1931	1,000,000–4,000,000
Flood	China	1887	900,000–2,000,000
Earthquake	China	1556	830,000
Cyclone	Bangladesh	1970	500,000
Cyclone	India	1839	300,000
Earthquake	Syria and Turkey	526	250,000
Earthquake	China	1976	242,000
Earthquake	China	1920	240,000
Tsunami	Indian Ocean	2004	230,000
Earthquake	Haiti	2010	50,000–300,000

Source: About.com

Main Idea Check

Here are the main ideas of paragraph 2–6 in Reading 1. Match each paragraph to its main idea. Write the number of the paragraph on the blank line.

_____ A Rain and wind from storms can cause a lot of damage.

_____ B Movement under the earth can result in earthquakes.

_____ C Human activity can be a factor in earthquakes.

_____ D Earthquakes can cause damage far away.

_____ E Strong storms in the mountains may cause mudslides.

A Closer Look

Look back at Reading 1 to answer the following questions.

1 According to the whole reading, what kind of natural disaster is each of the following events? Write _W_ on the line for an event caused by _weather_; write _ME_ for an event caused by _movement of the earth_.

   a _____ Cyclones

   b _____ Earthquakes

   c _____ Floods

   d _____ Hurricanes

   e _____ Mudslides

   f _____ Tsunamis

2 Match the type of storm in the left column to the location where the storm occurs in the right column. Some storms occur in more than one location. (Par. 2)

Storm	Location
_____ Cyclones	a Atlantic Ocean
_____ Hurricanes	b Eastern Pacific Ocean
_____ Typhoons	c Indian Ocean
	d Pacific Ocean near Asia
	e Pacific Ocean near Australia or Africa

3 More than half a million people died in the Haiti earthquake. **True or False?** (Par. 4)

4 Why was no one hurt at the center of the 2004 earthquake? (Par. 5)

   a It was not a very strong earthquake.

   b It was in the middle of the ocean.

   c The communities were prepared.

   d All of the houses were very strong.

5 Human activity may contribute to natural disasters. **True or False?** (Par. 6)

6 What factors may make a community vulnerable to a natural disaster? Circle three answers. (Par. 7)

a It is too near something dangerous.

b It has houses that are on very low land.

c It has very bad weather.

d It has houses that are not built very well.

7 The tsunami in the Indian Ocean in 2004 was one of history's five deadliest natural disasters. **True or False?** (Table 7.1)

8 According to the whole reading, which one of the following causes and effects is *not* true?

a Major storms may cause floods.

b Floods may cause mudslides.

c Human activity may cause hurricanes.

d Earthquakes may cause tsunamis.

Skill Review

In Skills and Strategies 13, you learned that some adjectives and nouns often appear together. Recognizing and learning these *collocations* can help you read more quickly.

A **Reread paragraph 2 from Reading 1 below. Highlight the adjective + noun collocations for** *storm, rain, wind, floods,* **and** *damage.*

Violent storms bring heavy rain and strong wind. So much rain can cause floods. The most serious violent storms begin over oceans. These are called *hurricanes, cyclones,* or *typhoons.* Their names depend on their locations. A hurricane is a massive storm in the Atlantic Ocean or the eastern Pacific Ocean. A cyclone is a severe storm that starts in the Indian Ocean or in the southwestern Pacific Ocean near Australia or Africa. A typhoon is a storm in the northwestern Pacific Ocean near Asia. In 2009, a typhoon hit Taiwan. Eighty inches (two meters) of rain fell in two days. Heavy floods destroyed bridges and roads and caused widespread damage.

B **Compare your answers with a partner.**

Definitions

Find the words in Reading 1 that complete the following definitions.

1 _____ means physical harm, usually to a thing, not a person. (n) Par. 1

2 Something that is very large is _____. (adj) Par. 2

3 _____ is a mix of dirt and water. (n) Par. 3

4 Something that is very dangerous and is likely to kill people is _____.
(adj) Par. 4

5 To _____ something means to help to cause it. (v) Par. 6

6 A/An _____ is a hole in the ground where you can find valuable
minerals, such as gold and coal. (n) Par. 6

7 A/An _____ is a wall across a river that stops the water. (n) Par. 6

8 A/An _____ is a group of people who live in the same area. (n) Par. 7

Words in Context

A Use context clues to match the first part of each sentence to its correct second
part and to understand the meaning of the words in **bold**.

_____ 1 The heavy rain and
strong wind

_____ 2 Last week's earthquake

_____ 3 The massive fire

_____ 4 The snow created

_____ 5 His leg was broken in three
places, which

_____ 6 We listened to the news
and heard

_____ 7 Engineers did a study and
found that the bridge

_____ 8 When the weather is dry,

a too much **pressure** on the bridge so it
fell into the river.

b caused him **extreme** pain for weeks.

c was **vulnerable**. They told residents not
to use it.

d caused **widespread** fear. People thought
there might be more tremors.

e **destroyed** many homes. They are now
just pieces of burned wood.

f forest fires become more **frequent**.

g the predictions of **violent** storms so we
moved everything inside.

h produced **floods** in several towns.

B Compare your answers with a partner's. Discuss what clues helped you match the
parts of the sentences and helped you understand what the words in **bold** mean.

Critical Thinking

At the end of Reading 1, the writer says that many communities are in areas that are vulnerable to natural disasters. As a result, many people die or lose their homes.

> **EXPLORING OPINIONS**
>
> Critical readers form their own opinions about important topics in a text.

A Discuss the following questions with a small group.

1 When a natural disaster, such as flood or earthquake, occurs in a vulnerable area, should the people who live there be allowed to return and rebuild their community?

2 Should their government help them to rebuild?

3 What would happen if there was another natural disaster after rebuilding? Should they rebuild again?

B Share your answers with the rest of the class.

Research

Do some research on a recent natural disaster. Find answers to the following questions.

- What happened? Describe it.
- Where did it happen?
- What caused it?
- Were people injured? How many? Did people die? How many?
- Was there any damage? Describe it.
- Who came to help after the disaster?

Writing

Write a short summary of your research.

Connecting to the Topic

Discuss the following questions with a partner.

1 Are you or your family prepared for a natural disaster? Explain your answer.

2 Does your country prepare for natural disasters? Explain your answer.

3 What does the government do to prepare for natural disasters in your community?

4 If there has been a natural disaster in your community, how has the government responded?

Previewing and Predicting

> Reading the title and the beginning of each paragraph can help you predict what a reading will be about.

A Read the first two sentences of paragraphs 2–7 in Reading 2, and think about the title of the reading. Then read the topics below. Write the number of the paragraph (*2–7*) next to the topic you think will be discussed in that paragraph.

PARAGRAPH	TOPIC
	Technology and prediction of natural disasters
	Disaster preparation
	Animals and earthquakes
	Education and disaster preparation
	Government warning systems
	Prediction of earthquakes

B Compare your answers with a partner's.

While You Read

As you read, stop at the end of each sentence that contains words in **bold**. Then follow the instructions in the box in the margin.

Predicting and Preparing for Natural Disasters

1   In 2011, there were 820 natural disasters all over the world. They killed more than 27,000 people and caused $380 billion in damage. In most years, an average of 65,000 people die in natural disasters. Many others lose their homes in the destruction. How can we prevent these terrible losses?

2   One way to prevent these losses is to predict natural disasters. With new technology, scientists can now predict some events. Satellites show massive storms as they develop over the oceans. Special equipment shows when there is movement under the earth. When there is an earthquake deep in the ocean, scientists can predict a **tsunami**.

3   Earthquakes are much more difficult to predict. Some people believe that animals know when an earthquake is coming. For example, in Haicheng, China, in February 1975, many animals began to behave strangely. Government officials believed this was a warning that an earthquake was coming. They ordered everyone to leave the city. A few days later, there was a strong earthquake. The next year, there was a stronger earthquake in another city in China. This time, however, animals did not behave strangely.

4   Most scientists believe that it is only possible to predict where an earthquake is likely to happen. They do not believe that it is possible to predict the precise date and time of an earthquake. Scientists know that before some earthquakes occur, there are often small movements, or **tremors**, that shake the earth. It is possible that animals

WHILE YOU READ 1

Look back in paragraph 2 for a collocation with an adjective and *storm*. Highlight the collocation.

WHILE YOU READ 2

Find a clue in this sentence that signals the definition of *tremors*. Highlight the definition.

Scientists are not able to make exact predictions about earthquakes.

may feel these movements and begin to act strangely. However, because earthquakes do not always follow these tremors, scientists cannot use these events to predict earthquakes accurately.

5   Although we cannot predict most natural disasters, it is possible to prepare for them. Many governments have warning systems. When a big storm or a tsunami is coming, the warning system can tell people to move away. This can save lives. Japan is a world leader in preparing for earthquakes and tsunamis. After an earthquake in Kyoto in 1975, they built an early warning system. When a massive earthquake hit Japan in 2011, there was a warning a few seconds after the first tremor. Although many people died, thousands of others lived because of the warning. They were able to escape the tsunami that followed the earthquake. Unfortunately, in many areas of the world, there are no warning systems. Scientists predicted the tsunami of 2004, but there was no warning system for thousands of people along the coast of the Indian **Ocean**.

A warning system can move people to a safer place before a disaster occurs.

6   The people who live in zones with frequent natural disasters should also prepare for them. They should store extra food and water. They should make a plan to contact and find the people in their family if there is a disaster. They should know where to find important news and information.

WHILE YOU READ ❸

What is the main idea of paragraph 5? Highlight it.

7   Education about natural disasters is crucial. Schools can teach children what to do in a disaster and to understand the warning signs of a disaster. An eleven-year-old tourist named Tilly Smith was on a beach in Thailand with her family on December 26, 2004. A lot of bubbles appeared in the water. Then the water went out very far. The beach was almost dry. Tilly remembered a school lesson about tsunamis, and she knew these were warning signs. She told her parents, and they told others. Many people were able to run to a safe place.

8   Natural disasters can cause terrible damage and loss of life. We cannot prevent them. However, we can predict some kinds of disasters, and our ability to predict other kinds of disasters is improving. We can also prepare for disasters. If people and governments prepare carefully, we can reduce the consequences of natural **disasters**.

WHILE YOU READ ❹

Look back in paragraph 8 to find a word that signals a contrast. Highlight the two ideas that are in contrast.

Main Idea Check

Match the main ideas below to five of the paragraphs in Reading 2. Write the number of the paragraph on the blank line.

_____ A Preparation can reduce damage and injuries in natural disasters.

_____ B Some people believe that animals know when an earthquake is coming.

_____ C People in vulnerable communities can plan for natural disasters.

_____ D Scientists cannot predict the exact day and time of an earthquake.

_____ E Schools can teach children what to do if there is a natural disaster.

A Closer Look

Look back at Reading 2 to answer the following questions.

1 In 2011, there were 65,000 natural disasters all over the world. **True or False?** (Par. 1)

2 What are successful methods of disaster prediction? Circle two answers. (Par. 2)
   a Equipment can sense movement under the earth.
   b Satellites show storm activity.
   c Animals can predict natural disasters.
   d Schools can tell children when a disaster is coming.

3 What are tremors? (Par. 4)
   a Natural disasters
   b Storm activity
   c Small movements of the earth
   d Strange animal movements

4 Which of the following statements is true about earthquakes and tsunamis? Write *T* on the blank lines before true statements. (Pars. 2 and 4)

   a _____ Scientists can predict the dates of earthquakes.
   b _____ Scientists can predict that a tsunami will follow an earthquake.
   c _____ Scientists can predict where earthquakes are likely to happen.
   d _____ Scientists can predict tremors in the earth.

5 How can governments and people prepare for natural disasters? Circle three answers. (Pars. 5 and 6)
   a People can store extra food and water.
   b Governments can use warning systems.
   c Governments can contact families.
   d People can move to a safer place.

6 Put a check (✓) next to the places where early warning systems saved lives in an earthquake or tsunami.

a _____ 1975 earthquake in China

b _____ 1975 earthquake in Kyoto, Japan

c _____ 2004 tsunami along the Indian Ocean

d _____ 2011 tsunami in Japan

Skill Review

In Making Connections on page 193, you learned that you should pay attention to words and phrases, such as *then, after that, before that,* or *since then,* that writers use to show time sequences. This will help you follow the order of events in a text.

A Reread these sentences from Reading 2. Highlight the words and phrases that show a time sequence. Then write *1* above the event that occurs first and a *2* above the event that occurs second. If there are three events, write *3* above the third event. The first one has been done for you.

1 Scientists know that before some earthquakes occur, there are often small movements, or tremors, that shake the earth.

2 After the earthquake in Kyoto in 1975, they built an early warning system.

3 When a massive earthquake hit Japan in 2011, there was a warning a few seconds after the first tremor.

4 A lot of bubbles appeared in the water. Then the water went out very far.

5 For example, in Haicheng, China, in February 1975, many animals began to behave strangely. Government officials believed this was a warning that an earthquake was coming. They ordered everyone to leave the city. A few days later, there was a strong earthquake.

B Compare you answers with a classmate's.

Vocabulary Development

Definitions

Find the words in Reading 2 that complete the following definitions.

1 A/An _____ is the usual number or amount. (*n*) Par. 1

2 Something that is very bad and very serious is _____. (*adj*) Par. 1

3 Something that is exact is _____. (*adj*) Par. 4

4 To _____ is to make movements from side to side. (*v*) Par. 4

5 A/An _____ is the shore between land and the ocean. (*n*) Par. 5

6 To _____ someone is to communicate with them. (*v*) Par. 6

7 Something that is very important and necessary is _____. (*adj*) Par. 7

8 To _____ is to make less or smaller. (*v*) Par. 8

Words in Context

Complete the sentences with words from Reading 2 in the box below.

accurately	loss	satellite	tremors
bubbles	prepares	signs	warning

1 There are often small _____ before a large earthquake.

2 The people in the town only had a few minutes of _____ before the tsunami came onto the shore.

3 She always _____ for examinations for a week. She reads all of her notes carefully.

4 The soap created lots of small _____ in the water.

5 A/An _____ above the earth sent information about weather back to officials on the ground.

6 It is important to report information _____ on government forms.

7 There was a significant _____ of jobs in the United States in the period between June and December.

8 Strong wind and dark clouds are often _____ that a storm is coming.

Critical Thinking

Reading 2 discusses ways to prepare for a natural disaster.

> **PERSONALIZING**
>
> Thinking about how new information applies to your own life can help you understand a text better.

A With a partner, complete the chart below. Put a check (✓) in the appropriate columns. Add two new ways in the chart in which people could prepare for a natural disaster.

WAYS TO PREPARE FOR A NATURAL DISASTER	I HAVE DONE THIS.	PEOPLE SHOULD DO THIS.
Store food and water		
Have a plan to contact family		
Find out where to get news and information		

B Share your chart with the rest of the class.

Research

Do some research on disaster preparation in your community. Find answers to the following questions.

- What kinds of natural disasters are most likely to happen in your community?
- Does your community have a plan for a natural disaster?
- Where should you go?
- Whom should you contact?

Writing

Write a short summary of your research.

Organizing Notes In Outlines

As you learned in Skills and Strategies 12 on page 181, good readers take notes to help them study for a test. Timelines are one way to organize your notes. Another way is to make an outline. In an outline, you can organize your notes about the main ideas and supporting details. Outlines can help you remember important information.

Examples & Explanations

Some of the effects of earthquakes occur right away; others last a long time. In March 2011, the strongest earthquake in recent history hit the Pacific coast of Japan. The earthquake led to a powerful tsunami that was more than 70 feet (21 meters) high in some places. The earthquake and tsunami caused widespread damage and loss of life. Officials say that more than 15,000 people died, and 120,000 buildings were destroyed. However, there were other important effects of the disasters: They caused accidents in nuclear energy plants. These accidents resulted in a lot of dangerous chemicals and gas in the area around the plants. Residents had to leave their homes because the chemical could harm them. Many people do not know when they will be able to return.

As the student read this paragraph, she looked for the main idea of the paragraph.

The main idea in this paragraph is: *Some effects of an earthquake occur quickly, but others last a long time.*

The student wrote the main idea in her outline. (See below.) Note that she didn't write a complete sentence. She wrote only the key words.

Then she found the two supporting details and put the important information and numbers into her outline.

A. *natural disasters effects – some short, some last long time – 2011 Japan earthquake*

   1. effects right after

      a. 15,000 deaths

      b. 120,000 buildings destroyed

   2. nuclear accident – effects last long time

      a. dangerous chemicals

      b. residents had to leave

Strategies

These strategies will help you organize your notes in an outline.

- As you read, look for the main ideas and supporting details. Make notes in the margins of the reading.
- When you make your outline, begin each section of your outline with the main idea of that section.

- Add the most important supporting details to your outline.
- Use a system of numbers and letters to show the difference between important and less important details.
- Keep your outline simple. Don't write too much detail.

Skill Practice 1

Read the following paragraph. In this case, the student wrote notes in the margin of the page to help her write an outline. Use these notes to help you complete the student's outline below.

Earthquakes are impossible to predict, but it is possible to prevent loss of life in an earthquake. Most of the damage in an earthquake does not result from the earthquake itself. It results from falling buildings, roads, and bridges. Therefore, the most important way to prevent deaths from an earthquake is to build better roads and buildings. The second important thing to help prevent death and injury is to teach people what to do in an earthquake. A final action that will help to save lives is to stop high-speed trains as soon as an earthquake happens.

poss. to prevent loss of life in earthquakes
①
②
③

A. *Possible to prevent loss of life in earthquakes – three ways*

1. _____

2. _____

3. _____

Skill Practice 2

Read the following paragraph. As you read, take notes in the margin. Find the main idea and number the supporting details. Then make an outline of the paragraph.

Most people think of a natural disaster as an event that happens suddenly with very little warning. This definition does not include drought, because a drought is a long period of time with no rain. A drought does not happen very suddenly. However, droughts are certainly natural disasters. First, they affect large numbers of people in one region. In 1920, a drought in China killed 500,000 people and affected 20 million others. In the early 1980s, severe drought in central Africa killed millions of people. Second, droughts cause severe damage. In a drought, the land gets so dry that it often blows away. No crops can grow. People have to leave their farms to try to find food and work in other areas. Last, local officials are rarely able to take care of people's needs during a drought. Officials need assistance from outside. In all of these ways, a drought is a natural disaster.

Connecting to the Topic

Discuss the following questions with a partner.

1 Some people worry that objects from outer space will hit Earth. Do you think this will happen? Explain your answer.

2 Do you think this has happened in the past? Explain your answer.

3 What do you think would happen if an object from outer space hit Earth?

Previewing and Predicting

Reading the title, section headings, and beginning of each paragraph can help you predict what a reading will be about.

A Read the title, the section headings, and the first sentence of each paragraph of Reading 3. Then read the questions below. Write the number of the section (*I*, *II*, or *III*) next to the question or questions you think the section will answer.

SECTION	QUESTION
	Have objects from outer space caused natural disasters in the past?
	Will any objects from outer space hit Earth in the future?
	Do objects fall from outer space?
	What can we do to prevent a natural disaster from outer space?
	How and why do objects fall to Earth from outer space?
	What happens when objects from outer space hit Earth?

B Compare your answers with a partner's.

While You Read

As you read, stop at the end of each sentence that contains words in **bold**. Then follow the instructions in the box in the margin.

A Natural Disaster from Outer Space?

I. Near-Earth Objects

1   Have you ever seen a falling star? Do you wonder what would happen if an object from space hit Earth? Would it be a disaster? Most natural disasters start on Earth, but some start farther away. They start in outer space. *Near-Earth objects* (NEOs) from outer space, such as *asteroids* and *meteoroids*, sometimes hit Earth. These objects are made of rock or metal. They move in an orbit around the sun. They vary in size. Meteoroids can be as small as a few feet wide. Asteroids are bigger and can be almost 600 miles (1,000 kilometers) wide.

2   Sometimes when the orbits of NEOs come near Earth, Earth's gravity pulls them toward us. Small meteoroids sometimes hit Earth's **atmosphere**, that is, the air and gas above Earth. However, when NEOs enter Earth's atmosphere, they start to burn. Most small NEOs burn up and disappear, so they never hit Earth. A few larger ones do not burn up completely, so they do hit Earth. What would happen if a large asteroid hit Earth? How real is the danger of a natural disaster from an asteroid?

WHILE YOU READ 1
Find a clue in this sentence that signals the definition of *atmosphere*. Highlight the definition.

II. When NEOs Hit Earth

3   It is possible that asteroids have already caused natural disasters. NEOs may help explain a great mystery in Earth's history. About 250 million years ago, all of the plants and animals began to die. They disappeared from Earth forever. In other words, they became **extinct**. Ninety-six percent of all the animals in the sea and 70 percent of all the animals on land at that time became extinct. Many scientists believe that one cause may be a giant asteroid that hit Earth. The

WHILE YOU READ 2
Highlight the words that help you understand the meaning of *extinct*.

Meteor Crater, Arizona, created by an asteroid strike 50,000 years ago

impact of a very large asteroid creates a lot of dust and gas above the Earth. This cloud of dust and gas can block the light from the sun. Without the light from the sun, plants cannot live. Without plants, all the animals will also die.

4   About 65 million years ago, another asteroid hit Earth. It was almost 6 miles (10 kilometers) wide. In the 1980s, scientists found the site of the impact in Mexico. This impact created a hole that is 112 miles (179 kilometers) wide. Scientists have studied rocks and soil from that period, 65 million years ago. Their analysis suggests that the impact of this asteroid caused huge tsunamis. It also created dust and gas in the atmosphere that blocked the sunlight for years.

5   When giant asteroids hit Earth, they can cause death and massive destruction. However, this destruction can lead to new life. When some plants and animals become extinct, other plants and animals begin to develop. For example, most scientists believe that dinosaurs developed after the first giant asteroid hit Earth. Asteroids are a natural part of how life on Earth **changes**.

6   Smaller NEOs hit Earth about every two or three hundred years. These can also cause major damage. The largest one in recent history was in Russia in 1908. It is called the *Tunguska explosion*. This explosion was many times more powerful than an atomic bomb.[1] Fortunately, it occurred in an area where no one lived. Scientists estimate that it burned 80 million trees across 830 square miles (2,150 square kilometers). This kind of explosion is big enough to destroy a major city.

7   Finally, there is *space junk* in orbit around Earth. Space junk is broken pieces of old satellites or other equipment. Do we need to worry

WHILE YOU READ ❸

Look back in paragraph 5 for a collocation with an adjective and *destruction*. Highlight the collocation.

---

[1] *atomic bomb:* a nuclear bomb that causes damage with a massive explosion and extreme heat

about space junk? Like other NEOs, most pieces of junk burn up in Earth's atmosphere and are not a danger to us. However, a few pieces have reached Earth. In 2012, 20 to 30 pieces of space junk from a Russian rocket fell into the Pacific Ocean.

III. Can We Prepare for an NEO Strike?

8   Some people worry that another giant asteroid will hit Earth in the future. This time, it may hit a large town or city. In 2002, a British scientist predicted that a large asteroid would hit Earth in 2019. Many other scientists immediately studied the NEO, and they disagreed. They do not think it will hit Earth. In their opinion, there is only one chance in a million that it will hit Earth. However, they predict it is more likely that another asteroid could hit Earth in 2880. They believe the chance is one in three hundred.

9   Our ability to predict these events is improving. We will probably have a warning many years before a large asteroid hits. The United States government has a project that follows 90 percent of all NEOs that are at least one kilometer wide. What would happen if one of these NEOs began to move toward Earth? What could we do to prevent a natural disaster? If there is enough time, scientists and engineers could build a special machine to change the NEO's orbit. Another possibility is that they could stop the asteroid before it entered Earth's atmosphere. They could send a rocket to destroy it. Governments could also help people leave the area. They could store food and water. These would help people survive if dust and gas blocked the light from the sun for a long **time**.

10   Should people worry about asteroids? Probably not. A large NEO that could cause a natural disaster only hits Earth once or twice in a million years. It is unlikely that an NEO will hit Earth soon. However, scientists will continue to keep track of the NEOs that could be a danger to us in the future.

WHILE YOU READ 4

Look back in paragraph 9 for a collocation with a verb and the noun *disaster*. Highlight the collocation.

Main Idea Check

Match the main ideas below to five of the paragraphs in Reading 3. Write the number of the paragraph on the blank line.

_____ A The impact of an asteroid caused massive destruction 250 million years ago.

_____ B Scientists follow NEOs and may soon be able to predict when they will hit Earth.

_____ C There is a lot of space junk in Earth's atmosphere.

_____ D An asteroid hit Earth 65 million years ago and caused widespread damage.

_____ E Destruction can lead to new forms of life.

A Closer Look

Look back at Reading 3 to answer the following questions.

1 Meteoroids are larger than asteroids. **True or False?** (Par. 1)

2 Why do NEOs sometimes hit Earth's atmosphere? (Par. 2)

  a Scientists are not sure why this happens.
  b They burn up so they do not hit Earth.
  c Gravity from Earth pulls them out of their orbit.
  d They are too large and heavy to stay in their orbit.

3 Put the events (A–E) in the correct order in which they happen. Write the correct letter in each box. (Pars. 3–5)

  A The explosion from the impact creates a lot of dust and gas in the air.
  B Plants and animals die.
  C Sunlight cannot reach Earth.
  D An asteroid hits Earth.
  E New and different plants and animals take the place of those that died.

4 The impact of an asteroid can cause a tsunami. **True or False?** (Par. 4)

5 What were the consequences of the Tunguska explosion? (Par. 6)

  a Dust blocked the sun for 200 years.
  b A major city was destroyed.
  c It created an atomic bomb.
  d Eighty million trees burned down.

6 Space junk never reaches the Earth. **True or False?** (Par. 7)

7 According to most scientists, what is the chance that an asteroid will hit Earth in the next thousand years? (Par. 8)

    a One in three hundred

    b One in a million

    c One in two million

    d There is no chance

8 If an asteroid is coming toward Earth, what can we do? Circle four answers. (Par. 9)

    a Scientists can try to destroy it.

    b People can prepare by storing food and water.

    c People can move to a safer place.

    d Scientists can try to change its orbit.

    e Governments can build a city under the ground.

Skill Review

> In Skills and Strategies 14, you learned that outlines can help you understand the organization of a text and help you find important information for a test.

A Complete these outlines of paragraphs 5 and 6 in Reading 3.

Paragraph 5 Main Idea:

Asteroids cause destruction but this is a natural part of how life on Earth changes.

    1 _____

    2 _____

    3 _____

Paragraph 6 Main Idea:

_____

    1 _____

    2 _____

    3 *The explosion was big enough to destroy a city.*

B Compare your outlines with a partner's.

Definitions

Find the words in Reading 3 that complete the following definitions.

1 _____ is the part of the universe that is farthest from Earth.
(*n 2 words*) Par. 1

2 _____ is the force that pulls things to the ground. (*n*) Par. 2

3 A/An _____ is something strange that has not been explained. (*n*) Par. 3

4 A plant or animal that no longer exists anywhere in the world is _____.
(*adj*) Par. 3

5 _____ is dry dirt. (*n*) Par. 3

6 To __ _____ is to stop something from passing through. (*v*) Par. 3

7 _____ is something useless that you throw away. (*n*) Par. 7

8 A/An _____ is a planned piece of work. (*n*) Par. 9

Word Families

A The words in **bold** in the chart are from Reading 3.
The words next to them are from the same word
family. Study and learn these words.

B Choose the correct form of the words from the
chart to complete the following sentences. Use the
correct verb tenses and subject-verb agreement.
Use the correct singular and plural noun forms.

NOUN	VERB
analysis	*analyze*
explosion	*explode*
impact	*impact*
orbit	*orbit*
suggestion	**suggest**

1 Scientists carefully _____ the chemicals
in their laboratory.

2 The _____ of the crash injured a passenger in the car.

3 After the accident, the car _____ in a ball of fire.

4 The moon _____ the Earth.

5 The study by the scientists _____ an important role for food in
our health.

6 Scientists are fairly certain that space junk will not _____ the Earth.

7 The scientists did a/an _____ of the NEOs that have hit Earth.

8 The people on the street were afraid when they saw the fire and heard the loud
_____ inside the factory.

9 Her teacher gave her some _____ about how to study more effectively.

10 The Earth's _____ around the sun is not quite a perfect circle.

Academic Word List

The following are Academic Word List words from all the readings in Unit 7. Use these words to complete the sentences. (For more on the Academic Word List, see page 260.)

accurately (*adv*)	community (*n*)	contributed to (*v*)	impact (*n*)	project (*n*)
analysis (*n*)	contacts (*v*)	crucial (*adj*)	precise (*adj*)	widespread (*adj*)

1 There was _____ unhappiness about the examination results. Everyone complained.

2 I cannot give you a/an _____ date for my visit because I am not sure when I am coming to your town.

3 Everyone in the _____ helped the survivors of the flood with food, clothes, and money.

4 The government is working on a/an _____ to bring new business and jobs to the city.

5 The teacher always _____ the parents of the children who are having problems in school.

6 She wanted to make sure she had done everything _____ so she read her homework again to find any mistakes.

7 Scientists believe that a NEO may have _____ the disappearance of dinosaurs.

8 The _____ of the meteoroid created a big hole in the ground.

9 The president is a very important person. He must make many _____ decisions every day.

10 A scientific _____ of the water showed that it contains harmful chemicals.

Critical Thinking

In the three readings of this unit, you read about different aspects of natural disasters and how governments and individuals can prepare for them.

SYNTHESIZING

Critical thinking includes connecting new information to information you learned in previous readings.

A Discuss the following question with a partner. Use your own ideas and opinions to explain your answers.

Most governments have a limited amount of resources to spend on natural disasters. How should they divide these resources among the following?

1 Predicting natural disasters
2 Preparing vulnerable communities for natural disasters
3 Following NEOs
4 Assisting in recovery after natural disasters

B Share your ideas with the rest of the class.

Research

Find out about NEOs in books and films. Survey some of your classmates. Find answers to the following questions.

- Have you ever seen a film or television show or read a book about an NEO that hit Earth? Describe the event in the film, television show, or book.

- Was the story based on any of the science that you read about in Reading 3?

- Why do you think people enjoy films and books about this topic?

Writing

Write two paragraphs. The first paragraph will describe some films or books about NEOs. The second paragraph will discuss why you think people enjoy them.

Improving Your Reading Speed

Good readers read quickly and still understand most of what they read.

A Read the instructions and strategies for Improving Your Reading Speed in Appendix 3 on page 273.

B Choose one of the readings in this unit. Read it without stopping. Time how long it takes you to finish the text in minutes and seconds. Enter the time in the chart on page 275. Then calculate your reading speed in number of words per minute.

REVIEW OF CONNECTORS

In Units 1–6, you learned that writers have several ways to make connections. To do this, they connect words and ideas in their writing using:

- pronouns to refer to previous things or ideas (See page 31.)
- words or phrases to signal addition (See pages 63 and 95.)
- words or phrases to signal contrast (See page 129.)
- words or phrases to signal causes and effects (See page 161.)
- words or phrases to signal time sequence (See page 193.)

Exercise 1

Read the following paragraphs. Highlight any pronouns, and underline what they refer to. Circle any words or phrases that signal addition, contrast, cause and effect, or time sequence. The first one has been done for you.

1   A tornado is a very strong and dangerous wind. It blows in a tight circle. If it contacts the ground, it can cause severe damage. For example, one tornado in 2010 in the southern region of the United States destroyed 700 houses.

2   Tornadoes occur all over the world. However, they occur most often in North America. Most of these occur between the Rocky Mountains and the Appalachian Mountains. For this reason, people call this area "Tornado Alley."

3   At one time, scientists were not able to predict when or where tornadoes would occur. Now, however, satellite images help them predict tornados. These images also can show when a tornado is nearby.

4   Emergency officials suggest the following steps to prepare for a tornado. First, decide which room in your building will give you the most protection. Next, buy flashlights and some emergency supplies. Finally, when you hear a tornado warning, move away from windows to the safest area of your building.

5   After a tornado hits, officials immediately go from block to block to help injured people. They try to contact all the residents in the area. Later, they survey the damage and try to figure out the losses and the precise costs of the damage.

Exercise 2

Make a clear paragraph by putting sentences A, B, and C into the best order after the numbered sentence. Look for pronouns and words or phrases that signal addition, contrast, cause and effect, or time sequence to help you. Write the letters in the correct order on the blank lines.

1 Natural disasters cause widespread destruction. ____ ____ ____

| A And, finally, there is often a harmful impact on the environment that can last a long time. | B In addition, there is damage to buildings, roads, and highways. | C Death and injuries are the most significant loss. |

2 There was, of course, no warning of the earthquake. ____ ____ ____

| A Next, the building began to shake. | B First, everyone felt slight tremors. | C The whole event seemed to last forever, but it only lasted for 15 seconds. |

3 In one part of the city, a fire destroyed an entire block. ____ ____ ____

| A This happened because a gas line broke. | B It took a long time to control the fire, but no one died. | C The gas caused a huge explosion and started a fire. |

4 Rockets lift the weather satellite into outer space. ____ ____ ____

| A They can even watch the storms move around the world. | B When it is in orbit, it starts to send photos back to Earth. | C Weather officials use these to predict storms. |

5 Before the hurricane, the road went along the coast. ____ ____ ____

| A Because this could happen again, city officials do not want to rebuild the road. | B People who live nearby, however, want the city to start rebuilding it immediately. | C Now, after the hurricane, there is no sign of the road. |

8

LEISURE

SKILLS AND STRATEGIES

- Phrases
- Reading Quickly

Phrases

As you learned in Skills and Strategies 7 on page 98, some words always go together to form a fixed phrase. You must learn the meaning of these phrases as a unit, not as individual words. Another group of words that you must learn as a unit is *phrasal verbs*. Phrasal verbs are a combination of a verb plus one or more prepositions. For example, *take off* and *check in* are phrasal verbs. Good readers notice phrasal verbs and learn them. If you can find phrasal verbs in a reading, it can help you understand a reading better and read more quickly.

Examples & Explanations

The plane **took off** late but **got in** early.

A phrasal verb often has a different meaning from the individual words.

take off = to leave
get in = to arrive

We will **pick** the rental car **up** in Paris and **drop** it **off** in Marseilles.

Some phrasal verbs are *separable*. In other words, the object of these verbs can come between, or separate, the two parts of the phrasal verb. In this example, *the car* and *it* are the objects of *pick up* and *drop off*.

pick the car up (or *pick up the car*) = go to get the car

However, when the object of a separable phrasal verb is a pronoun, the pronoun must always come between the verb and the preposition.

drop it off = deliver something (You cannot say, "drop off it.")

The teenager couldn't go to the party because she had to **look after** her little brother.

Some phrasal verbs are *inseparable*. In other words, the object of these verbs must always go after the whole phrasal verb. In this example, *her little brother* is the object.

look after her little brother = watch and make sure that nothing bad happens to her little brother

They tried to **put** the fire **out**, but it was too big.

Phrasal verbs usually have a one-word equivalent, but the phrasal verb is usually more common.

put out (a fire) = extinguish

Put out is more common than *extinguish*.

The Language of Phrasal Verbs

Here are some common phrasal verbs and their meanings.

PHRASAL VERBS	MEANINGS
catch up	*to do what you have not had time to do*
check in	*register (for example, at a hotel)*
cut back (on)	*reduce*
drop off (separable)	*deliver; leave someone*
figure out (separable)	*understand; find; solve*
get in	*arrive*
look after	*take care of*
make up (separable)	*invent*
move out	*leave one home and go to another one*
pick up (separable)	*go to get; collect; take into a vehicle*
put away (separable)	*save*
put out (separable)	*stop, especially a fire*
run out (of)	*use up; not have any more*
show up	*appear*
take off	*leave*

Strategies

These strategies will help you identify and learn phrasal verbs.

- When you read, look for words that often go together.
- When you make a list of new vocabulary to study, write words that go together, not just the single words.
- When you look up a verb in a dictionary, notice if the dictionary lists a special meaning for the verb when it combines with a preposition.
- Notice whether phrasal verbs are separable or inseparable.

Skill Practice 1

Read the following paragraphs. Fill in the blank lines with phrasal verbs from the box above each paragraph. If you need help, use the Language of Phrasal Verbs chart on page 229. The first one has been done for you.

| figure out | look after | move out | pick up |

1   Parents are very busy when their children are young. They do not have a lot of

free time, because they have to ____*look after*____ their children. When they are
                                      a

older, parents have to _____ their children at the end of the school day
                              b

and take them to different activities. When children finally _____, this is
                                                                    c

called "an empty nest." Parents often have to _____ new ways to spend
                                                    d

their time.

| cut back on | put away | run out of | show up |

2   Usually, when people work, they _____ money for retirement. They
                                            a

dream about the time when they won't have to _____ for work every
                                                      b

day. Many people hope to travel at that time. However, as people live longer lives,

they worry about whether they might _____ money in retirement.
                                            c

Therefore, they often decide to _____ their expenses.
                                      d

Skill Practice 2

Read the following paragraphs. Highlight any phrasal verbs you see. Then write the phrasal verbs on the blank lines next to their meanings. The first one has been done for you.

The couple planned a short trip to get away for a short vacation. They took off
on Friday immediately after work, and drove to the hotel. Unfortunately, at the
hotel, they found out that the hotel mixed up the dates of their reservation. So,
they went back home. They were very unhappy that their plans for a wonderful
weekend did not work out.

a confused _____   d left _____

b discovered _____   e returned _____

c leave or escape *get away*   f succeed _____

Connecting to the Topic

Read the definition of *leisure*, and then discuss the following questions with a partner.

> **leisure** (*n*) the time when you are free from work, school, and other responsibilities and can relax

1 Do you think people have more leisure now, or did they have more in the past? Explain your answer.

2 In what parts of the world do you think people have the most leisure?

3 Do you think leisure is important for people? Explain your answer.

Previewing and Predicting

> Reading the title and the first sentence of each paragraph and looking at graphic material can help you predict what a reading will be about.

A Read the title and the first sentences in each paragraph in Reading 1, and look at Figure 8.1 on page 233. Then put a check (✓) next to the topics you think will be discussed in the reading.

_____ a Work and leisure around the world

_____ b The connection between work and leisure

_____ c Leisure activities

_____ d Reasons why people don't like to work

_____ e The history of leisure

_____ f The best places to go in your leisure time

B Compare your answers with a partner's.

While You Read

As you read, stop at the end of each sentence that contains words in bold. Then follow the instructions in the box in the margin.

◄» Work and Leisure

1   People often complain that they work too hard. They complain that they don't have enough time for leisure. Leisure is what you do when you are not working, studying, or looking after your home and family (for example, cooking and **cleaning**). It is what you do when you relax and enjoy yourself. Most people have leisure time at the end of the workday or school day or on weekends.

WHILE YOU READ 1

Look back in this sentence for a phrasal verb. Highlight it.

2   The amount of time we have for leisure has changed throughout history. In the past, most people worked on the land, so their work depended on the weather and the seasons. For example, in western countries – Europe and North America, people did most of the work during the late spring, summer, and early fall. They did not do as much work during the winter.

3   The amount of time that people have for leisure changes when their work changes. In the late eighteenth century and early nineteenth century, industrialization transformed many western countries. Thousands of people left their farms and small villages. They went to work in factories in towns and cities. Their work in factories was very hard, and both the workday and workweek became longer. Many people worked for 16 hours a day, 6 days a week. They only took off one day a week from work – Sunday.

4   In the middle of the nineteenth century, **factory work began to change in two ways.** First, the machines in the factories became faster and more efficient, so that workers did not need to work as many hours. They had more free time. Second, the factories began to pay their workers more money. As a result, workers had more money to spend.

WHILE YOU READ 2

As you read this paragraph, look for words and phrases that signal cause and effect. Highlight the effects.

5   With more time and money, workers had more opportunity for leisure activities. People who worked in or near cities in the second half of the nineteenth century had many new choices about how

In the nineteenth century, many people had more time for leisure.

Figure 8.1 Number of Work Hours Per Week

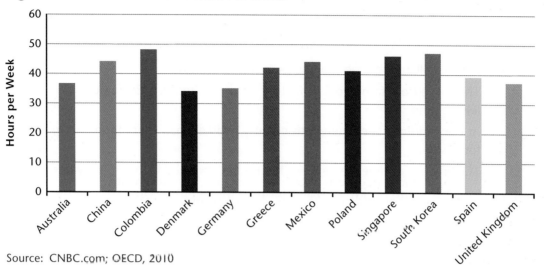

Source: CNBC.com; OECD, 2010

to spend their time and money. Western countries were changing rapidly. Transportation was continuing to improve, so people could get around more **easily**. Streetcars could take people into the city for entertainment. In the cities, there were new public parks and gardens. Workers could go out with their families to the city for games, picnics, and concerts. The first movies and professional baseball games appeared at this time. They were both very popular. There were also trains so that people could get away from the city and spend the day in the country or at the beach.

WHILE YOU READ ③

Look back in this sentence for a phrasal verb. Highlight it.

6 As people moved from farms to cities to work in factories, at first the number of hours people worked went up. However, as a country's economy develops, average working hours start to decrease. As a result, by the middle of the twentieth century, the eight-hour workday and the five-day workweek became typical in most western countries. Today, the average workweek in most countries of western Europe is about 35 **hours**.

WHILE YOU READ ④

What is the main idea of paragraph 6? Highlight it.

7 In many parts of the world, however, people continue to work much longer hours. In many Asian and Latin American countries, many people work more than 45 hours per week. (See Figure 8.1.) They also get less time off from work. Workers in many western European countries get more than 30 days off every year. In contrast, North American, South American, and Asian workers have fewer days off. In general, the pattern around the world has been similar: Both work hours per week and the number of weeks worked per year have decreased in the last 50 years. However, there is still significant variation in the number of work hours across different regions of the **world**.

Main Idea Check

Match the main ideas below to five of the paragraphs in Reading 1. Write the number of the paragraph on the blank line.

_____ A People still have a long workweek in many countries.

_____ B The move from farm work to factory work resulted in a decrease in leisure time.

_____ C In the middle of the nineteenth century, workers had more time and money for leisure.

_____ D The amount of time we have for leisure has changed through the years.

_____ E In general, the workweek is shorter now than in the past.

A Closer Look

Look back at Reading 1 to answer the following questions.

1 In the past, the amount of work often depended on the following factors. Circle two answers. (Par. 2)

　a Seasons

　b Location

　c Factories

　d Weather

2 When people moved from farms to factories, their leisure time increased. **True or False?** (Par. 3)

3 In the middle of the nineteenth century, how did the machines in factories change? Circle two answers. (Par. 4)

　a They became less dangerous.

　b They got faster.

　c They got cheaper.

　d They became more efficient.

　e They became easier to use.

4 What did workers do in their leisure time in the nineteenth century? Circle three answers. (Par. 5)

　a They went to the beach.

　b They went to parks.

　c They listened to music.

　d They listened to the radio.

　e They played music.

5 Put the events (A–D) in the correct order in which they happened. Write the correct letter in each box. (Par. 6)

◯ → ◯ → ◯ → ◯

A Work hours decreased.
B People moved from farms to factories.
C Factories became more efficient.
D Work hours increased.

6 According to Figure 8.1 on page 233, people in western Europe generally work for fewer hours than people in Asia. **True or False?**

Skill Review

In Skills and Strategies 15, you learned that phrasal verbs are a combination of a verb and one or more prepositions. Since it is often difficult to figure out their meaning from their individual parts, it is important to learn phrasal verbs as a unit.

A Find the phrasal verbs in Reading 1 that mean the same as the words and phrases in parentheses in the sentences below. Write the appropriate phrasal verb on the blank line.

1 I stay home in the evening during the week, but on weekends, I prefer to (leave the house) _____. Perhaps I might go to a restaurant or a movie. (Par. 5)

2 During the winter, it is more difficult to (move from place to place) _____ because of the snow. (Par. 5)

3 Some people decide to ride bicycles when gasoline prices (increase) _____. (Par. 6)

4 Many people like to (escape) _____ from the city when the weather is hot. They go to the mountains or to the beach. (Par. 5)

5 Some people (take care of) _____ other children in their homes to make some extra money. (Par. 1)

6 I'm going to have to (not go to work) _____ Friday, because it is my sister's wedding. (Par. 3)

B Compare your answers with a partner's.

Vocabulary Development

Definitions

Find the words in Reading 1 that complete the following definitions.

1 _____ are places where things are made by machines. (*n pl*) Par. 3

2 A/An _____ is a chance to do or get something. (*n*) Par. 5

3 Something that is open and available to everyone is _____. (*adj*) Par. 5

4 _____ are meals that you eat outside, often in parks. (*n pl*) Par. 5

5 _____ are performances of live music. (*n pl*) Par. 5

6 A/An _____ is the area of land next to the sea or a lake. (*n*) Par. 5

7 The _____ is the system in which a country makes and uses things and money. (*n*) Par. 6

8 Two things that are almost the same are _____. (*adj*) Par. 7

Word Families

A The words in bold in the chart are from Reading 1. The words next to them are from the same word family. Study and learn these words.

NOUN	VERB
appearance	*appear*
enjoyment	*enjoy*
entertainment	entertain
improvement	*improve*
transformation	*transform*

B Choose the correct form of the words from the chart to complete the following sentences. Use the correct verb tenses and subject-verb agreement. Use the correct singular and plural noun forms.

1 I _____ many leisure activities, but listening to music is my favorite one.

2 The president wants to _____ her small company into a large international one.

3 After she stopped smoking, her health began to _____.

4 Films, concerts, and games are all forms of _____.

5 The musicians played in the park for the _____ of the tourists.

6 The sun _____ for a few minutes, and then went behind the clouds.

7 The children _____ their parents with their musical performance.

8 The _____ of the president surprised all of the people who were waiting at the train station.

9 His parents were very happy with the _____ in his grades in math.

10 Industrialization brought the greatest _____ in 100 years. It changed many things about how people lived and worked.

Critical Thinking

Reading 1 states that people worked more hours during the period of industrialization than when they worked on farms.

ANALYZING INFORMATION

Critical thinking involves thinking carefully about important topics that the writer has not completely explained.

A Discuss the following questions with a partner.

1 How do you define "hard work"? What makes a job hard? For example, which do you think is harder: farm work or factory work?

2 Why do you think so many people chose to leave the land and go to work in factories?

3 Today, a lot of people work for long hours in offices, often in front of computers. Do you think their work is as hard as the factory work of the nineteenth century? As hard as earlier farm work? Explain your answers.

B Share your discussion with the rest of the class.

Research

Do some research on work hours in your country or another country that interests you. Find answers to the following questions.

- How long is the average workday?
- How long is the average workweek?

Writing

Use your class's results to create charts like the one below. Use answers to one of the questions above to create your chart. Then write a few sentences about the information in the chart.

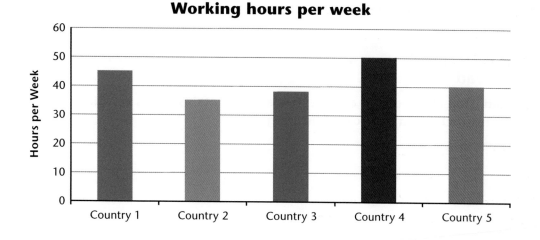

Working hours per week

Connecting to the Topic

Discuss the following questions with a partner.

1 How do you spend your leisure time?

2 Do you prefer to spend your leisure time by yourself or with other people? Explain your answer.

3 Do you enjoy sports or games of competition? Which ones?

4 Do you spend some of your leisure time on the Internet? Explain your answer.

Previewing and Predicting

Reading the title and first sentence of each paragraph and looking at the photographs in a reading can help you predict what the reading will be about.

A The following are the first one or two sentences of paragraphs 2–6 in Reading 2. Read these sentences and look at the photographs on pages 239 and 240. Then, with a partner, discuss what you think these paragraphs will be about.

a Today, many people use their leisure time to do something productive. Perhaps because they work only with their minds all day, they want to do something with their hands. (Par. 2)

b For some people, the most important thing about leisure time is to spend it with other people. (Par. 3)

c Technology has transformed how we spend our leisure time. (Par. 4)

d Games sites are not the only online communities. (Par. 5)

e Facebook, the most popular social network site, started in 2004. At that time, most of the members were from the younger generation – people under 30 living in western countries. (Par. 6)

B After discussing the paragraphs, discuss with a partner what you expect the *whole* reading to be about.

While You Read

As you read, stop at the end of each sentence that contains words in **bold**. Then follow the instructions in the box in the margin.

◀)) Leisure Activities

1   Most people today have more time for leisure than people had in the past. What are they doing with this time? Some people just want to relax. They watch television, read, or listen to music. Others want to be more active and productive with their leisure time. They want to learn something new or develop a new skill. Other people want to participate in activities with people who have similar **interests**.

WHILE YOU READ ①

Look back in paragraph 1 for a collocation with a verb and the noun *television*. Highlight the collocation.

2   Today, many people use their leisure time to do something productive. Perhaps because they work only with their minds all day, they want to do something with their hands. They want to do something very different from their office jobs or schoolwork. Some enjoy working in a garden. Others like to build or fix things in their leisure time. For example, they may want to work with wood, build furniture, or paint. Others learn how to cook foods from other countries.

3   For some people, the most important thing about leisure time is to spend it with other people. **This** is especially true for those people who like to play sports. All over the world, soccer, basketball, tennis, and other sports unite people. Other games of competition also bring

WHILE YOU READ ②

Look ahead for a collocation with a verb and the noun *sports*. Highlight the collocation.

people together. Card games, such as poker, are popular in the United States. Dominos are popular in Latin America and the Caribbean. Many people in Asian countries, especially in China, enjoy mahjong.

People around the world enjoy games.

4   **Technology has transformed how we spend our leisure time.** For example, it has made it possible to play games on computers. Today, you can play card games, word games and even sports on your computer or smart phone. You can play by yourself or with other people. Internet technology also makes it possible for people who are far apart to play games together online. People all over the world play online games such as *Happy Farm* and *World of Warcraft*. People who play games together form an online community, that is, a group of people who have similar interests.

WHILE YOU READ ③

As you read, find and highlight the supporting details of this main idea.

5   Game sites are not the only online communities. Technology has made it possible for people with similar interests, such as music, gardening, and politics, to establish online communities. However, the most popular are social network sites like Orkut, Mixi, Xiaonei, and Facebook. People join social network sites to stay in touch with old friends and make new friends.

6   Facebook, the most popular social network site, started in 2004. At that time, most of the members were from the younger generation – people under 30 living in western countries. By 2009, it had more than 100 million members of all ages from all over the world. Three years later, the number reached 850 million – more than 10 percent of the world's population. More than 80 percent of Facebook members live outside of the United States. **Facebook** users spend almost 10 billion hours a month online. It is likely that the popularity of these leisure activities will keep growing because more people are using the Internet. Experts predict there will soon be a billion Facebook members.

WHILE YOU READ ④

Look ahead for a collocation with a noun and the verb *spend*. Highlight the collocation.

7   People spend their leisure time in many different ways. Some people want to learn. Others just want to have fun. Some want to spend their time alone. Others prefer social activities during their leisure time. The most important recent development in leisure activities is in technology. More and more people depend on technology for their leisure activities today.

Many people spend their free time online.

Main Idea Check

Here are the main ideas of paragraphs 2–6 in Reading 2. Match each paragraph to its main idea. Write the number of the paragraph on the blank line.

_____ A Facebook is the most popular social network site.

_____ B Sports and other games are popular leisure activities.

_____ C Some people prefer productive activities.

_____ D Technology makes it possible to play games online.

_____ E Social network sites are becoming more popular.

A Closer Look

Look back at Reading 2 to answer the following questions.

1 Why do some people like to do leisure activities that require them to use their hands? Circle three answers. (Par. 2)

   a They want to do something different from their daily jobs.
   b They want to get some exercise.
   c They work with their minds most of the day.
   d They want to be productive in their leisure time.

2 Why do people like leisure activities such as sports and games? (Par. 3)

   a They get to spend time with other people.
   b They like to compete with other people.
   c They like to meet people from different countries.
   d They like to use technology.

3 How does technology expand leisure opportunities? Circle three answers. (Pars. 4 and 5)

   a It allows people to communicate when they are far away.
   b It helps create online communities.
   c It increases competition.
   d It allows people all over the world to play games together.
   e It increases the time for leisure.

4 When Facebook began, most of the members were professionals, like teachers and engineers. **True or False?** (Par. 6)

5 In 2012, about how many Facebook members lived in the United States? (Par. 6)

   a Less than 200 million
   b Between 300 and 400 million
   c Between 500 and 600 million
   d About 800 million

6 Fill in the chart to show the features of leisure activities according to Reading 2. Put a check (✓) in the appropriate boxes.

LEISURE ACTIVITY	FEATURE			
	It is productive	It requires other people	There is competition	It uses technology
Basketball				
Building furniture				
Mahjong				
Online games				
Social networks				

Skill Review

In Skills and Strategies 12, you learned that a timeline is a useful way to organize notes about when events happened.

A Look back in Reading 2, then make a timeline that shows the history of Facebook and its users. Include the events and the dates when they occurred.

B Compare your timeline with a partner's.

Definitions

Find the words in Reading 2 that complete the following definitions.

1 A / An _____ is the ability to do something well because you have practiced it. (*n*) Par. 1

2 To _____ something means to repair it. (*v*) Par. 2

3 _____ includes tables, chairs, beds, and desks. (*n*) Par. 2

4 _____ are a leisure activity that includes competition. (*n pl*) Par. 3

5 _____ are a place, especially on the Internet. (*n pl*) Par. 5

6 To _____ is to become a member. (*v*) Par. 5

7 A / An _____ is a group of people who are about the same age. (*n*) Par. 6

8 To _____ doing something is to continue doing it. (*v*) Par. 6

Words in Context

Complete the sentences with words from Reading 2 in the box below.

apart	in touch	productive	social
established	network	reached	united

1 My brother always wants to do something _____ with his free time. He likes to paint and fix things, but I prefer to relax and read a book.

2 I stay _____ with my best friend from high school. We send each other e-mail messages every week.

3 Facebook is the most popular social _____ site in the world.

4 The world's population _____ seven billion in 2011.

5 Everyone in the country _____ to support their leaders.

6 The two brothers live far _____, but they talk on the phone every Sunday.

7 My grandfather _____ the company in 1951.

8 I prefer _____ activities because I like to spend my time with other people.

Critical Thinking

Reading 2 describes one of the most popular leisure activities today, especially among young people: social networking on the Internet.

EXPLORING OPINIONS

Critical readers form their own opinions about important topics in a text.

A Fill out the chart below with a partner.

What are some valuable aspects of social networking?	What are some negative aspects of social networking?

B Then discuss the following questions with your partner.

1 Look at your chart. Do your answers suggest that that social networking is mostly a valuable activity or a waste of time? Explain your answer.

2 How much time do you spend on social networking sites every day? Every week?

3 What do you think is the future of social networking?

C Share your answers with the rest of the class.

Research

Do some research on how your friends spend their leisure time. Ask at least three of your friends the following questions.

- How do you spend most of your leisure time?
- Do you prefer to spend it alone or with other people?
- Do your leisure activities use technology, such as music players, cameras, computers, or the Internet?

Writing

Write a short summary of your class research.

Reading Quickly

Throughout this book you have been developing your reading speed, or fluency. The best way to improve your fluency is by reading material that is familiar, that is, texts you have read before. However, you will also have to learn how to read unfamiliar material quickly. Good readers use an important strategy when they need to read new material quickly. They don't read every single word. They let their eyes find and focus on the most important words in a sentence – usually the nouns, verbs, adjectives, and adverbs. When you do this, you read more quickly, and you usually can still understand the most important ideas in the reading.

Examples & Explanations

Most people in the United States say that reading is their favorite leisure time activity. However, reading is not the most common way that people actually spend their time. For example, one study asked people, "How did you spend your free time last night?" The number of people who spent the evening reading was half the number who spent the evening watching television. In this case, people's actions tell a different story than their words. They would like to spend more time reading, but they actually spend more time watching television.

Try reading only the "important" words in this paragraph. Time yourself. Then answer the two questions below.

Start time: _____

End time: _____

Total time: _____

- Which leisure activity do Americans say is their favorite?
- Which leisure activity do Americans actually do most?

You probably answered these questions correctly. In other words, you could get the most important ideas of the paragraph.

Most people in the United States say that reading is their favorite leisure time activity. However, reading is not the most common way that people actually spend their time. For example, one study asked people, "How did you spend your free time last night?" The number of people who spent the evening reading was half the number who spent the evening watching television. In this case, people's actions tell a different story than their words. They would like to spend more time reading, but they actually spend more time watching television.

Now read the paragraph again. Read every word. Put your finger under each word as you read. Time yourself.

Start time: _____

End time: _____

Total time: _____

You probably read more slowly but understood the same amount as before.

Strategies

These strategies will help you read more quickly.

- Look quickly at paragraphs to identify the topic, main ideas, and supporting details.
- As you read, let your eyes focus on the "important" words in a sentence, not every single word.
- Do not use a pencil or finger under the words as you read. This slows you down.
- Do not speak the words as you read. This will also slow you down.
- Time yourself sometimes as you read. Try to read fast. Reading more quickly can then become a habit.

Skill Practice 1

Read each paragraph below as quickly as you can. Try to focus only on the words in bold – the most important words – as you read. After you read a paragraph, look at the three possible main idea choices for the paragraph. Circle the best choice.

1   There is a **big difference** between the **way people** would **like** to **spend** their **free time** and the **way** they **actually spend** it. For **example**, in a **research study**, **cleaning** the **house** was **not** on the **list** of **favorite ways** to **spend leisure time**. **However**, it was **number eight** on a **list** of **how people actually spent their time**. This **shows** that **people** do **not always have a choice** about **how** they **spend** their **leisure time**.

Main idea:
a Cleaning the house is a favorite activity of many people.
b People often have to do things in their leisure time that are not favorite activities.
c People tell researchers things that are not true about the way they spend free time.

2   **Teenage girls** and **boys like** to **spend** their **free time** in **different ways**. In a **research study**, **43 percent** of the **teenage girls said** that their **favorite way** to **spend** an **evening** was to **hang out** with **friends** and **family**. In **contrast**, **only 26 percent** of the **teenage boys said** this was their **favorite way** to **spend** an **evening**. **Fifteen percent** of the **teenage boys said** they would **like** to **play video games**. **However**, **no girls gave** this **answer**. There is **clearly** a **difference** in the **activities** that **teenage girls** and **boys like** to **do** in their **free time**.

Main idea:

a There are differences in the ways that teenage girls and boys like to spend their free time.

b Teenage girls don't like to play video games.

c Teenage boys and girls like to do a lot of things.

Skill Practice 2

Read the paragraph below. Time yourself. Try to read the paragraph in 45 seconds (a rate of about 150 words a minute). As you read, focus only on the most important words in each sentence. Then look at the three possible main idea choices for the paragraph. Circle the best choice.

Research shows that teenagers spend a lot of time in front of a computer or television screen. Researchers in Canada did a study of 1,300 teenagers. They wanted to know how much time the teens spent watching television or looking at a computer. They called this "screen time." On average, the teens' screen time was 20 hours a week. The screen time of some of the teenagers in the group was much higher. For example, 30 percent of the teens spent about 40 hours a week at a television or computer. Seven percent of the teens spent more than 50 hours a week doing these things. Most of the screen time was at the television.

Main idea:

a Teenagers spend a lot of time watching television.

b Teenagers spend a lot of time in front of a television or a computer.

c Researchers studied a group of teenagers in Canada.

Connecting to the Topic

Discuss the following questions with a partner.

1 What do you usually do on your vacations?

2 Do you travel to different places? Explain your answer.

3 Is this different from what your parents did on their vacations when they were your age? Explain your answer.

Previewing and Predicting

> Reading the title, section headings, and beginning of each paragraph can help you predict what a reading will be about.

A Read the title, the section headings, and the first sentence of each paragraph in Reading 3. Then read the questions below. Write the number of the section (*I*, *II*, or *III*) next to the question or questions you think the section will answer.

SECTION	QUESTION
	Do some companies try to stop their workers from taking vacations?
	How do most people choose to spend their vacations?
	Why do some people keep working on their vacations?
	What are some less traditional choices for vacations?
	What is the history of vacations?
	Are decisions about vacations connected to the economy?
	Do some vacations require special knowledge?

B Compare your answers with a partner's.

While You Read

As you read, stop at the end of each sentence that contains words in **bold**. Then follow the instructions in the box in the margin.

◄)) Vacations

I. Vacations and the Economy

1   Vacations are a fairly new idea. Until the twentieth century, most people worked every day except on Sundays and religious holidays. Even students had to work when they were not in school. Today, many people have more time for leisure activities in the evenings and on weekends. They also have time for vacations, that is, days when they do not have to go to school or to their jobs.

2   Vacation trends are closely related to the economy. If people don't make much money, they don't think about vacations, they think about providing a home for their family and education for their children. As a country's economy develops, its citizens have more money and more leisure time so they can take vacations. Today, tourists are from all over the world, not just from the United States, Europe, and Japan but also from countries with developing and strong economies such as Brazil and China. Brazilians spent more money in New York City than

Some people enjoy extreme leisure activities, like exploring caves.

tourists from any other country in 2011. The Chinese now spend $232 billion a year on their vacations. Experts predict that these numbers will **increase**.

II. Vacation Choices

3   People choose different ways to spend their vacations. Some people stay home and relax or visit people in their family. However, more and more, people choose to travel on their vacations. For example, they may go camping in the mountains or go swimming at a beach. Some people want to explore somewhere new and exciting. They want to visit another country. In 2010, Paris was the most popular city for tourists, followed by London, New York, and Istanbul. Tourists want to visit famous attractions like the Statue of Liberty, Buckingham Palace, and famous museums like the Louvre.

4   Some people want less traditional vacations. They want to do something physical and active on vacation. Some of them want vacations that are more than just active. They want an *extreme* vacation. An extreme vacation has activities that are physically difficult and also risky. Some extreme vacation activities are more than risky. They are dangerous. Examples of extreme vacation activities are skiing in high mountains and exploring caves. Some people like to do dangerous things because they think danger is exciting.

5   Traditional and extreme vacations are not the only choices. Some people choose volunteer vacations. On volunteer vacations, people do things to help other people, animals, or the environment. For example, they may teach children in developing countries or build houses in communities that need help. Some people want to work with scientists on a project. For example, they may help injured birds or plant trees in a **forest**.

6   Most of these volunteer vacations do not require special knowledge. However, there are also volunteer vacations for people who want to continue to work during their vacations. They find great satisfaction in their work. They do not want to relax during their vacations. They do not want to go to a

WHILE YOU READ **1**

What is the main idea of paragraph 2? Highlight it.

WHILE YOU READ **2**

Look back in paragraph 5 for a collocation with an adjective and *countries*. Highlight the collocation.

On green vacations, people enjoy nature and protect the environment.

beach or the mountains on their vacations. Every year, for instance, hundreds of dentists and doctors leave their office and work in other places during their vacations. They go to places where people need their assistance.

7   Most people do not want to work on their vacations, however. They just want to relax, but they do not want their vacation activities to harm the environment. Unfortunately, this has happened, especially in popular tourist locations where there are lots of big hotels and shopping malls. For example, some people worry that too many tourists have damaged the environment in places like Hawaii. As a result of these concerns, many people choose "green" vacations. On green vacations, people can enjoy the natural beauty of the places they visit, but they will not damage the environment. On green vacations, tourists can learn about nature. They can find out about the birds or other wild animals that live **there**. If they visit wild and fragile places, "green" tourists stay in small, simple places that do not use a lot of resources like water and energy.

III. The Disappearing Vacation

8   Many workers now have more time for vacations, and they have more options for their vacation time. However, a global study of workers shows that not all of them take their vacations. Many workers just keep working. They do not use all of the vacation days that they have earned on their **job**. (See Figure 8.2.)

WHILE YOU READ 3

Look back in this sentence for a phrasal verb. Highlight it.

WHILE YOU READ 4

Look back to find a word that signals a contrast. Highlight the two ideas that are in contrast.

Figure 8.2 Number of Vacation Days per Country – 2011

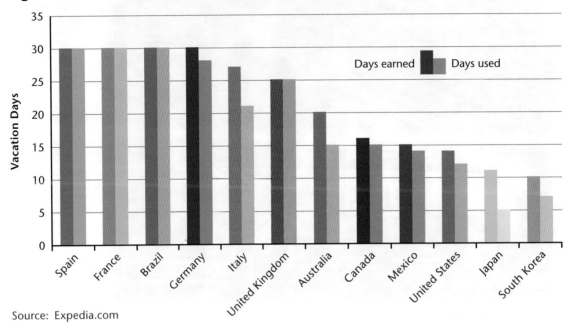

Source: Expedia.com

9   Even when some people do take a vacation, they often keep working during their vacation. They answer their e-mail, or they call their office to check on their work. They do this because they are afraid something important might happen during their vacation. They do not want to miss anything. They cannot completely relax and enjoy their leisure time. Many workers say that it is too stressful to take a long vacation. When they return to work, they have to catch up on all of the work that they did not do when they were on vacation. This means they have to work even **harder**.

10   Some people are also afraid their bosses will think they are not good workers if they take a vacation. However, research shows that most workers feel better after they return from a vacation. They return to the office with new ideas and lots of energy. Workers who spend time away from the office and relax are better workers. Some companies, like *Hewlett Packard* and *PricewaterhouseCoopers* understand this. They require their employees to take a vacation. Workers may not check their e-mail or cell phones while they are away.

11   There are many different kinds of vacations: traditional, extreme, volunteer, and green, among others. It does not matter what kind of vacation people choose, as long as they take their vacation. They should not put it off. They should relax and forget about their work or their studies for a while. They might feel better when they return to work or school, and they may be more productive.

> **WHILE YOU READ 5**
>
> Look back in paragraph 9 for a word that signals cause and effect. Highlight the effect.

Main Idea Check

Match the main ideas below to five of the paragraphs in Reading 3. Write the number of the paragraph on the blank line.

_____ **A** Some people enjoy dangerous activities on their vacations.

_____ **B** Some people use their knowledge to help others on their vacations.

_____ **C** Some people continue to work on their vacations.

_____ **D** Green vacations are a good choice for people who do not want to harm the environment.

_____ **E** Vacation trends are connected to economic development.

A Closer Look

Look back at Reading 3 to answer the following questions.

1 What are some examples of traditional vacations? Circle two answers. (Par. 3)
   a Going swimming at the beach.
   b Exploring caves
   c Visiting famous attractions
   d Planting trees

2 London was the most popular city for tourists in 2010. **True or False?** (Par. 3)

3 What are some examples of extreme vacation activities? Circle two answers. (Par. 4)
   a Climbing the Great Wall
   b Exploring caves
   c Skiing in high mountains
   d Camping in the mountains

4 How can you describe extreme vacation activities? Circle two answers. (Par. 4)
   a They are physically active.
   b They are expensive.
   c They are far away.
   d They are dangerous.

5 What are some things that people do on volunteer vacations? Circle three answers. (Pars. 5 and 6)
   a They help sick people.
   b They help scientists.
   c They explore the environment.
   d They plant trees.
   e They meet people.

6 Who might choose a green vacation? Circle two answers. (Par. 7)

    a People who think danger is exciting.

    b People who like to learn about nature.

    c People who are worried about the environment.

    d People who want to help others.

7 Why do some people continue working on vacation? Circle two answers. (Pars. 9 and 10)

    a They think they will miss something important.

    b They think vacations are stressful.

    c They think they will feel better.

    d They are afraid they will have to catch up on a lot of work when they return.

8 Workers who take a vacation are often more productive than workers who do not. **True or False?** (Par. 10)

9 In what country do workers use the smallest number of vacation days? (Fig. 8.2)

    a South Korea

    b United States

    c Japan

    d Australia

Skill Review

In Skills and Strategies 16, you learned that it is important to develop strategies for reading unfamiliar texts more quickly. One of these strategies is focusing on important words in a reading, not every word.

A Focus on the "important words" in Reading 3, and read it as quickly as possible. Time yourself. Put your time into the first blank, and then calculate your reading speed.

    980 words ÷ _____ minutes = _____ words per minute

B Now try the same strategy on an unfamiliar text. Choose a text that is about 600–800 words long. Focus on the "important" words, and read it as quickly as possible. Time yourself. Put your time into the first blank, and then calculate your reading speed.

    _____ words ÷ _____ minutes = _____ words per minute

C With a partner, discuss the difference between reading a familiar and unfamiliar text quickly.

Definitions

Find the words in Reading 3 that complete the following definitions.

1 Something that is _____ is very dangerous. (*adj*) Par. 4

2 A/An _____ is a person who does work without payment. (*n*) Par. 5

3 _____ is a good feeling you get when you do something well. (*n*) Par. 6

4 _____ is help or support. (*n*) Par. 6

5 The _____ is the natural world all around us. (*n*) Par. 7

6 Something that helps protect nature is _____. (*adj*) Par. 7

7 A/An _____ is a person who is in charge and tells other people what to do. (*n*) Par. 10

8 A/An _____ is a worker. (*n*) Par. 10

Words in Context

Complete the passages with words or phrases from Reading 3 in the box below.

attraction	catch up	mall	put off
camping	earn	option	trend

1   A new _____ in vacations is the "staycation." On staycations people

                   a
do not go anywhere on a vacation. They stay at home. They try to

    _____ on their sleep and visit friends that live nearby. They go to the

        b

    _____ and do some shopping. It is a much cheaper _____

       c   d
than a real vacation, and some people say it is less stressful, too.

2   If you do not _____ a lot of money, you cannot take an expensive

                        e
vacation. You could _____ your vacation until you save enough money

                  f
to visit a popular tourist _____ like the Grand Canyon or the Eiffel Tower.

                        g
However, a less expensive possibility is _____. You sleep outside and

                        h
cook over a fire. You can hear the birds sing in the morning and see the stars
at night.

Academic Word List

The following are Academic Word List words from all the readings in Unit 8. Use these words to complete the sentences. (For more on the Academic Word List, see page 260.)

assistance (*n*)	environment (*n*)	generation (*n*)	similar (*adj*)	trends (*n*)
economy (*n*)	established (*v*)	options (*n*)	transform (*v*)	volunteers (*n*)

1 We can do many things to protect the _____. For example, we can save water and energy.

2 It is important for teachers to learn about new _____ in technology in education.

3 When the _____ is growing, there are more jobs, and people spend more money.

4 My friend and I have _____ coats, so I took hers by mistake.

5 Hundreds of _____ went to Haiti to help victims of the earthquake.

6 The technology company Google was _____ in 1998.

7 The English program offers several different _____. Students can take classes during the day, at night, or on the weekends.

8 The new leader's energy _____ the country. Everyone sensed that a change was coming.

9 Every new _____ has new ideas. Young people do not like to follow their parents' ideas.

10 Communities often need _____ after natural disasters.

Critical Thinking

From Figure 8.2 on page 253, you learned the number of vacation days that people earn and use varies across countries.

EVALUATING INFORMATION

Critical thinkers ask themselves if there is enough information to support the points a writer makes in the text.

A Review Figure 8.2, and discuss the following questions with a partner.

1 Does the writer explain why employees in different countries earn a different number of vacation days? Why do you think this is the case?

2 Do you see any patterns in the graph from one part of the world to another? Does the writer explain them?

3 Why do you think people do not take all of the vacation days that they earn? Does the writer explain why this varies across countries? Why do you think this is the case?

B Share your answers with the rest of the class.

Research

Do a survey of your classmates about how they like to spend their vacations. Find answers to the following questions.

- What do you like to do most on a vacation? Go to the beach? Go to a new city? Explore nature? Explain your answer.

- If you could do anything on your next vacation, what would it be? Explain your answer.

Writing

Write a short description of what you like to do on your vacations.

Improving Your Reading Speed

Good readers read quickly and still understand most of what they read.

A Read the instructions and strategies for Improving Your Reading Speed in Appendix 3 on page 273.

B Choose one of the readings in this unit. Read it without stopping. Time how long it takes you to finish the text in minutes and seconds. Enter the time in the chart on page 275. Then calculate your reading speed in number of words per minute.

MAKING CONNECTIONS

REVIEW OF CONNECTORS

In Units 1–6, you learned that writers have several ways to make connections. To do this, they connect sentences using:

- pronouns to refer to previous things or ideas (See page 31.)
- words or phrases to signal addition (See pages 63 and 95.)
- words or phrases to signal contrast (See page 129.)
- words or phrases to signal causes and effects (See page 161.)
- words or phrases to signal time sequence (See page 193.)

Exercise 1

Read the following paragraphs. Highlight any pronouns, and underline what they refer to. Circle any words or phrases that signal addition, contrast, cause and effect, or time sequence. The first one has been done for you.

1   As people change their ideas about vacations, new types of travel companies start up. They offer tourists opportunities to participate in many different types of activities on their vacation trips. For example, "wilderness" travel companies take people to spend time in rainforests or mountains.

2   Many hotels around the world are trying to be green. They hope to have a smaller impact on the environment than in the past. For example, most hotels give guests an option to use their towels more than once before washing them.

3   The first home video game, *Pong*, appeared in 1972. People played it on their television sets. Then, when personal computers became popular, companies started to develop new games for computers. Now, home video games are very common. The Nintendo Wii, for example, is in 80 million homes.

4   Many people just want to relax on their vacations. Therefore, they choose vacations where they can stay home and visit local attractions. In contrast, other people give up their comfortable homes and go camping outdoors.

5   What is the healthiest way to spend leisure time? Most experts say that it is important to be active. In addition, communication with friends and family is also important. For these two reasons, a walk in the park together is a great way to spend free time.

Exercise 2

Make a clear paragraph by putting sentences A, B, and C into the best order after the numbered sentence. Look for pronouns and words or phrases that signal addition, contrast, cause and effect, or time sequence to help you. Write the letters in the correct order on the blank lines.

1 As employees, many people spend all day on the computer. ____ ____ ____

A	B	C
A For example, you can play card games without a partner or participate in online games.	**B** Therefore, it is surprising that they also spend a lot of their leisure time on the computer.	**C** However, at home, people use their computers for entertainment more than for work.

2 The first games appeared on computers many years ago. ____ ____ ____

A	B	C
A At that time, many people only had computers at work.	**B** When their boss came in, they pretended to be working, but they really were not very productive.	**C** Because of this, employees sometimes played computer games at work.

3 A group of teenagers decided they were spending too much time on Facebook, so they closed their accounts. ____ ____ ____

A	B	C
A So after a few weeks, they reopened their accounts.	**B** Instead, they decided to use only e-mail and their phones.	**C** However, they found these methods of communication were not as good as Facebook.

4 Volunteer vacations are becoming more and more popular. ____ ____ ____

A	B	C
A The volunteers learn about different cultures, and the community gets economic help.	**B** For example, they may build new schools or help communities start new businesses.	**C** On these vacations, people go to different communities in the world that need help.

5 Many people take vacations in campers. ____ ____ ____

A	B	C
A They enjoy driving to see things in the daytime.	**B** Then, at night, they spend the night in the camper.	**C** This simple way to travel is popular in many countries.

Key Vocabulary

The Academic Word List is a list of words that are particularly important to study. Research shows that these words frequently appear in many different types of academic texts. Words that are part of the Academic Word List are noted with an Ⓐ in this appendix.

UNIT 1 • READING 1

Borders on the Land, in the Ocean, and in the Air

airspace *n* the air above a country • *The government did not allow planes from other countries to fly into its* **airspace**.

area Ⓐ *n* a particular part of a place • *This* **area** *is too dangerous for swimming.*

border *n* the line where one country touches another country. • *The* **border** *between the United States and Canada is the longest one in the world.*

check *v* to take a careful look at • *The police officer* **checked** *the man's identification card.*

control *v* to make someone or something do what you want • *The government* **controls** *the border.*

cross *v* to go from one side of something to the other side. • *She* **crossed** *the street at the corner.*

feature Ⓐ *n* an important part of something • *The map shows* **features** *such as mountains very clearly.*

freely *adv* without limit or restriction • *The room was large so people could move around* **freely**.

official *n* someone who has an important position in an organization such as the government • *Government* **officials** *watch who comes into the country.*

permission *n* when you allow someone to do something • *You need* **permission** *to enter the building.*

physical Ⓐ *adj* relating to real things that you can see and touch • *The* **physical** *border is the river between the two countries.*

request *v* to ask for something • *She e-mailed the university to* **request** *information about a new program.*

resource Ⓐ *n* a valuable thing that belongs to a person, group, or country • *Water is an important natural* **resource**.

shore *n* the land at the edge of an ocean, lake, or large river • *The border of the country is a few miles from its* **shore**.

straight *adj* not curved or bent • *The students walked in a* **straight** *line from the library to their classroom.*

tax *n* money that you have to pay to the government, for example, when you buy, sell, or own something • *The dress cost fifty dollars plus three dollars in* **tax**.

UNIT 1 • READING 2

Walls as Borders

agree *v* to have the same opinion or idea • *The two governments* **agree** *on many things.*

attempt *v* to try to do something, especially something difficult • *The man* **attempted** *to cross the border without a passport, but the officials stopped him.*

divide *v* to separate into more than one part • *The officials* **divided** *everyone into two groups, one for tourists and the other for citizens.*

electronic *adj* using computers or parts of computers • *The* **electronic** *door only opens after you type in your identification numbers.*

enemy *n* a person or army you don't like • *The country fought against its* **enemies**.

entrance *n* a door or opening • *We walked through the* **entrance** *of the building.*

fence *n* a wall made of metal or wood • *There is a* **fence** *around the building. We can't go in.*

guard *n* a person who watches or protects a person or place • *The* **guard** *asked me for my identification and then let me go inside the building.*

invasion *n* the arrival of enemies • *The government was worried about an* **invasion** *on its northern border.*

major Ⓐ *adj* more important or more serious than other things or people of a similar type • *The* **major** *problem is the length of the border. It's very long.*

prevent *v* to stop something from happening or to stop someone from doing something • *The official* **prevented** *her from entering the country.*

purpose *n* a reason for doing something • *The official asked, "What's the* **purpose** *of your visit?"*

recent *adj* happening or starting a short time ago • *Look at the Internet for news about* **recent** *changes at the border.*

search *v* to try to find someone or something • *Guards are* **searching** *for the man who entered the country without stopping at the border.*

several *adj* an amount that is more than a few but less than many • *The president gave* **several** *reasons for his decision.*

suddenly *adv* very quickly and without warning • *The change happened* **suddenly**. *They didn't tell us about it before it happened.*

Border Control

advantage *n* something that is good about a situation and that helps you • *When Mei Ling visits the United States with her friends, she has an **advantage**. She speaks excellent English.*

brief Ⓐ *adj* short, not lasting a long time • *The business trip was very **brief** – just 36 hours.*

citizen *n* someone who was born in a particular country or who lives in a particular country and has special rights to live and work there • *He was born in Turkey, but he became a German **citizen** after living in Germany for many years.*

depend on *v* to be influenced by something or change because of something • *The amount of time it takes to cross the border **depends on** the number of people who are crossing.*

disappear *v* to stop appearing, to go away • *After he crossed the border, he **disappeared**. No one saw him, and no one knows where he went.*

document Ⓐ *n* a piece of paper with official information on it • *When I got my passport, I had to show several **documents**.*

examine *v* to look at someone or something very carefully • *At the border, the official **examined** our passports.*

fake *adj* not real, but made to look real • *He was arrested for having a **fake** passport.*

identification Ⓐ *n* an official document that proves who you are • *A driver's license is the most common type of **identification**.*

require Ⓐ *v* to need or demand something • *The law **requires** all drivers to pass a driving test before getting a license.*

store *v* to keep information on a computer • *With computers, it is easier to **store** and find information.*

technology Ⓐ *n* knowledge, equipment, and methods that are used in science and industry • *New **technology** makes it easier to see who enters or leaves a country.*

tourist *n* someone who visits a place for pleasure and does not live there • *The **tourists** needed visas to enter the country.*

trick *v* to make someone believe something that is not true and to do something that the person does not want to do, often as a part of a plan • *The young men tried to **trick** the guard by using fake documents.*

twin *n* one of two children who are born to the same mother at the same time • *They are **twins**, but they do not look exactly alike.*

unique Ⓐ *adj* different from everyone and everything else • *No one has exactly the same face. Each face is **unique**.*

Where Does Your Name Come From?

clan *n* a large group of people who are related • *The whole **clan** is gathering at my house for the holidays.*

common *adj* frequent and usual • *My name is not **common**, so I always have to spell it for people.*

culture Ⓐ *n* the way of life, including customs and beliefs, of a particular group of people • *Each **culture** has different traditions for naming children.*

custom *n* a belief or way of behaving that has a long history • *At Chinese New Year, it is the **custom** to give money to children and young people.*

embarrassment *n* a feeling of discomfort in front of other people • *She loved to sing but her fear of **embarrassment** stopped her from singing in public.*

generally *adv* usually • *In the United States, parents **generally** choose names for their babies before they are born.*

honor *n* to show respect • *They built a monument to **honor** the soldiers who died in the war.*

invent *v* to create something new • *No one has my name because my parents **invented** it. They wanted a unique name for me.*

leader *n* a person who controls a group or country • *He was a wonderful speaker, but he wasn't a great **leader**. He tried to do too many things by himself.*

lucky *adj* having good things happen to you • *The number seven is a **lucky** number in many countries.*

member *n* a person who is part of a group • *All the **members** of the basketball team wear red shirts and white shorts.*

origin *n* the beginning or cause of something; the way something began • *We have had that name in our family for a very long time, but I don't know its **origin**.*

popular *adj* liked by many people • *Michael is a very **popular** name for boys in the United States.*

professional Ⓐ *n* a person who uses special knowledge and training in a job • *I have no training in computers. I'm not a **professional**.*

select Ⓐ *v* to choose someone or something • *It's difficult to **select** a child's name because there are so many choices.*

share *v* to have the same thing as another person • *The girls in the family **share** the same first name: Maria.*

Changing Names

boxer *n* a person who fights as a sport • *Mohammed Ali was one of the most famous **boxers** of the twentieth century.*

childish *adj* when an adult acts like a child • *No one wants to work with him because of his **childish** behavior. He always wants to be first, and he never shares anything.*

conflict Ⓐ *n* a serious disagreement between people or groups • *The **conflict** started because the two groups had different ideas.*

couple Ⓐ *n* two people, usually a husband and a wife • *After they got married, the **couple** lived in a small apartment.*

discrimination (A) *n* when people are treated badly because of their sex, race, or religion • *When the manager offered the job to a man instead of a woman, the woman thought this was because of discrimination.*

entire *adj* whole, complete • *He ate the entire pizza by himself.*

ethnic (A) *adj* relating to the same race or cultural group • *The city has a lot of ethnic groups, so it has a lot of different types of restaurants.*

face *v* to deal with something difficult. • *He could not face seeing his son in the hospital.*

fit in *v* to be accepted by other people, to belong to a group • *She tried to fit in to the new culture, but she did not know how to act.*

identity (A) *n* who someone is • *The identity of the man in the photo is not clear, and there is no name on the photo.*

immigrant (A) *n* a person who comes from one country to live in another country • *Some immigrants change their names when they move to another country.*

ordinary *adj* not special, different, or unusual in any way • *In Latin America, Jesus is an ordinary name, but it is not common in Britain or Canada*

period (A) *n* a fixed time during the life of a person or in history • *Names change according to the values of the period. For example, at one time many girls were named Patience and Grace.*

reveal (A) *v* to give someone a piece of information that is surprising or that was previously secret • *The names Garcia and Patel reveal different family backgrounds: one is probably Spanish, and the other is probably Indian.*

serious *adj* thinking carefully about everything and not laughing a lot • *When she was a little girl, her name was Susu. When she became an adult, she changed her name to Susan because it sounded more serious.*

simplify *v* to make easier to understand • *The teacher simplified the scientific ideas so the young children could understand them.*

UNIT 2 • READING 3

Names in Business

advertisement *n* a picture, song, or other information that may make people buy something • *Most companies spend a lot of money on television advertisements.* **advertise** *v* to tell the public about something in order to sell it • *They wanted to sell their business so they advertised it in the newspaper.*

advice *n* an idea or opinion someone gives you to help you make a decision • *The company needed advice about what to name its product.* **advise** *v* to give your opinion to help someone make a decision • *His doctor advised him to eat more fruit and vegetables.*

consider *v* to spend time thinking about a decision • *It is important to consider how a product name will sound in a different language.* **consideration** *n* careful thought • *She gave the idea a lot of consideration before she made a decision.*

customer *n* a person who buys something from a store or a business • *It was already 10:00 at night so there were not very many customers in the store.*

emotion *n* a strong feeling such as love or anger, or strong feelings in general • *A good name may be connected to a positive emotion such as happiness.*

factor (A) *n* a fact or situation that influences a result • *Cost was the main factor in whether the company would change its name.*

influence *v* to change what people think or do • *A good name may influence a shopper's decision to buy a product.* **influence** *n* the power to have an effect on someone or something • *Parents often have a lot of influence on their children's behavior.*

modern *adj* using the most recent ideas, design, and technology • *A name such as Tech Shop sounds more modern than Record Store.*

product *n* something that companies make and sell • *The company sold its products in 12 different countries.*

research (A) *v* to find information about something • *The company researched what names sounded best to people.*

response (A) *n* an answer or reaction to something that has been said or done • *People had a negative response to the new name, so the company stopped using it.* **respond (A)** *v* to answer something that has been said or asked • *The student responded to the teacher's questions.*

successful *adj* getting the results you want • *A good name may make a product more successful because people will notice or try it.*

victory *n* when you win a race or a game • *The company used the V sign for victory to show that the company was a winner.*

UNIT 3 • READING 1

Food from the Old World and the New World

available (A) *adj* able to be used or found • *Fresh fruits and vegetables are available in the summer.*

chili *n* a pepper that makes food spicy • *Some cultures use a lot of chili in their food, which makes it hot and spicy.*

crop *n* a plant that is grown in large amounts on a farm • *The farmer planted his crop in April when the weather got warmer.*

exchange *n* when you give something to someone and they give you something in return • *After all of the new students met one another, there was an exchange of phone numbers and email addresses.*

explore *v* to travel to a new place in order to learn about it • *It is interesting to walk around different areas and **explore** when you go to a new city.*

familiar *adj* something you have often seen or heard before • *After traveling to other countries, it feels good to eat **familiar** food when you are back home again.*

flavor *n* the taste of a particular type of food or drink • *Chocolate is a very popular ice cream **flavor**.*

insect *n* a very small animal with six legs • *Some **insects**, such as flies and mosquitoes, sometimes carry dangerous diseases.*

occur Ⓐ *v* to happen • *When bad weather **occurs**, the price of food usually goes up because the farmers lose some of their crops.*

population *n* the number of people living in a particular area • *The **population** in China is the largest in the world.*

produce *v* to make or create something • *Brazil **produces** most of the world's coffee.*

rare *adj* unusual and hard to find • *The fruit was expensive because it was very **rare**.*

snack *n* a small amount of food that is eaten between meals • *She was hungry at 3:00 so she ate a **snack**.*

soil *n* the top part of the earth where plants can grow • *The **soil** near the river is very good for farming.*

valuable *adj* worth a lot of money • *The land was very **valuable**, so it sold for $1,000,000.*

wild *adj* living in nature; not controlled by humans • *At night, they could hear **wild** animals in the forest.*

UNIT 3 • READING 2

Fast Food

consumption Ⓐ *n* eating or using something • ***Consumption** of sugar in the United States is very high.*

continent *n* one of the seven main areas of land on the Earth, such as Asia, Africa, or Europe • *Apples are common now in North America, but at one time there were no apples on that **continent**.*

convenient *adj* easy to use, helpful • *Fast-food restaurants are very **convenient**.*

effect *n* a result; an impact • *Eating too much fat and sugar can have a bad **effect** on people's health.*

expand Ⓐv to increase in size or amount • *The fast-food restaurant **expanded** to Asia in 2009 when it opened a store in Seoul, South Korea.*

gain weight *v* to become heavier and bigger • *Eating cheese and ice cream every day will make you **gain weight**.*

global Ⓐ *adj* relating to the whole world • *A lot of fast-food restaurants are now **global**; they are all over the world.*

instead of *prep* in the place of someone or something else • *In Asia, most fast-food restaurants serve rice **instead of** potatoes.*

likely *adj* will probably happen • *Fast food is more **likely** to have a lot of fat in it than food at a regular restaurant.*

majority Ⓐ *n* most of the people or things in a group • *The **majority** of the class wanted to visit the zoo.*

offer *v* to give or provide something • *The new restaurant **offers** a variety of seafood at a low price.*

percentage Ⓐ *n* an amount of something, often stated as a number out of 100 • *Today, people eat a higher **percentage** of meals at fast-food restaurants than they used to.*

satisfy *v* to please someone by giving them what they want or need • *Restaurants that can **satisfy** their customers are successful.*

serve *v* to give someone food or drink, especially guests or customers in a restaurant • *The restaurant **serves** dinner from 5:00 p.m. until 10:00 p.m.*

tasty *adj* having a good flavor • *I think Mexican food is very **tasty**, so I often eat at Mexican restaurants.*

worry *v* to feel uncertain or nervous; to think about problems or unpleasant things that might happen in a way that makes you feel nervous • *Government officials **worry** about the number of people who are not healthy because they weigh too much.*

UNIT 3 • READING 3

Table Manners

appreciation Ⓐ *n* value; when you understand and enjoy something or someone • *She sent a thank-you letter to show her **appreciation** for the dinner.* **appreciate** Ⓐ *v* to say or show thanks • *I really **appreciate** all of your help.*

behavior *n* the way a person acts or responds • *His **behavior** is surprising. He acts more like a nine-year-old than a fifteen-year-old.* **behave** *v* to act • *He **behaved** very badly at the party, so no one wanted to invite him again.*

final Ⓞ *adj* last in a series or coming at the end of something • *Our **final** project in the speech class was to give a presentation about table manners.*

germ *n* a very small living thing that causes disease • *Wash your hands to get rid of **germs**.*

hide *v* to put something in a place where no one can see it • *Instead of putting my money in a bank, I **hid** it under my bed.*

host *n* someone who organizes a party and invites the guests • *I called the **host** to get directions to his house before the party.*

observe *v* to watch someone or something carefully • *If you don't know what to do, **observe** other people.* **observation** *n* the act or process of watching carefully • *After several weeks of **observation** in another teacher's classroom, she was ready to begin teaching her own class.*

offend *v* to make someone upset or angry • *He offended everyone when he yelled in the restaurant.* **offense** *n* a feeling of hurt or anger because of something someone has said or done • *In some cultures you may cause offense if you touch another person's head.*

order *n* a strong request or demand • *The restaurant manager gave an order to the servers to make sure that they picked up the food while it was still hot.*

protection *n* keeping someone or something safe and away from danger • *The fence gives the home protection from people walking along the road.* **protect** *v* to keep someone or something safe • *It is important to protect your skin when the sun is very strong.*

spread *v* to move across a bigger area and have a stronger effect • *The illness spread quickly through the city.*

visible Ⓐ *adj* able to be seen • *My friend was clearly visible in the large crowd because she was wearing a red coat..*

weapon *n* something you use to fight with • *Knives and guns are dangerous weapons.*

operate *v* to make a machine do what it is designed to do • *You have to have training and a special driver's license to be able to operate a truck.* **operation** *n* the process of doing something; the way something works • *When you buy a motorcycle, you get a book that explains its operation.*

pollution *n* damage caused to water, air, or land by harmful substances or waste • *A lot of pollution in the cities is caused by cars sitting in traffic.* **pollute** *v* to make water, air, or soil dirty or harmful • *New cars do not pollute the air as much as older cars used to because new cars have cleaner engines.*

system *n* a set of connected things or pieces of equipment that work together • *The subway system in Paris is called the Metro.*

tunnel *n* a long road or passage under the ground or through a mountain • *Buses usually travel on city streets, but the subway travels through an underground tunnel.*

wide *adj* not narrow; measuring a long distance or longer than usual from one side to the other • *It's easy to drive on modern streets because they are wide enough for trucks and buses.*

UNIT 4 • READING 1

A Short History of Public Transportation

competition *n* when a company or a person is trying to win something or be more successful than someone else • *Car makers now have more competition from motorcycle makers.* **compete** *v* to try to be more successful than someone or something else; to take part in a race or competition • *The store competed for customers by cutting its prices.*

crowded *adj* very full of people or things • *The roads are much more crowded in the afternoons than they are in the middle of the night.*

decline Ⓐ *n* a change to a lower amount • *There has been a decline in rice production this year.* **decline** Ⓐ *v* to go down, to decrease • *The population of some U.S. cities has declined in the last 10 years.*

efficient *adj* quick; effective; in an organized way; without waste • *The public transportation system in Tokyo is very efficient.*

encourage *v* to make someone more likely to do something • *High gas prices encourage people to ride bicycles instead of driving cars.* **encouragement** *n* when you give someone the confidence or interest to do something • *Some companies offer their workers free bus passes as encouragement to ride the bus.*

energy Ⓐ *n* the power from something like oil or electricity, which makes things work • *Large cars and trucks use a lot of energy.*

location Ⓐ *n* a specific place • *Public transportation is best in locations such as New York and Tokyo.*

narrow *adj* not wide; measuring a small distance from one side to the other • *The streets in the old part of the city are very narrow.*

UNIT 4 • READING 2

Bicycles for City Transportation

annual Ⓐ *adj* happening every year • *She went to the doctor for her annual examination.*

beneficial Ⓐ *adj* having a good or helpful effect • *Thirty minutes of exercise every day is beneficial for your health.*

concern *n* a feeling of worry about something, or the thing that is worrying you • *Safety is a big concern of bicycle riders because drivers cannot always see them well, especially at night.*

contrast Ⓐ *n* something that shows that someone or something is different from someone or something else; an obvious difference between two people or things • *The traffic on Sunday mornings is very light in contrast to traffic on weekday mornings.*

create Ⓐ *v* to make something happen or exist; to make something new • *The city created a special road for bicycles along the side of the highway.*

decrease *v* to become less; to go down • *The number of cars on the road decreased after gas prices went up.*

expert Ⓐ *n* a person with special knowledge or skill • *The city invited transportation experts to help them plan the new bus system.*

helmet *n* a strong, hard hat that protects your head • *In many locations, helmets are required for all motorcycle and bicycle riders.*

issue Ⓐ *n* an important subject or problem that people are discussing • *In some places, people can talk on cell phones as they drive. This is a public safety issue that the police are worried about.*

path *n* a small road, usually for walking, biking, or riding a horse. • *You have to park your car on the road and walk along the **path** to her house.*

predict Ⓐ *v* to say what will happen in the future. • *Scientists use new technology to **predict** dangerous storms.*

rate *n* the number of times something happens or how fast it happens in a period of time • *The birth **rate** in Japan is going down.*

separate *v* to divide and put or go into different places • *The teacher **separated** the students into three different groups.*

significantly Ⓐ *adv* in an important or noticeable way • *The number of bicycles on the road increased **significantly** when gas prices went up.*

solution *n* an answer to a problem • *Perhaps bicycle use is the **solution** to traffic problems everywhere.*

traffic *n* all the cars, trucks, and buses on a road • *There is a lot of **traffic** in the mornings and afternoons when people go to work or back home.*

UNIT 4 • READING 3

The Dangers of Driving

avoid *v* to stay away from a person, place, or situation • *It is hard to **avoid** driving at the busiest times of the day when you have a job.*

ban *v* to say that something cannot be seen, heard, or done • *In the 1960's, BBC radio **banned** several songs by the Beatles, but people found ways to listen to them.*

brake *n* equipment on a machine, such as car or plane, that makes it slow down and then stop • *It is important to check your **brakes** in bad weather to make sure you can stop quickly if you have to.*

conversation *n* a talk between two or more people, usually an informal one • *It's difficult to pay attention to the road when you are having a **conversation** with someone.*

distraction *n* something that stops you from paying attention • *Children in the backseat can be a big **distraction** to the driver, especially when the children are noisy.*

estimate Ⓐ *v* to guess the cost, size, or value of something • *The government **estimated** that it would cost about $11.2 million to build the road.*

injury Ⓐ *n* the physical harm or damage done to a person or animal • *She had a lot of **injuries** after the accident, so it took a long time for her to feel better.*

lead to *v* to cause something to happen • *Her car accident **led to** many serious medical problems.*

makeup *n* something that a woman puts on her face to make herself look prettier • *Putting on **makeup** while you are driving a car seems very dangerous to me.*

miss *v* to not be present at an activity or event • *My flight was cancelled so I **missed** my sister's wedding.*

obey *v* to do what you are told to do by a person, rule, or instruction • *If you **obey** the laws and drive carefully, the police won't stop your car.*

passenger *n* a person in a car, train, bus, or plane who is not driving • *There were too many **passengers** and not enough seats on the bus, so I had to stand.*

recommend *v* to say that something would be good • *I would like to see a movie tonight. Could you **recommend** one?*

seat belt *n* a strap or belt used to hold you safely in a car or airplane • *Everyone needs to wear a **seat belt** in the car.*

shave *v* to cut hair off your face or body • *He **shaves** every weekday but not on weekends.*

teenager *n* someone who is between 13 and 19 years old • *Some **teenagers** are not good drivers, and they have a lot of accidents.*

UNIT 5 • READING 1

The Importance of Sleep

adult Ⓐ *n* an animal that is fully grown; a human who is 18 years or older • *Adults do not need as much sleep as children.*

breathe *v* to take air in and out of your body • *People **breathe** more slowly when they are sleeping.*

concentrate Ⓐ *v* to think very carefully about something you are doing • *You can **concentrate** better when you get enough sleep.*

development *n* when someone or something grows or changes and becomes more advanced • *Doctors can see if a baby's **development** is slower than normal.*

dream *n* a series of events and images that happen in your mind while you are sleeping • *When you sleep, you have **dreams**. However, you usually can't remember your **dreams** when you wake up.*

inactive *adj* not moving or doing anything • *People who are **inactive** often gain weight.*

muscle *n* the part of the body that makes you move • *The day after she ran in a race, all of her **muscles** were very sore.*

normal Ⓐ *adj* usual and expected • *Eight hours of sleep is **normal** for most people.*

paralyzed *adj* not able to move all or part of your body • *When you are in a deep sleep, your muscles are **paralyzed**.*

pattern *n* the particular way that something occurs; something that occurs in the same way over and over • *The sleep **pattern** of babies is different from the sleep **pattern** of older children.*

rapidly *adv* quickly • *He is breathing **rapidly** because he ran all the way home.*

restore Ⓐ *v* to make something the way it was earlier • *After a race, runners sometimes use special drinks to **restore** their energy.*

snake *n* an animal with a long thin body and no legs • *The little boy would not walk in the garden because he was afraid of snakes.*

stage *n* a specific period during an activity • *When you sleep, you go through five different stages.*

strange *adj* very unusual • *Sometimes when people are sick, they have very strange dreams.*

variation Ⓐ *n* something that is slightly different from the usual form • *There is a lot of variation in sleep patterns among animals.*

Getting Enough Sleep

ability *n* the physical or mental skill or qualities that you need to do something • *The ability to remember changes as we grow older.*

alcohol *n* a liquid, such as wine, that can make you drunk • *You should not drive after you drink alcohol.*

aspect Ⓐ *n* a feature or part of a situation or plan • *The engineer explained the technical aspects of the bridge design.*

at least *adv* as much as, or more than, a number or amount • *Most adults need at least 8 hours of sleep each night.*

comfortable *adj* relaxed and having no pain • *It is important to have a comfortable place to sleep.*

consequence Ⓐ *n* the result (often bad result) of a situation or activity • *Falling asleep in class is a possible consequence of not getting enough sleep the night before.*

essential *adj* very, very important • *Getting enough sleep is essential to human health.*

fall asleep *v* to begin to sleep • *Some people think that a glass of milk helps them to fall asleep quickly.*

judgment *n* the ability to make decisions • *People who do not get enough sleep often have poor judgment.*

memory *n* the ability to remember • *Getting too little sleep can have a bad effect on your memory.*

mental Ⓐ *adj* related to thinking and to the brain • *Sleep is important for mental and physical health.*

nap *n* a short period of sleep during the day • *Every day he took a nap on the bus on the way home from work.*

realize *v* to come to understand something, often quickly • *She finally began to realize that her lack of sleep was causing her a lot of problems.*

stress Ⓐ *n* great concern and worry about a difficult situation • *The stress about taking an exam the next day can make it difficult to fall asleep at night.*

sufficient Ⓐ *adj* as much as is necessary • *It is difficult for students to get sufficient sleep when they have exams.*

unfortunate *adj* used to show that you wish something was not true or had not happened • *It is unfortunate that the garbage truck makes noise outside her window so early in the morning.*

Your Body Clock

adjust Ⓐ *v* to change something a little so that it works better in a new situation • *When you travel to a different time zone, your body has to adjust to the new time.* **adjustment** Ⓐ *n* a small change • *He made an adjustment to the engine and now the car is running very well.*

affect Ⓐ *v* to cause something to change • *Noise can affect your body clock.*

alert *adj* awake and having enough energy to understand and learn • *Most teenagers are not alert in the morning.*

alter Ⓐ *v* to make something change • *They had to alter their travel plans because they were so tired on the first day in the different time zone.* **alteration** Ⓐ *n* a minor change • *They made some alterations in their plans in order to be in New York on New Years Eve.*

complain *v* to say that you don't like something • *The people next door called us to complain about the loud music at our party.* **complaint** *n* a statement about what is wrong or not good enough • *There have been a lot of complaints from the students about their chemistry teacher. They say he does not explain things very well.*

confusion *n* when a person doesn't understand what is happening or doesn't know what to do • *The school wanted to hold classes in the afternoon and early evening. However, there was a lot of confusion, and some students went to class in the morning instead.* **confuse** *v* to cause someone to feel unclear about something • *All of these narrow streets confuse me. I don't know where I am going.*

disturb *v* to interrupt what someone is doing by making noise or annoying them • *The loud noises on the busy street outside disturb the parents every night, but the baby sleeps well.* **disturbance** *n* interruption • *She turned off her phone so she could study without any disturbance.*

exhausted *adj* very tired • *When you don't get enough sleep, you will feel exhausted the next day.*

habit *n* an action you do over and over again, often without really thinking about it • *She had the habit of waking up early in the morning and then taking a short nap in the afternoon.*

mood *n* the way you feel at a certain time • *If you don't get enough sleep, it may affect your mood.*

permanent *adj* going on forever • *This work schedule is permanent, so you'll have to get used to working late at night.*

plant *n* a large factory • *People on the night shift in a plant often work all through the night.*

typical *adj* having all the qualities you expect a particular person, group, object, or place to have • *What is your typical schedule for waking up and going to sleep?*

The Power of Music

alphabet *n* a set of letters that are used for all the words in a language • *The English **alphabet** goes from A to Z.*

cell *n* the smallest unit of living things; skin, muscles, and your brain are all made of these • *Some people think music may change the **cells** in the brains of babies and young children.*

comfort *v* to make someone feel better when they are worried or sad • *A familiar song may **comfort** you if you are not feeling well.*

department store *n* a store that is divided into areas where different kinds of things are sold • *You can buy many different things in a **department store**, such as clothing, kitchen equipment, and furniture.*

energetic Ⓐ *adj* very active • *The children were very **energetic** in the morning but they were tired after lunch.*

instrument *n* An object that produces music • *The violin is my favorite **instrument**.*

patient *n* a person who goes to a doctor or hospital because he or she is sick • *Doctors try to help their **patients** feel better.*

recognize *v* to realize that you have seen or that you know the person or thing • *We all **recognize** songs even though we don't know the name of the song or all the words in the song.*

recover Ⓐ *v* to become healthy again after an illness or injury • *After a bad car accident, she stayed in the hospital for two months while she **recovered**.*

relax Ⓐ *v* to become comfortable and less worried or nervous • *After his test was over, he began to **relax** and enjoy himself.*

release Ⓐ *v* to let something go • *Our brains **release** chemicals when we exercise or when we hear music.*

relieve *v* to make pain or a bad feeling less • *Soft music may **relieve** the pain of a headache.*

repetition *n* when something is repeated • *Practicing music requires a lot of **repetition**.*

rhythm *n* a regular pattern of sounds in music • *Everyone likes to dance to fast music because it usually has a great **rhythm**.*

role Ⓐ *n* the use or function that something has • *The university's music program played a big **role** in the student's decision to study there.*

survive Ⓐ *v* to continue to exist after being in a difficult or dangerous situation • *The man's knowledge of how to live in the woods helped him **survive** when he got lost*

Can Anyone be a Musician?

access Ⓐ *n* the chance to use or have something • *On the Internet, you can have **access** to a lot of music. However, you have to pay to download it.*

band *n* a group of musicians who play together • *The **band** played soft music while the guests ate dinner.*

complicated *adj* having many parts, difficult to understand • *The math problem was very **complicated**, so it took a long time to understand it.*

consumer Ⓐ *n* a person who buys things to use • *Research showed that **consumers** are more likely to buy things when they are happy.*

distance *n* the amount of space between two places or things • *The **distance** between Riyadh and Jeddah is just over 500 miles.*

equipment Ⓐ *n* a set of tools or machines that you need for a special purpose • *When rock bands travel around the world to give concerts, they need to have a lot of **equipment** at each place they play.*

industry *n* a business that sells a particular kind of product or service, such as oil, food, or electronics • *The electronics **industry** employs millions of workers around the world.*

mobile *adj* able to move or be moved • *Today most people want all of their electronics, such as computers, telephones, and music players, to be **mobile**.*

note *n* a musical sound • *The teacher sang the first **notes** of the song, and then children began to sing with her.*

participate Ⓐ *v* to be involved with other people in an activity • *A lot of people from the school **participated** in a discussion about plans for the new building.*

portable *adj* easy to carry • *Before the Sony Walkman music player, music was not **portable**.*

practice *n* when you do something over and over in order to do it better • *Becoming a good musician or athlete requires a lot of **practice**.*

record *v* to store words, sounds, or pictures • *The official **recorded** the names of all the people on the plane.*

talent *n* a natural ability to do something well • *Some nicknames are given because of a person's **talent**. For example, a good card player might have the name Ace.*

the rest *n* the people, things, or amount that remain • *They ate half of the pizza but left **the rest** for their friends.*

unlock *v* to open, usually with a key • *She tried to **unlock** the door but the key did not work.*

The Music Industry

challenge Ⓐ *n* a very difficult situation or problem • *Music companies face a **challenge** today because people can copy music so easily and not pay for it.*

collection *n* a group of objects of the same type that have been collected by one person or in one place • *He loves jazz, so he has a very large **collection** of jazz CDs.* **collect** *v* to bring together things of the same time in one place • *When she was young girl, she **collected** butterflies.*

copy *n* something that is exactly like something else • *The teacher made copies of the homework and gave them to her students.* **copy** *v* to produce something that is exactly like something else • *She copied the math problems that the teacher wrote on the blackboard.*

distribute Ⓐ *v* to give products to different stores and companies so they can sell them • *Apple only distributes its computers to a small number of stores.* **distribution** *n* that act of supplying products to stores and businesses. • *Part of the manager's job is the distribution of the company's products in Canada and South America.*

download *v* to take something (for example, a document, photo, or song) from the Internet and put it on your own computer • *When you download music from the site, you pay for each song.*

fragile *adj* easily broken, damaged, or destroyed • *Records were more fragile than CDs, so people often bought new ones when the music on the records wasn't clear any more.*

method Ⓐ *n* a way of doing something, often one that involves a system or plan • *Downloading is a method of getting music from the Internet onto a music player.*

positive Ⓐ *adj* showing without any doubt that something is true • *People immediately had a positive feeling about CDs when they first appeared because the sound was very clear.*

profit *n* the money that you get from selling a product or service after costs have been paid • *We made a big profit when we sold our boat. It was worth 50 percent more than it was 5 years ago.* **profit** *v* to make money from something • *The company has profited from the public's interest in mobile electronics.*

punish *v* to do something to someone that they won't like because they have done something wrong • *Sometimes the government catches people who copy music without paying for it and punishes them by making them pay a lot of money.* **punishment** *n* some sort of bad treatment or bad experience for a person because he or she has done something wrong • *The punishment for serious crimes is usually a period of time in prison.*

record *n* a flat circle of plastic on which music is stored • *In the 1990s, CDs replaced records as the best way to play music.*

scratch *v* to make a slight cut or long, thin mark with a sharp object • *When you scratch a record, it sounds terrible or repeats the same sound every time you play it.*

share *v* to have or use with others; to let other people use something • *Parents often teach their children to share their toys.*

UNIT 7 • READING 1

The Dark Side of Nature

community Ⓐ *n* a group of people who live in the same area • *The whole community came together to rebuild the town after the flood.*

contribute to Ⓐ *v* to be a factor in, to help make something happen • *Bad weather often contributes to car accidents.*

dam *n* a wall that is built across a river to stop the water • *Three Gorges Dam, on the Yangtze River, produces a great deal of electricity.*

damage *n* harm or injury • *There was a lot of damage from the hurricane, and a few people got hurt. However, no one died.*

deadly *adj* very dangerous and likely to kill people • *A deadly storm came through the area killing 28 people.*

destroy *v* to damage something so badly that it does not exist or cannot be used • *The tornado destroyed the house completely, but it didn't touch the garage.*

extreme *adj* more than expected; more than usual; very severe • *The weather forecast calls for some extreme weather this weekend with high winds and a lot of rain.*

flood *n* when a lot of water covers an area that is usually dry, especially when a river becomes too full • *The flood caused a great deal of damage in the neighborhood near the river.*

frequent *adj* common, happening often • *Hurricanes in the United States are more frequent in the second half of the year than in the first half of the year.*

massive *adj* very large • *A massive hurricane hit the coast and caused damage to many communities.*

mine *n* a large tunnel in the ground where people dig for rocks that contain something valuable, for example coal or gold • *It can be dangerous to work underground in a coal mine.*

mud *n* soil or earth mixed with water • *The mud came all the way down the river after the volcano erupted.*

pressure *n* the force or weight that is put on something • *During a fire, the pressure from hot air can break windows and even doors.*

violent *adj* sudden and powerful • *The violent movement of the earth caused a lot of damage.*

vulnerable *adj* able to be hurt or influenced easily • *Areas along the coast are vulnerable to severe storms called hurricanes, cyclones, or typhoons.*

widespread Ⓐ *adj* happening in many places • *The huge storm caused widespread flooding in the area.*

UNIT 7 • READING 2

Prediciting and Preparing for Natural Disasters

accurately Ⓐ *adv* correctly or exactly • *It is very difficult to predict the weather accurately.*

average *n* the usual number or amount • *There were more hurricanes this year than on average.*

bubble *n* a ball of air or gas with liquid around it • *Before a tsunami, there are a lot of bubbles in the water on the beach.*

coast *n* the shore between land and the ocean • *Severe weather that starts in the ocean often hits the coast.*

contact Ⓐ *v* to communicate with someone • *After a natural disaster, it can be difficult to* **contact** *friends and relatives.*

crucial Ⓐ *adj* very important and necessary • *A plan for a response to an emergency is* **crucial** *for every community.*

loss *n* a thing or a number of related things that are lost, destroyed, or killed • *A lot of houses and buildings fell down, but there was no* **loss** *of life.*

precise Ⓐ *adj* exact • *It is impossible to know the* **precise** *number of people who died in the disaster.*

prepare *v* to get someone or something ready for something that will happen in the future • *People can* **prepare** *for a hurricane. They can cover the windows in their houses and move away from dangerous areas.*

reduce *v* to make something smaller in size or amount • *We must* **reduce** *pollution in our air and water.*

satellite *n* a piece of equipment that is sent into space around the earth to receive and send signals or to collect information • **Satellites** *help people predict where storms will cause problems.*

shake *v* to move something in one direction and then the other direction many times • *Everything in the house started to* **shake** *when the earthquake began.*

sign *n* something that shows that something is happening • *The bubbles in the water are a* **sign** *of a tsunami.*

terrible *adj* very bad and very serious • *The storm caused* **terrible** *damage to the coast.*

tremor *n* an uncontrolled shaking; a slight earthquake • *After a big earthquake, there are often smaller* **tremors**.

warning *n* something that tells or shows you that something bad may happen • *There was no* **warning** *before the earthquake.*

UNIT 7 • READING 3

A Natural Disaster from Outer Space?

analysis Ⓐ *n* a careful study • *A scientific* **analysis** *showed that a disaster was not very likely to happen in that area.* **analyze** Ⓐ *v* to study carefully • *The doctor* **analyzed** *the patients' blood in her laboratory.*

block *v* to stop or prevent anyone or anything from moving from one place to another • *The dust from the volcano explosion* **blocked** *the sunlight.*

dust *n* dry dirt • *What would happen if* **dust** *blocked the sun for a long time?*

explosion *n* a burst with a loud noise when something such as a bomb explodes • *An asteroid can cause a huge* **explosion** *if it hits the earth.* **explode** *v* to burst with a loud noise. • *The windows in the burning house* **exploded**.

extinct *adj* no longer existing anywhere in the world (describing plants or animals) • *Dinosaurs are* **extinct**.

gravity *n* the force that pulls things to the ground • *Earth has* **gravity** *that pulls asteroids towards it.*

impact Ⓐ *n* the force or action of one object hitting another object • *The* **impact** *of the explosion caused severe damage.* **impact** Ⓐ *v* to have a strong influence on something or someone • *The decisions you make today will* **impact** *your choices in the future.*

junk *n* things that have no value • *When we moved to a new house, we threw out all the* **junk** *we did not need anymore.*

mystery *n* an unknown thing that people do not understand • *No one really knows the answer to the* **mystery** *of why there are no dinosaurs on Earth any more.*

orbit *n* the path that objects travel around the sun or a planet • *The earth travels in an* **orbit** *around the sun.* **orbit** *v* to move in a path around the sun or a planet • *The Earth* **orbits** *the sun once a year.*

outer space *n* the part of the universe that is farthest from Earth • *A near-Earth object is something that is in* **outer space** *and comes in an orbit near the Earth.*

project Ⓐ *n* a carefully planned piece of work that has a particular purpose • *Several governments are working on a* **project** *to identify all the near-Earth objects.*

suggest *v* to point to • *Research* **suggests** *there is a way to solve this problem.* **suggestion** *n* an idea or plan that someone mentions • *His father gave him several* **suggestions** *about how to find a summer job.*

UNIT 8 • READING 1

Work and Leisure

appear *v* to become noticeable or to be present • *The first televisions* **appeared** *in homes in the 1930s.* **appearance** *n* when you arrive somewhere or can be seen somewhere • *His* **appearance** *at the party surprised everyone. He usually doesn't go to parties.*

beach *n* the area of land next to the sea or a lake • *They stayed at a hotel near the* **beach**, *so they went swimming every day.*

concert *n* a performance of live music • *Many people go to* **concerts** *outdoors in the summer.*

economy Ⓐ *n* the system in which a country makes and uses things and money • *The* **economy** *is not growing as fast as it was a few years ago, so it is more difficult to get a job today.*

enjoy *v* to get pleasure from something • *The young children* **enjoy** *swimming at the beach.* **enjoyment** *n* the pleasure you get from something • *The singer's music brought* **enjoyment** *to millions of people.*

entertainment *n* shows, films, television, or other performances or activities that people enjoy • *As people get older, their favorite* **entertainment** *is often watching other people, especially at parks or shopping centers.* **entertain** *v* to keep someone interested and help them to have an enjoyable time • *Electronic games are a good way to* **entertain** *children on long trips.*

factory *n* a place where things are made by machines • *The shoe* **factory** *employed 60 people.*

improve *v* to get better or to make something better • *Speech classes help people **improve** their ability to speak in public.*
improvement *n* when something gets better or when you make it better • *Everyone noticed the **improvement** in air quality after the plant closed.*

opportunity *n* a chance to do or get something • *The students had an **opportunity** to travel during the summer.*

picnic *n* a meal that you eat outside, often in a park • *It rained yesterday, so we did not have our **picnic**.*

public *adj* open and available to everyone • *There are **public** parks in almost every city and town in France.*

similar Ⓐ *adj* almost the same • *The two hotels are **similar** in price, but one is closer to the center of the city.*

transform Ⓐc *v* to change completely • *Computers and other technology have **transformed** education in many countries.*
transformation ⒶC *n* a complete change • *The government plans a **transformation** in the national economy.*

UNIT 8 • READING 2

Leisure Activities

apart *adj* living or staying in a different place from other people • *The twins live far **apart** from each other, so they can only see each other once a year.*

establish ⒶC *v* to start a company or organization • *The United Nations was **established** in 1945.*

fix *v* to repair something • *It was not possible to **fix** the car because it had so much damage from the crash.*

furniture *n* things such as tables, chairs, beds, and desks • *Very few people make their own **furniture** today, but it is possible to take classes to learn how to do it.*

game *n* an activity in which people play against each other • *Some people like quiet **games** like cards; others prefer active games, like tennis or football.*

generation ⒶC *n* members of a family or community who are about the same age • *Each new **generation** creates its own music and styles in clothing.*

in touch *adv* in contact by talking or writing • *I will be in **touch** with you after I return from my trip.*

join *v* to become a member of an organization • *When he moved to a new city, he **joined** the football club so he could make new friends.*

keep *v* to continue • *They had walked all day, but they **kept** walking until 10:00 at night.*

network ⒶC *n* a group of people who know each other or who work together • *Facebook is a very well-known social **network** that many people participate in.*

productive *adj* producing a good or useful result • *Some people get bored if they are not **productive** on vacations.*

reach *v* to come to a certain point • *After traveling for 30 hours, they finally **reached** Australia.*

site ⒶC *n* a place on the Internet • *There are many different **sites** on the Internet where you can buy inexpensive books.*

skill *n* the ability to do something well because you have practiced it • *During her vacation, she took a class to improve her tennis **skills**.*

social *adj* related to the way people live together and interact • *He had many professional relationships but not as many **social** relationships.*

unite *v* bring together • *The workers at the factory **united** to fight for higher pay.*

UNIT 8 • READING 3

Vacations

assistance ⒶC *n* help • *She was lost so she asked the police officer for **assistance**.*

attraction *n* a place that a lot of people want to visit • *The Taj Mahal is a famous **attraction** in India that many tourists visit.*

boss *n* the head of a company • *The employees asked their **boss** for an extra week of vacation.*

camping *n* sleeping and eating outside on vacation • *I don't think anyone enjoys **camping** in the rain.*

catch up *v* to do something that you have not been able to do until now • *After he was sick for a week, it took him a long time to **catch up** on his work.*

earn *v* to get money for doing work • *Teenagers usually don't **earn** very much money in their jobs.*

employee *n* a worker • *The factory did not need as many **employees** because fewer people were spending money on the company's products.*

environment ⒶC *n* the natural world all around us • *Eco-tourism is popular with people who are interested in saving the **environment**.*

green *adj* helping to protect nature • *Hotels try to be **green** by asking guests to use their towels more than once and to recycle glass, plastic, and paper.*

mall *n* a large, covered shopping area • *The largest **mall** in the United States is in King of Prussia, Pennsylvania.*

option ⒶC *n* a choice • *The travel company offered a lot of **options** for ways to visit Europe, but the most popular one was a group tour.*

put off *v* to wait until later to do something • *If you **put off** making your plane reservations, you will probably have to pay more for your ticket.*

risky *adj* very dangerous • *Some people like to go rock climbing, but I think it's too **risky**.*

satisfaction *n* pleasure • *Volunteer work gives people **satisfaction** because they are able to help other people.*

trend ⒶC *n* the general way or direction that things are changing • *The news reported on recent **trends** in the price of houses: They are lower than they were 5 years ago.*

volunteer ⒶC *n* a person who does work without payment • *Many **volunteers** came to help rebuild the city after the earthquake.*

Index to Key Vocabulary

Words that are part of the Academic Word List are noted with an Ⓐ in this appendix.

Improving Your Reading Speed

Good readers read quickly and understand most of what they read. However, like other skills, reading faster is a skill that requires good technique and practice. One way to practice is to read frequently. Read about topics you are interested in, not just topics from your academic courses. Reading for pleasure will improve your reading speed and understanding.

Another way to practice is to choose a text you have already read and read it again without stopping. Time yourself, record the time, and keep a record of how your reading speed is increasing.

These strategies will help you improve your reading speed:

- Before you read a text, look at the title and any illustrations. Ask yourself, *What is this reading about?* This will help you figure out the general topic of the reading.

- Read words in groups instead of reading every single word. Focus on the most important words in a sentence – usually the nouns, verbs, adjectives, and adverbs.

- Don't pronounce each word as you read. Pronouncing words will slow you down and does not help you to understand the text.

- Don't use a pencil or your finger to point to the words as you read. This will also slow you down.

- Continue reading even if you come to an unfamiliar word. Good readers know that they can skip unfamiliar words as long as they understand the general meaning of the text.

Calculating Your Reading Speed

After you have completed a unit in this book, reread one of the readings. Use your cellphone or your watch to time how long it takes you to complete the reading. Write down the number of minutes and seconds it took you in the chart on the following pages.

You can figure out your reading speed; that is your words per minute (wpm) rate by doing the following calculation:

First, convert the seconds of your reading time to decimals using the table to the right.

Next, divide the number of words per reading by the time it took you to complete the reading. For example, if the reading is 525 words, and it took you 5 minutes 50 seconds, your reading speed is about 90 words per minute (525 ÷ 5.83 = 90).

Record your wpm rate in the chart on the following pages.

Seconds	Decimal
:05	.08
:10	.17
:15	.25
:20	.33
:25	.42
:30	.50
:35	.58
:40	.67
:45	.75
:50	.83
:55	.92

UNIT	READING TITLE	NUMBER OF WORDS IN READING	YOUR READING TIME minutes:seconds 00:00	READING SPEED (WPM)
Unit 1 Crossing Borders	Borders on the Land, in the Ocean, and in the Air	523	_____ : _____	
	Walls as Borders	607	_____ : _____	
	Border Control	782	_____ : _____	
Unit 2 Names	Where Does Your Name Come From?	577	_____ : _____	
	Changing Names	614	_____ : _____	
	Names in Business	855	_____ : _____	
Unit 3 Food	Food from the Old World and the New World	515	_____ : _____	
	Fast Food	582	_____ : _____	
	Table Manners	813	_____ : _____	
Unit 4 Transportation	A Short History of Public Transportation	586	_____ : _____	
	Bicycles for City Transportation	666	_____ : _____	
	The Dangers of Driving	893	_____ : _____	
Unit 5 Sleep	The Importance of Sleep	500	_____ : _____	
	Getting Enough Sleep	634	_____ : _____	
	Your Body Clock	793	_____ : _____	

UNIT	READING TITLE	NUMBER OF WORDS IN READING	YOUR READING TIME minutes:seconds 00:00	READING SPEED (WPM)
Unit 6 Music	The Power of Music	558	_____:_____	
	Can Anyone Be a Musician?	590	_____:_____	
	The Music Industry	802	_____:_____	
Unit 7 Natural Disasters	The Dark Side of Nature	525	_____:_____	
	Predicting and Preparing for Natural Disasters	602	_____:_____	
	A Natural Disaster from Outer Space?	899	_____:_____	
Unit 8 Leisure	Work and Leisure	587	_____:_____	
	Leisure Activities	554	_____:_____	
	Vacations	978	_____:_____	

UNIT 1, READING 1

Territorial waters, *Britannica Concise Encyclopedia*. http://www.answers.com/topic/territorial-waters.

United Nations, Convention on the Law of the Sea, http://www.un.org/Depts/los/convention_agreements/texts/unclos/closindx.htm.

UNIT 1, READING 2

Berlin Wall Online, http://www.dailysoft.com/berlinwall/history/index.htm.

Frontiers of the Roman Empire, World Heritage, UNESCO, http://whc.unesco.org/en/list/430.

UNIT 1, SKILLS AND STRATEGIES 2

Basic Information sheet about SARS. 2005. Centers for Disease Control. May 3. http://www.cdc.gov/ncidod/sars/factsheet.htm.

UNIT 1, READING 3

Lee, Jennifer. 2003. Threats and responses: Identity documents. *New York Times*, February 12.

McGeever, J. 2006. Computer chips get under skin of enthusiasts. *Reuters*, January 6.

South Korean woman tricked fingerprint scanner at Japanese airport. 2009. *Chicago Tribune*, January 2.

UNIT 2, SKILLS AND STRATEGIES 3

Top 10 Most Interesting Place Names. VirtualTourist.com. http://members.virtualtourist.com/vt/t/1eb/.

UNIT 2, READING 1

List of most common surnames. http://en.wikipedia.org/wiki/Lists_of_most_common_surnames

UNIT 2, READING 2

Sochaczewski, P. 1994. The guts of a name change. *International Herald Tribune*, March 24. Wong, W. 2009. What's in a name? *Chicago Tribune*, August 9.

WuDunn, S. 1996. Korea's Romeos and Juliets, cursed by their name. *New York Times*, September 11.

UNIT 2, SKILLS AND STRATEGIES 4

Boring Oregon. http://www.oregoncities.us/boring/index.htm.

Inbar, M. 2009. Top 10 "bad boy" baby names. *The Today Show*, July 17. http://www.msnbc.msn.com/id/31960846/ns/today-parenting_and_family/.

Thompson, A. 2008. Your initials may spell success. *LiveScience*, January 11. http://www.livescience.com/health/071210-name-letter.html.

UNIT 2, READING 3

Altman, D. 2009. Renaming your way out of a swamp. *On the button*, June 15. http://onthebutton.wordpress.com/2009/06/15/gm_renaming/.

Dahle, C. 2000. How to make a name for yourself. *Fast Company*, 38, August . Deluzain, H. (no date). http://www.behindthename.com/articles/1.php.

Reebok history. http://corporate.reebok.com/en/reebok_history/default.asp.

UNIT 3, READING 1

Crosby, A. 1988. *The Columbian exchange*. New York: Greenwood.

Foster, N., & Cordell, L. 1992. *Chilies to chocolate: Food the Americas gave the world*. Tucson, AZ: University of Arizona Press.

UNIT 3, READING 2

Griffin, W. 2008. McDonald's has big appetite for China. MSNBC, August 15. http://www.msnbc.msn.com/id/26226387/ns/business-cnbc_tv/.

Noreen. 2009. What you can and can't get at McDonald's India. *Indiamarks*, February 26. http://www.indiamarks.com/guide/What-You-Can-and-Can-t-Get-at-McDonalds-India-/1739/.

Praetorius, D. 2011. Subway passes McDonald's to become world's largest restaurant chain. March 7. http://www.huffingtonpost.com/2011/03/07/worlds-largest-restaurant-chain-subway_n_832511.html

UNIT 3, READING 3

Romagnoli, D. 1996. "Mind your manners" Etiquette at the table. In J-L. Flandrin & A. Sonnenfeld. *Food: A culinary history* (pp. 328–338). New York: Penguin.

UNIT 4, SKILLS AND STRATEGIES 7

New York Transit Museum. History of public transit in New York City. http://www. transitmuseumeducation.org/trc/background.

Wikipedia. http://en.wikipedia.org/wiki/List_of_metro_systems.

Wikipedia. http://en.wikipedia.org/wiki/Metro_systems_by_annual_passenger_rides.

UNIT 4, READING 1

Transitpeople. http://www.transitpeople.org.

UNIT 4, READING 2

Austen, I. 2009. Montreal inaugurates continent's most ambitious bike-sharing program. *New York Times*, May 13. http://greeninc.blogs.nytimes.com/2009/05/13/montreal-inaugurates-continents-most-ambitious-bike-sharing-program/.

Bicycles produced in the world. *Worldometers*. http://www.worldometers.info/bicycles/.

Fong, C. 2009. City bike-sharing picks up speed. CNN.com, April 26. http://edition.cnn.com/2009/

Rosenthal, E. 2008. European support for bicycles promotes sharing of the wheels. *New York Times*, November 10. http://www.nytimes.com/2008/11/10/world/europe/10bike.html?_r=1.

UNIT 4, SKILLS AND STRATEGIES 8

Wikipedia. http://en.wikipedia.org/wiki/DeLorean_Motor_Company.

UNIT 4, READING 3

Distracted Driving Major problem 2011. December 8. http://www.reuters.com/article/2011/12/08/us-usa-autos-distraction-idUSTRE7B718H20111208?feedType=RSS

Grover, C. 2009. Asleep at the Wheel: New technologies to help drivers stay in control. *Thatcham Research News*, February.

Madden, M., & Lenhart, A. 2009. Teens and distracted driving. Pew Internet and American Life Center, November 16.

Mohin, T. 2009. Group warns of global road-death "epidemic." *New York Times*, September 22. http://wheels.blogs.nytimes.com/2009/09/22/group-warns-of-global-road-death-epidemic/.

Richtel, M. 2009. U.S. withheld data on risks of distracted driving. *New York Times*, July 21. http://www.nytimes.com/2009/07/21/technology/21distracted.html.

UNIT 5, READING 1

National Institutes of Health. Brain basics: Understanding sleep. http://www.ninds.nih.gov/disorders/brain_basics/understanding_sleep.htm.

University of Washington. How much do animals sleep? http://faculty.washington.edu/chudler/chasleep.html.

What is sleep and why do we need it? *Neuroscience for Kids*. http://faculty.washington.edu/chudler/sleep.html.

UNIT 5, READING 2

APA online. Why sleep is important and what happens when you don't get enough. http://www.apa.org/topics/whysleep.html.

Jones, M. 2011. How little sleep can you get away with? *New York Times*, April 15.

Roberts, S. 2009. Can you die from lack of sleep? *Slate*, May 11. http://www.slate.com/id/2218092.

UNIT 5, READING 3

Kreizman, L. 2009. Larks, owls and hummingbirds. *New York Times*, April 21. http://judson.blogs.nytimes.com/2009/04/21/guest-column-larks-owls-and-hummingbirds/?emc=eta1.

National Sleep Foundation. Sleep drive and your body clock. http://www.sleepfoundation.org/article/sleep-topics/sleep-drive-and-your-body-clock.

UNIT 6, READING 1

LeTrent, S. 2010. Restaurants' table turnover tricks boost business. *CNN Living*, April 30. http://www.cnn.com/2010/LIVING/04/30/noisy.restaurant.business/index.html.

Lloyd, R. 2008. The amazing power of music revealed. *Live Science*. http://www.livescience.com/health/081015-music-power.html.

Shulman, M. 2008. Music as medicine for the brain. *U.S. News and World Report*, July 17. http://health.usnews.com/articles/health/brain-and-behavior/2008/07/17/music-as-medicine-for-the-brain.html.

UNIT 6, READING 2

Walker, R. 2011. A machine that makes you musical. *New York Times*, Nov. 23 http://www.nytimes.com/2011/11/27/magazine/smule.html?_r=1&ref=mobileapplicationsnewsandamusements

UNIT 6, SKILLS AND STRATEGIES 12

History of the piano. http://www.essortment.com/all/historypiano_resc.htm.

Mad About Mozart: W.A. Mozart – a Timeline. *ABC Classic FM*. http://www.abc.net.au/classic/mozart/timeline.htm.

UNIT 6, READING 3

Stone, B. 2009. The music streams that soothe an industry. *New York Times*, July 26. http://www.nytimes.com/2009/07/26/business/26stream.html.

UNIT 7, READING 1

Karpilo, J. 2010. World's worst disasters. January 25. http://geography.about.com/od/hazardsanddisasters/a/worstworlddisasters.htm.

MCEER. Haiti Earthquake Facts 2010. http://mceer.buffalo.edu/infoservice/disasters/Haiti-Earthquake-2010.asp.

UNIT 7, READING 2

British schoolgirl Tilly Smith saves hundreds of lives. 2005. *Yahoo Thailand News*, January 1. http://www.thaipro.com/thailand_00/320-tsunami-tilly-smith.htm.

Mott, M. 2003. Can animals sense earthquakes? *National Geographic News*, November 11. http://news.nationalgeographic.com/news/2003/11/1111_031111_earthquakeanimals.html.

UNIT 7, SKILLS AND STRATEGIES 14

Padgett, T. 2010. How to Survive an Earthquake: Two Schools of Thought. Time.com, February 1. http://www.time.com/time/specials/packages/article/0,28804,1953379_1953494_1958235,00.html.

Verma, S. 2005. *The Tunguska fireball: Solving one of the great mysteries of the 20th century*. Cambridge: Cambridge University Press.

UNIT 7, READING 3

Cuk, M. 2002. How dangerous are asteroids? Curious about Astronomy, *How Stuff Works*, November http://www.howstuffworks.com/framed.htm?parent=peru-meteor.htm&url=http://curious.astro.cornell.edu/question.php?number=215.

Geologist Gets To The Bottom Of Chicxulub Impact Crater. 2007. *Science Daily*, January 22. http://www.sciencedaily.com/releases/2007/01/070118094039.htm.

The Great Dying. http://science.nasa.gov/headlines/y2002/28jan_extinction.htm.

What killed the dinosaurs? Evolution. PBS. http://www.pbs.org/wgbh/evolution/extinction/dinosaurs/low_bandwidth.html.

UNIT 8, READING 1

OECD Stats references http://stats.oecd.org/Index.aspx?DataSetCode=ANHRS

UNIT 8, READING 2

Facebook. 2012. http://www.facebook.com/press/info.php?timeline.

McGuire, J. 2009. Volunteer vacations. *Time Magazine*, March 13. http://www.time.com/time/travel/article/0,31542,1885136,00.html.

The serious leisure perspective. http://www.soci.ucalgary.ca/seriousleisure/

UNIT 8, SKILLS AND STRATEGIES 16

How do Americans spend their leisure time? http://www.libraryindex.com/pages/1947/How-Americans-Spend-Their-Time-HOW-DO-AMERICANS-LIKE-SPEND-THEIR-LEISURE-TIME.html.

Many Teens Spend 30 Hours A Week On "Screen Time" During High School. 2008. *ScienceDaily*, March 14. http://www.sciencedaily.com/releases/2008/03/080312172614.htm.

Pong Story. http://www.pong-story.com/intro.htm.

UNIT 8, READING 3

Do us a favor, take a vacation. 2007. *Business Week*, May 21. http://www.businessweek.com/magazine/content/07_21/b4035088.htm.

Expedia.com – 20011 International Vacation Deprivation™ Survey Results. http://www.expedia.com/daily/promos/vacations/vacation_deprivation/default.asp.

CREDITS

Page 1: ©Paulo Whitaker/Reuters/Landov; page 13: ©lily/fotolia/AP; page 14 top: ©Time & Life Pictures/Getty Images; page 14 bottom: ©David Turnley/Corbis; page 18: ©Mark Ehrman; page 23: ©Bloomberg/Getty Images; page 24 top: ©Kitch Bain/fotolia/AP; page 24 bottom: ©Minerva Studio/fotolia/AP; page 25: ©Ivan Bliznetsov/iStockphoto; page 33: ©John Griffin/The Image Works; page 38: ©Bob Daemmrich/PhotoEdit; page 45 top: ©Fawan-CNImaging/Newscom; page 45 bottom: ©Adam Orchon/Everett Collection/Glow Images; page 46: ©Michael Newman/PhotoEdit; page 55: ©kurmyshov/iStock Editorial/Getty Images Plus/Getty Images; page 56 left: ©Peter Chadwick/Getty Images; page 56 right: ©Dea/Archivio J. Lange/De Agostini Editorial/Getty Images; page 57 left: ©Bernard Classen/Alamy; page 57 right: ©Boston Globe/Getty Images; page 65: ©marlee/Shutterstock; page 70: clockwise from top ©mates/fotolia/AP, ©rimglow/fotolia/AP, ©nenovbrothers/fotolia/AP. ©sergign/fotolia/AP; page 71 top: ©picsfive/fotolia/AP; page 71 bottom: ©Oleksiy Ilyashenko/fotolia/AP; page 77: ©Tom Cockrem/Lonely Planet Images/Getty Images; page 87: ©Visual &Written/SuperStock; page 88 top: ©Bombaert Patrick/fotolia/AP; page 88 center: ©Picture Contact BV/Alamy; page 88 bottom: ©Nikolai Sorokin/fotolia/AP; page 89: ©BLOOM images/Getty Images; page 97: ©Thomas Lottermoser/Getty Images; page 102: ©Bettmann/Corbis; page 102 frame: ©rangizzz/fotolia/AP; page 103 top: ©Corbis; page 103 top frame: ©sirylok/fotolia/AP; page 103 bottom: ©Christian Delbert/fotolia/AP; page 110: ©Jake Wyman/Getty Images; page 111: ©Harris Shiffman/fotolia/AP; page 112 top left: ©Alvey & Towers Picture Library/Alamy; page 112 top right: ©venca/fotolia/AP; page 112 bottom: ©Jacek Chabraszewski/fotolia/AP; page 121: ©JGI/Blend Images/Corbis; page 122: ©Chris Rout/Alamy; page 123: ©Tom Merton/Getty Images; page 131: ©Thinkstock Images/Getty Images; page 143: ©Fuse/Getty Images; page 144: ©David De Lossy/Getty Images; page 153 left: ©Stewart Cohen/Blend Images/Getty Images; page 154: ©Peter Macdiarmid/Getty Images News/Getty Images; page 158 right: ©Arrows/fotolia/AP; page 163: ©Siegfried Layda/Getty Images; page 168: ©Guido Mieth/Taxi/Getty Images; page 169: ©Image Source/Getty Images; page 175 left: ©Image Source/iStockphoto; page 175 right: ©ashumskiy/fotolia/AP; page 176: ©Frances Roberts/Alamy; page 185: left to right ©Redfx/Alamy, ©Marushin/Dreamstime.com, ©Jaap2/iStockphoto; page 186: ©SuperStock/PKS Media/Getty Images; page 187: ©photocreo/Fotolia/AP; page 195: ©Gandee Vasan/Getty Images; page 200: ©AFP/Getty Images; page 201: ©JIJI Press/Stringer/AFP/Getty Images; page 202: ©Mark Pearson/Alamy; page 208: ©iStockphoto/Thinkstock; page 209: ©Craig McCausland/iStockphoto; page 217: ©Panoramic Images/Getty Images; page 218: ©mediacolor's/Alamy; page 219: ©Manamana/Shutterstock; page 227: ©iStockphoto/Thinkstock; page 232: ©Bettmann/Corbis; page 239: clockwise from top ©Yellow Dog Productions/Getty Images, ©Mike Goldwater/Alamy, ©Hans Neleman/Getty Images; page 240: ©kiankhoon/iStock/Getty Images Plus/Getty Images; page 249 top: ©Henrik Sorensen/Getty Images; page 249 bottom: ©VRD/Fotolia/AP Images; page 250: ©mk-perspective/Fotolia/AP; page 251: ©Ryan McVay/Getty Images

Pages 30, 62, 94, 128, 160, 192, 224, 257: Nick Koudis/Getty Images

Layout services, book design, and photo research: Page Designs International, Inc.

Cover design: Studio Montage

Audio production: John Marshall Media